QUEST FOR TRIBAL ACKNOWLEDGMENT

QUEST FOR TRIBAL ACKNOWLEDGMENT

CALIFORNIA'S
HONEY LAKE MAIDUS

SARA-LARUS TOLLEY

FOREWORD BY GREG SARRIS

UNIVERSITY OF OKLAHOMA PRESS : NORMAN

Library of Congress Cataloging-in-Publication Data

Tolley, Sara-Larus, 1973–
    Quest for tribal acknowledgment : California's Honey Lake Maidus /
Sara-Larus Tolley ; foreword by Greg Sarris.
        p.   cm.
    Includes bibliographical references and index.
    ISBN 0–8061–3748–7 (alk. paper)
        1. Maidu Indians—Government relations. 2. Maidu Indians—Legal
status, laws, etc. 3. Federally recognized Indian tribes—California. I. Title.

E99.M18T65 2006
323.1197'41—dc22
                                                              2005054868

1 2 3 4 5 6 7 8 9 10

This book is dedicated to Neil Tolley, my brother, and to Viola Williams and Carole Mickens, who you will meet in the pages that follow.

CONTENTS

ILLUSTRATIONS

MAPS

FIGURE

FOREWORD

I am a writer. I am also chairman of my tribe, the Federated Indians of the Graton Rancheria. When I was in my hometown—Santa Rosa, California—filming an HBO miniseries based on my novel *Grand Avenue*, the town exulted in me. Local papers hailed me as their "Native Son." When I announced, some years later, that my tribe planned to build a casino, I was called a devil. The same newspapers cast me as public enemy number one. Bumper stickers exhorted, "Not Here Tonto."

The American Indian has been represented—and hence understood—as either a fallen nature god or a wagon-burner. These two stereotypes, flip sides of the same coin that undermine any complex understanding of us as human beings, let alone genuine respect, are directly connected to power relations. When we are defeated completely, separated from our homeland and any heretofore meaningful—translate "empowered"—relationship to it, we are pitied. When we are a threat, when we possess the means to fight, whether for that same homeland, or even for an idea of ourselves, we are scourged.

Representations of us as fallen nature gods began to appear regularly in the early part of the nineteenth century in the form of biographies of Indians (mostly written by non-Indians) from tribes east of the Mississippi River—tribes that had suffered military defeat. Meanwhile, where "Indian wars" raged elsewhere, the Indian was seen as inhuman, an animal-like threat to Western civilization, a notion Buffalo Bill perpetuated in his extremely popular traveling circus, later appropriated by Hollywood for even greater profit and lasting effect.

Often, particularly in very recent history, a political entity, or even an individual, will deem the Indian a nature god one moment and then a wagon-burner the next. This stereotyping is, as it always was, directly related to the viewer's purpose and position of power. Environmental groups, sometimes bolstered by narratives they create with regard to Indians' relationship to a landscape, not only consult the Indian, of course desiring reaffirmation of their narratives, but then use the Indian in their political battles with developers and government policies. Yet the same environmentalists will cast us as enemies when we violate their engrained notion of who or what we are, especially when the violation threatens their purpose. They declare war when we chop down a tree or build a casino. We are not "real Indians" then. Likewise, a community's non-Indian citizens may admire examples of our artwork behind glass in a museum—baskets, beads, pots—but those same citizens are too often on the front lines against us when they sense a possible shift in power relations that may arise due to our economic—translate "empowerment"—plans.

The essential problem—good Indian, bad Indian—is that neither of the notions is ours. Our legitimacy as well as our illegitimacy is determined by others. Nowhere is this problem more poignant than with the federal government, whose prescribed notions—amended at will and, as in the wider culture, determined by the entity's purpose and position of power—define "Indian." Based on the federal government's need, often calculated by pressure from local constituents, tribes not only exist or don't exist but eat or don't eat. Federally recognized tribes eat, those not recognized don't—at least not at the table of government helpings. Only federally recognized tribes are allowed a land base, trust land that is held by the government, which means that non-recognized tribes don't have the means for shelter and sustenance from a collective land base either.

Tribes have been created—and destroyed—with the stroke of a pen. In 1958 Congress passed the California Indian Rancheria Termination Act, an updated version of the earlier Dawes Act. It granted Indian tribes the option of private ownership of their reservation (trust) land in exchange for their status as a recognized sovereign nation, meaning all ties and responsibilities on the part of the government as a result of treaties and other agreements become null and void should the Indians choose the option to privately own the land. In essence Indians, should they choose the private land option—would no longer be Indians in the eyes of the government.

That year, in August, a federal agent came to the Graton Rancheria with his offer. In August, our people harvested crops in the nearby Santa Rosa plain; only two elderly men were on the reservation at the time. Neither read English particularly well, nor did they comprehend the meaning and consequences of the agent's proposal. To them owning land sounded like a good thing, so they "signed the piece of paper." We not only lost our land, but our rights as an Indian nation—no longer were we "legally" Indians.

Of course the agent's actions were illegal. The Termination Act specified that any action taken by a respective tribe required tribal consensus. Over thirty years later, in 1991, I began the tribe's struggle to right this wrong. We were looking for ways in accordance with narrow government definitions to prove we were Indians. Ironically, my great-great-grandfather Tom Smith, a Coast Miwok medicine man, was the principal informant for a dissertation on the Coast Miwoks written by Isabel Kelly, a student of Alfred Kroeber at the University of California, Berkeley. The government helped fund this study utilizing, and thus recognizing, Tom Smith as a Coast Miwok. Because the Federated Indians of the Graton Rancheria are comprised of Coast Miwoks and Southern Pomos, this evidence directly supported our case.

The Graton tribe was lucky—we were able to get a bill through Congress and signed by President Clinton on December 27, 2000, declaring the U.S. government's action on behalf of Graton Rancheria illegal and restoring us to full status as a recognized American Indian tribe and sovereign nation.

Part of our luck was due to the fact that we had once been recognized, or, in the current term, Acknowledged, by the government as a distinct nation of Indian people. During the early part of the twentieth century, the federal government, under pressure from California's growing non-Indian citizenry, many of whom were farmers who didn't need nor want Indian workers living permanently on their property, established reservations for the "homeless Indians," locally known as "rancherias," de facto creating tribes often made from two or more distinct aboriginal tribes (such as the Graton Rancheria, with Coast Miwoks and Southern Pomos).

Dozens of tribes were never recognized—or created—under this process. Often they were tribes with very few survivors and/or located in remote areas not impacted by California's growing non-Indian population. The Honey Lake Maidus were one such tribe left off the government's list. Hence, the tribe is not an "acknowledged tribe." This despite the fact that anthropologists documented in studies the tribe's distinct status as a culturally autonomous nation of Indians in the same way and according to the same criteria they documented other distinct tribes in California. It means that the tribe, in its historic attempt to be acknowledged, has been at the mercy of the U.S. government's whim as to who is and who is not an Indian. The struggle brilliantly recorded by Sara-Larus Tolley thus illuminates not just the history of a distinct American Indian nation but, at the same time, the larger history of U.S.–Indian relations, in which that nation struggles to do what it, like other nations, has done since time immemorial—that is, to define itself.

The situation isn't getting any less difficult. As I sit writing today, legislation is being pushed around Congress that would make it more difficult—if not legally impossible—for a tribe to get "acknowledged." The controversy surrounding American Indian gaming has cast us once again as an enemy, as wagon-burners. Before any of the very few successful American Indian tribes—those with successful casino operations—appeared and, for a variety of reasons, threatened the general public and hence its opinion about us, we were seen in a more sympathetic light, poverty-stricken and so forth, yes, tragic, fallen nature gods. Now, too often we are associated with corruption, greed, and environmental degradation. Our motives for acknowledgement are suspect—Why else would Indians want to be recognized by the federal government if that wasn't the only way they could get the right to build a casino?

Read on for a bigger picture—an accurate answer.

GREG SARRIS
Los Angeles, California

ACKNOWLEDGMENTS

My acknowledgments go first and foremost to the Honey Lake Maidu Tribe. (If only my own counted for as much as the federal government's did!) I was privileged to work with and for its members. Particular thanks go to Ron Morales and Viola Williams, and all those who shared their stories with me. Viola Williams passed on in April of 2005 and this loss reminds me all the more of the import of telling her story.

Words of gratitude go, too, to my grandmother, Alma Wies (now deceased), for her tireless, intellectual scissor-work, and to Melanie and William Tolley, who helped me get started on this route and who served as the Connecticut front. Shep Kreck III guided me with my ideas in the earliest stages in ways that would carry me through; Bill Simmons very generously showed me around both the academic and Indian worlds; Helen McCarthy, Jenny Kim, and Jay Petersen inspired and encouraged me; my writing group, including Kira Foster, Amy Gardner, Benedito Dos Santos, Peter Cahn, Damani Partridge, Karen Greene, Nancy Scheper-Hughes, and Stanley Brandes helped me express "what's at stake"; Nelson Graburn, Donald S. Moore, and Leanne Hinton offered their invaluable comments; and Amy Hofer edited a later draft. The Wenner Gren Foundation and the Department of Anthropology at the University of California, Berkeley funded this research. The American Indian Studies Center at UCLA provided a grant and a place to write—special thanks to Heather Valdez Singleton, Kasey McMurray, and Ken Wade. Jessica Manlin was a supportive editor; Crystal Mustric's activism and energy were inspirations; my housemates used early drafts as scrap paper, inspired my pseudonyms, and never failed to encourage me; and Nik Putnam listened tirelessly to my thoughts, feelings, and struggles with this work. Thank you!

Some names and facts have been changed to protect people's identities.

QUEST FOR TRIBAL ACKNOWLEDGMENT

INTRODUCTION

Working for the Honey Lake Maidus

THE ANTHROPOLOGIST
AND THE HONEY LAKE MAIDU TRIBE

THE FIRST TIME I MET RON MORALES, WHO WAS TO BECOME THE
Honey Lake Maidu tribal chair, was in Sacramento in October
1997 at the state of California's Heritage Commission's Native
American Graves Protection and Repatriation Act (NAGPRA)
hearing. NAGPRA, enacted in 1990, is a set of national procedures by which a tribe can reclaim its ceremonial items,
ancestors' bones, and "associated funerary objects" from federally
funded museum collections. I had been invited to come to the
hearing by my Ph.D. advisor from the UC Berkeley Anthropology Department, anthropologist Bill Simmons, who had
done some ethnohistorical work with a tribe from rural northeastern California, the Honey Lake Maidus. Without much more
information than this, I went along with him to the hearing.
Unwittingly, I was inserting myself into a very complicated set
of relationships. Eventually I would be thoroughly entangled.

I remember that after the morning's introductory discussions I ate my lunch with a group that included Bill, Ron
Morales, Ron's sister, Viola Williams, and her daughter and
granddaughter, Wanda and Season Brown. Ron asked boldly if
I was going to come work for the Honey Lake Maidus on their
Federal Recognition project. I was only politely responsive,
although I do remember some kind of a spark: these were
three generations of Leona Morales's descendants, and I'd heard

Leona's *voice* . . . spent hours with it transcribing it from tape for the regional ethnohistory Bill had been working on. But I was also nervous. Perhaps I was absorbing some of Simmons's anxiety about "testifying" against the archaeologist Fritz Riddell (using his own work against him) at the hearing. Riddell was well respected throughout California for the publications resulting from his work as archaeologist for the state Parks and Recreation Department. At this point in his life he had cancer, the outward sign of which was a large bandage wrapped over his head and around his jaw; I couldn't help but notice that he was looking wizened and fragile. Nonetheless, Ron cursed Riddell, who sat apart from us. My overall impression of Ron, whose relatives called him Comanche, was that he was loud, angry, and absolutely confident I was going to work for him.

Throughout lunch, Ron referred to the representatives of the Federally Recognized Susanville Indian Rancheria—who, at this meeting, were Northern Paiute and Mountain Maidu individuals—as "old coyotes, . . . sneaking, lying son-of-a-guns."[1] Ron and his family were trying to claim California State Museum bones that Ron said were not "Federally Recognized" bones, but non-Recognized, Honey Lake Maidu bones. Simmons was there to say that the Honey Lake Maidus were indigenous to the area from which the bones were collected. It appeared to be a losing battle though: the Rancheria was Recognized by the government as the tribe indigenous to Honey Lake Valley, and so the bones would go to them. But it became clear to me that Ron and his family were testing the state of California's NAGPRA mechanism, daring it to exclude them. And they were staking this dare on much more than just legal Recognition, a word I capitalize to refer to the government's use of its status as a political technology of exclusion, via the Federal Acknowledgement Process. At the crossroads of Federal Acknowledgment policy and the Native American Graves Protection and Repatriation Act, they were daring the state Heritage Commission to deny them their history.[2] What they were asking for was lowercase r *recognition*, as the word is used in plain English to mean accepting responsibility for something.

In the end, what impressed me most was how each "side," the Honey Lake Maidus and the Susanville Indian Rancheria, had brought its own anthropologist. What I had witnessed was Indians battling for their identities—to a large extent through anthropology.

The second time I met Ron Morales my scholarly fascination had won out, and I was ready to work for him and his tribe. Why were the Honey Lake Maidus not Recognized? And how had Ron come to the point of such animosity with the Susanville Indian Rancheria? At the end of the summer of 1998, Bill and I traveled to Susanville, on the dry side of the Sierras, an hour and a half north of Reno, Nevada, for a visit. Ron's house was welcoming and full of Indian artifacts and crafts, organized museum style: a tall glass case with dusty photographs from the old days, pieces of bone, and elaborate "cut" bead purses, bottles and key chains. There were metates and arrowheads, pestles, paintings, manos, feathers, Indian motif calendars from years past, dolls, a badger skull, and what seemed to be a do-it-yourself taxidermy project involving a bear's paw. There was also an "Indian Rottweiler" named *Pano*, Bear, who was sleeping on the rug in a distinctly aggressive manner. A framed photo of Ron's maternal grandmother, Roxie Peconom, held a prominent place. Ron pointed to the picture and told me that many of the things in his home had been hers. Roxie had died in 1956 at the age of 105 or 106. She had lived through major changes in the Mountain Maidu world, and he explained that today the knowledge and experience she passed on serve as a guide for all of her relatives, tribe members, and some of the greater Indian community.

We moved outside to the backyard and sat down near the garden and vast woodpile, Ron in a La-Z-Boy recliner and Bill, Viola, and myself in lawn chairs. As night fell, he rigged a floodlight to a ladder, adjusting its distance from us to discourage an assembly of hopping bugs, which flitted and settled all around and on top of us nonetheless. Viola was going slowly through the text Bill had brought, a transcription of her mother's telling of the Creator's journey through Mountain Maidu country: through American and Indian valleys, on through Big Meadows and Mountain Meadows, and covering ground across Honey Lake Valley until He disappeared beyond the Skedaddle Mountains that frame its eastern edge. Soon, she and Ron were complaining about the person who had done the transcription—a person who didn't know Mountain Maidu, that's for sure! I thought of my long hours at the keyboard trying to capture the way Leona spoke as exactly as I could, thinking I was doing right by her and her descendants. But here they were reversing, cursing my work, smoothing over the memories, the sounds.

The next time I visited Susanville, I drove up from Sacramento with a California Housing and Community Development/Indian Assistance Program grant writer, Jim Reid. We were hoping to win a grant for Federal Recognition from the Administration for Native Americans, part of the Department of Health and Human Services. Ron greeted us with Indian tacos and spicy salsa from that summer's garden. Now it was deep fall and the wood stove was so hot my shirt almost burst into flames as we sat on stools at the kitchen counter. I jumped to open the door. There weren't as many kittens crawling up the screen begging for food as there had been last time. Perhaps they'd all grown too big.

Jim Reid wanted to know if he would be able to write a compelling grant: were the Honey Lake Maidus good candidates for Federal Recognition? Would he be able to convince the Administration for Native Americans they would be funding a winner? Ron was evasive in a studied way. But he did convince Reid—in the same way that I later noticed he would tell someone he wanted to impress a bit of some secret, emphasizing the part that let them know it *was* a secret. He told Reid, "I'm hiding the Maker's Footprint—from everyone."

The Maker's Footprint is, literally, the enormous footprint left by the World Maker (also called the Creator) as He journeyed through Mountain Maidu country. It is said to have curative powers if a person lies down in it. Secrets such as this one are often mentioned but rarely revealed in the Honey Lake Maidu community; tribe members sometimes complain that Ron has hidden the footprint from *them*. This is part of a pervasive, old-time pattern of closed knowledge in the community, which extends from the (purposefully unfiled?) papers under Ron's bed or in his locked back room to the previous generation's reluctance to exert their identity in public arenas in town.

Reid was satisfied with Honey Lake Maidu "Indianness" by this and other evidences. Most compelling, we noted as we drove past the Central Valley rice fields, closing in on Sacramento, was the degree of organization of family and tribal leadership evidenced by the Honey Lake Maidus' staging of the Bear Dance every spring.

On my third visit, Ron drove Pano and me around the high desert valley in which Susanville is located. (See Map 1.) The rabbitbrush was blooming and the valley had an appealing chartreuse glow. We stopped by Peter Lassen's gravesite. Peter Lassen was the prospector/businessman/adventurer for whom the county was named. Ron showed me the old ranches as we continued driving in his huge GMC truck—the old white people's ranches, where the (older) Indian villages used to be. Roxie Peconom was born on the land now called Rousche's Ranch, a quarter mile back, which was also near where *her* grandmother, Momolo, had been born in the late 1700s. We drove around checking on the black oak on different people's properties, but the acorns were not ready, and dogs barked at us though we backed out before the little boy could find his

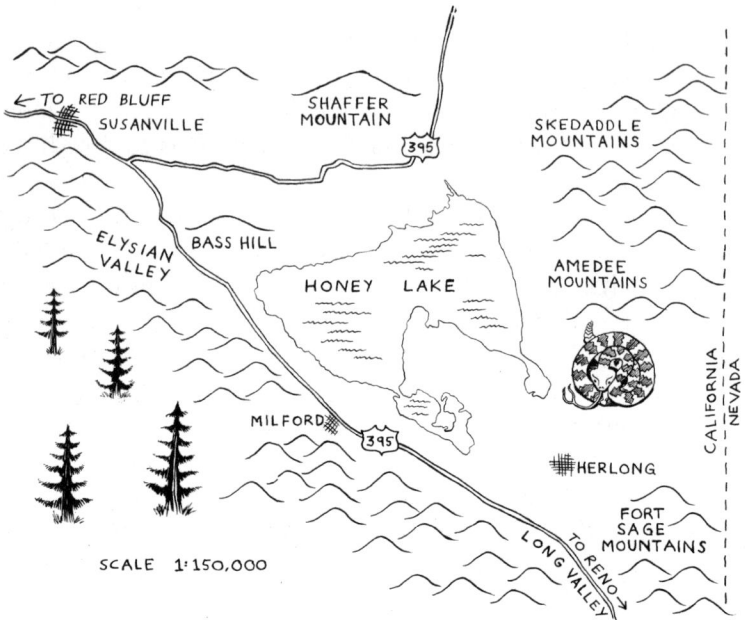

Honey Lake Valley. Illustrated by John Isaacson, © 2005.

father and tell him we'd driven up their long, winding driveway. Then we drove on to the "hanging tree," where various people had been hanged, and, as the plaque read, "The first white man was killed." Comanche dug some medicine. When I left, he sent me off with a whole bunch of it. He said I'd need it, living as I did in the city—where "life is rough."

At the end of the summer of 1999, I moved to Susanville. Ron had first asked me to come work for the tribe's Federal Recognition nearly two years before, and there I finally was, with a laden pickup truck, ready to test whether I could be accountable both to the Honey Lake Maidus and to my academic colleagues. Being accountable to the Honey Lake Maidus meant understanding and explaining how they were a tribe that should be acknowledged as such by the U.S., the state, and the local governments. Being accountable to the academics might mean scrutinizing the meaning of *tribe* and taking on the body of literature on its invention. If so, this second responsibility could also mean a disengaged or even active skepticism of the Honey Lake Maidus that I already knew I could not assume, simply because of my connections to Ron and his family.

Instead, I chose another route and put the Honey Lake Maidu perspective first in order to reflect upon the insults and provocations they experienced in undertaking Federal Acknowledgment. What I have found is that my critique of the Federal Acknowledgment process's arbitrary, bureaucratic definitions of Indianness has good company among academics—see, for example, Barsh (1991), Cramer (2001), Davis (2001), Duthu (2001), Grabowski (1994), Greenbaum (1985), Schiedermair (1990). The book in your hands begins with the colonial imposition of *tribe*, emphasizing the twentieth century Acknowledgment process's awkward and continuing redefinitions of the concept by looking honestly toward an understanding of twenty-first century Indianness, as explained by Indian people themselves. This book also reaches for something more: what if anthropologists, employed by tribes, worked for transformation of their subjects' life experiences, instead of simply for documentation? This might mean, as it does here, a new ethics, hard to handle though it may be. The reader will find that in this text, with tribal permission, I reveal Honey Lake Maidu strategies in petitioning for Federal Acknowledgment, specifically because we hope to make an impact upon the reader and then the Acknowledgment system itself.

This can certainly be tricky. As I learned outside Ron's house that summer under the flood lamp, my sense of responsiveness often needs to be checked by Honey Lake Maidu understandings of the same. The problem of translation (or, as mentioned earlier, even transcription!) occurs on many levels in this book. First, there is the translation that occurs as the Honey Lake Maidus narrate themselves as a tribe. Second, there is the federal imposition, the strangeness of the government's ideal form or narration of tribe, as it is reflected in the Federal Acknowledgment procedures. And third, there is the problem of how, under my direction as an anthropological consultant to the Honey Lake Maidu tribe, the petition took shape in consideration and studied ignorance of bits of each of these narratives and translations of their experience.

My opening vignette—with its dueling anthropologists, Riddell versus Simmons, with Tolley in the wings—points to the way that anthropology has come to matter and even act as the mediator in the instatement of federal relationships with Native peoples: anthropological pronouncements have real-life effects when it comes to proving aboriginality in NAGPRA hearings and for Federal Recognition cases. But anthropological pronouncements are also contentious—the products of histories that are often not exclusive in their affirmations, for, again, the anthropological project concerns itself with the translation (and editing and analysis) of what Native peoples have chosen to report. What I emphasize is that the context of such work matters; all anthropology has been "applied anthropology," or anthropology applied in one theoretical or political context or another. To be clear, the political context of *this* work stems from my belief that the power of anthropological analysis is significant, not only because it gets taken up in various ways by the government, but because it can influence public opinion, which has the potential to challenge and change government policy.

The reader will find this book to be an essential guide to understanding the situation of non-Recognized peoples throughout the United States, but particularly in California. The California story is the story of hundreds of very small, often landless tribes of great linguistic variety that remain, for the most part, off the non-Indian radar, unacknowledged. Their experiences of initial contact with Europeans—Spaniards, Russians, Americans—were especially brutal. Indeed, California's Indian peoples have been emblemized in the non-Indian imagination best by Ishi, a Yahi survivor of vigilante extermination campaigns in northern California, who appeared in 1911 in the dry foothills town of Oroville as an emaciated ghost-man not sure he was alive or dead.[3] Eventually, he was taken in by University of California anthropologists as a friend and informant because his people were supposedly no more.

In this way, extinction looms large in the non-Indian imaginary of California's peoples. If they are considered at all today, California Indians are called remnant tribes or landless tribes, or they are remembered as squatters, or as an esurient workforce, illegitimate according to society's rules. Historically, what this perception meant on the national level was that their particular forms and stories were not considered when the Federal Acknowledgment process was being created, and so they remain . . . illegitimate.

At the same time—a great contradiction contained within this non-Indian imaginary—California's Indian peoples are a rising power, driving gaming law and regulation and negotiating Federal Acknowledgment in creative ways such as through statewide coalition and legislative action. In a jolting manner, the "last of his tribe" scenario is being replaced with a perception of tribes coming out of the woodwork to take on, with their new casinos, the sacred pastoral presence of California's ranchers and farmers. In short, because of gaming, California Indian people have new power in the non-Indian imagination and in reality. Californians' eyes are on the tribes, and this interaction may well be shaping the future of federal-Indian relationships and law, nationwide. We should not forget that the treatment of California Indians on the national level has always been an important indicator of political commitment to Indians. California was where the reservation system was pioneered, and today, because it has the most non-Recognized peoples of any state, we should recognize that California may well be the place where a regional solution to the Federal Acknowledgment bottleneck is designed and forwarded.

In the meantime, California Indians hold fiercely to their tribal differences and their particular claims to California's places. (This is often perceived as "factional" by non-Indians who like their Natives to take predictable positions.) In part because of this spirit, but mostly because I believe that anthropology's greatest impact is achieved through careful attention to the details of people's lives in context, I have chosen to employ a traditional anthropological form, the monograph, and to focus upon a single tribe, the Honey Lake Maidus. Details lead to connection, and connection is necessary for moving toward resolution of conflict: what I hope is to reach the reader by making vivid the experiences of Ron, Viola, and other tribe members. My greatest aspiration is that the Honey Lake Maidu case, which is certainly similar to other tribes' situations but at the same time quite unique, might become a heuristic for connecting empathetically to the intricacies and complications of the relationships between Native peoples and the state that are described by the U.S. Acknowledgment system— in California, across the nation, and beyond.[4]

FEDERAL ACKNOWLEDGMENT

The Federal Acknowledgment process is a set of administrative procedures by which the U.S. government "Acknowledges" Indian tribes. Petitioning tribes must submit evidence of their social, political, and cultural continuities over time. An office of the Bureau of Indian Affairs (BIA) called the Branch of Acknowledgment and Research (BAR) evaluates the merit of tribal petitions. BAR makes recommendations as to what kind of Final Determination the Assistant Secretary–Indian Affairs should make—whether or not a petitioner should be included into the suite of legal impositions, protections, and privileges afforded Native peoples in this country.[5] Repatriation of ancestral bones and grave goods, religious and cultural protections, federal housing, education monies, trust land, and casinos are some of the benefits of official tribalness. Yet undertaking Federal Acknowledgment means that a tribe must engage intensely with a set of Acknowledgment procedures founded and limited by the racial biases of the majority, non-Indian culture. Because of this, Federal Acknowledgment should be thought of as a crucial reckoning point for liberal political systems and the possibility of multicultural inclusion.

Liberal political systems, such as exist in the United States, are founded on an orientation to individual rights and equalities in the public sphere. In such systems, cultural differences—and the notion of collective rights—are relegated to the private sphere, which lies (in privacy) beyond the law. This book is about the borderlands of the public and the private spheres, where racial and cultural differences emerge at times as publicly acceptable and at other times as repugnant. It is at such limits and edges of liberal political recognition that national stereotypes—expectations—of Indianness impact constructions of difference (see Povinelli 2002). From the Honey Lake Maidu perspective, why the tribe participates with the state reveals what is valuable about the status quo of its relation to the U.S. government, as well as what needs to be changed. One conclusion I have come to is that, in the current climate, the Honey Lake Maidu sense of belonging seems to come from finding a sustainable antagonism.

THE WORK OF PETITIONING

For the Honey Lake Maidus, gaining Federal Acknowledgment would mean having a federally sanctioned means—with a full set of legal teeth behind it—of protecting burial grounds and cultural sites in their homeland from federal, state, and corporate development. It would also mean having a way of protecting their right to use lands that they themselves no longer own for gathering acorns and other plant materials. Federal Recognition would mean literal recognition: a place in local histories and non-Indian consciousness. Further, Federal Recognition would offer the possibility of tribal economic endeavors—or at least federal support for taking good care of its children and elders.

But to achieve either Federal Recognition or just plain recognition, the Federal Acknowledgment procedures demand disclosure. In order to have a hearing—the goal of which is someone's *listening*—there has to be a telling: in legal-bureaucratic form, a petition must be produced. To do so, decisions about what shape the telling will take need to occur. These pages will describe the Honey Lake Maidu struggles over how to share but still keep traditional knowledge, and detail the Honey Lake Maidu transformation from a non-Recognized tribal people to the Honey Lake Maidu Tribe, modeled according to the government's definition. I pay close attention to what gets reproduced in the process of the tribe's articulation with the government's criteria of Indianness, and in those aspects of the criteria that are themselves transformed. In sum, this book describes the goal of winning Federal Recognition as a response to the state's projects of politico-economic domination in the twentieth century. As such, it considers seriously how Federal Recognition draws a tribe closer to the state in potentially destructive ways, acknowledging that this choice is made by people like the Honey Lake Maidus with lasting survival foremost in mind.

Coyote's image and imagery will shadow these inquiries into tribe. The Maidus say that it was Coyote who created death and hunger out of the perfect world the Maker intended. Perhaps Coyote also created miscommunication and its twin possibility of reinterpretation to contradictory ends—resistance.

THEORETICAL UNDERPINNINGS

I locate the Federal Acknowledgment procedures and continuing state violence to Indian communities at the crossroads of Michel Foucault's decentered or authorless investigations into governmentality and the kind of analysis that emphasizes a clear vision of justice such as Antonio Gramsci's. Observing how Foucault's and Gramsci's ideas intersect one another on their routes to different places casts light upon the Honey Lake Maidu experience as petitioners.

The Foucaultian project is one of uncovering the intricacies of state and institutional power through genealogical analysis. A genealogical analysis of power is opposed to a traditional historical analysis, seeking not power's origins but the details of the many lines of the construction of its broad discourses—which can be found, for instance, in individuals' often-unconscious ways of thinking, speaking, or acting. Foucault argued that power is achieved through discourse applied to the end of defining the abnormal and via the science of government, statistics. He pointed out that the discipline of the state is today worked less frequently than it has been in the past through physical manipulations such as torture. Instead, control over the conduct of the populace is exercised through "techniques of the self"—through internalizations of bodily discipline, schedules, examinations, and through the inculcation of habit. Criticized for creating his own powerful discourse from which escape is nearly impossible, Foucault's approach is quite distinct from one that focuses upon envisioning alternatives to power using binary or antagonistic propositions such as justice/injustice. Yet his genealogical technique, valuably, enables insightful analysis of the effects of state control. A self-described "specific intellectual," Foucault was able to offer political intervention through critical knowledge, without posing as the sole possessor of truth, or claiming to know the route to justice.

Antonio Gramsci was concerned with power on a material rather than discursive plane. And rather than genealogy, Gramsci was interested in history. He based his elaboration of social change on his experience with the Communist Party's struggle against Fascism in Italy: why had a revolution of the workers not succeeded? Facing the ideological problem of how to make unfree subjects free, Gramsci theorized (from his prison cell) that the bourgeois state is composed of two realms: political society and civil society. The ruling powers of the political society control the meanings circulated within civil society. Yet room remains there for the rise of organic intellectuals who might lead the working classes from whom they come in either a traditional military war (a war of maneuver) or a war of position against the dominant political regime. Gramsci's war of position, at its most basic, is a conception and description of a protracted struggle over all the ordered meanings of society into which the (in this case, non-Indian) hegemony has been inculcated. This is truly an ideological battle, fought on many fronts. Such a contest entails a long-term assault on the consensual basis of power that can remain in contradiction fairly stably over time.

At the intersection of these two approaches and in my consideration of the intersection of the Honey Lake Maidu Tribe and the U.S. government—the tribe's Acknowledgment petition—I will offer an analysis of the way that the freedom of the liberal state is the procedural freedom, in actuality, to be controlled, even as I keep an eye on the ultimate justice that the Honey Lake Maidus hope will come of the Federal Acknowledgment proceedings. Another important aspect of this intersectional analysis is that it focuses as much upon how the Honey Lake Maidus engage anthropology and politics to argue their own identity as upon how anthropologists and the state have attempted to do the same with definitions of *tribe*. While the Honey Lake Maidus recognize the symbolic violence of petitioning, they also claim this violence and pin it to the state. This act opens up avenues for critiquing the Federal Acknowledgment process's discourse of its nonconfrontational administration of Acknowledgment.

CHAPTER ONE

ETHNOGRAPHY AFTER GENOCIDE: THE UNMENTIONED IN CALIFORNIA'S KROEBERIAN ANTHROPOLOGY

ALFRED KROEBER'S 1925 HANDBOOK OF THE INDIANS OF CALIFORNIA begins with his admission of hesitation before the topic of California's Indian genocide and then his final decision to ignore it.

After some hesitation I have omitted all directly historical treat-ment in the ordinary sense; that is, accounts of the relations of the natives with the whites and of the events befalling them after such contact was established. It is not that this subject is unimportant or uninteresting, but that I am not in position to treat it adequately. It is also a matter that has comparatively slight relation to the aboriginal civilization. It presupposes, indeed, some understandings of that civilization; but it requires also a thorough knowledge of the local history as well as of the institutions of the superior race. It involves prolonged study and acquaintance with Spanish and mission archives, with Government documents, with early California events and pioneer conditions. In all these things many others are more proficient than I can hope to become; and it has seemed that I might better contri-bute to the future writing of such a history by concentrating effort in the field into which training and predilection have led me, and endeavoring to render the California Indian, as such, a more familiar object to the future historian of his political and economic relations with ourselves. (1925, vi)

Kroeber's reasoning does not negate the fact that in writing of California Indian customs, he was ignoring how genocide may have affected them. Of his work among the Yoruk people, Thomas Buckley, for instance, has written, "Although Kroeber was avowedly apolitical in his ethnology, his reconstruction of a Yoruk culture caught in static balance and free of the contaminating influences of traumatizing contact with whites was profoundly political. . . . The Yoruks that Kroeber constructed were a people outside of—or before—time, and most especially before genocide" (1977, 288).

Following Buckley's lead, as well as Kroeber's call for a more proficient scholarship, my work begins with genocide.[1] For the Honey Lake Maidus, genocide—and anthropological and historical oversight thereof—is necessarily the starting point of the story of their contemporary experience as petitioners to the government for Federal Acknowledgment. They can feel the continued reverberations of genocide today in the Bureau of Indians Affairs' Federal Recognition process, through which groups apply to be Recognized as official Indians. The process places the burden of proving Indianness upon the non-Recognized groups themselves, taking little or no responsibility for the state's own part in the history that has left them un-Recognized in the first place. The skeptical assumption is that the non-Recognized are not Indians until *proven* Indians.

What California's non-Recognized tribes contribute to the national critique of Federal Acknowledgment is a clear depiction of how the ways the tribes of this state found for surviving through the years make the uniform application of the Acknowledgment procedures untenable. Painting a stark picture, the Bureau of Indian Affairs estimates that two-thirds of all California tribes are not Recognized.[2] As of February 2004, there were sixty-four California petitioners for Federal Recognition in the nation's 235-tribe queue at the Branch of Acknowledgment and Research. Despite the bottleneck of the restrictive Federal Acknowledgment procedures, Federal Recognition is valued by its petitioners in California and across the nation because it offers a glimmer of hope for a real base upon which a tribal future can grow—sanctioned, sovereign, and protected once and for all. In this sense, Federal Recognition represents a refutation of genocide.

What we will begin to see, though, is that Federal Recognition, according to the Bureau of Indian Affairs' Branch of Acknowledgment and Research guidelines, necessitates that a tribe simplify its historical experience so that it is, in critical ways, unrecognizable to its own members: at times, petitioning means contracting the very history of dislocation and abuse that is, in part, what confirms their knowledge of themselves as an Indian people.

GENOCIDE

My uncle George took me around to where the whites killed Indian people. You can still see the bullet casings today.
—Ron Morales

Sherburne Cook (1978) has estimated that the death toll of Native persons at Contact in California between 1770, the date of the establishment of the first Spanish mission, and 1900 was over 90 percent of the original population of 310,000. Accordingly, the near-destruction of the Indians of California meant that *only 20,000 Indian people remained by the turn of the century.* Cook explains this near-devastation in three waves. The first wave came following the development of the Spanish missions project in 1769. A system of twenty-one Spanish missions was built throughout southern and central California, where religious conversion and forced labor were emphasized as a means for transforming Indian people from something akin to animals into *gente de razon.*[3] The second wave of destruction extended from the end of the mission period in 1821 to the Mexican-American War in 1845, when ranching and trading brought brutal economic exploitation as well as a series of epidemics to ravage Indian communities. The third wave followed the gold rush settlement of the Sierra Nevada, Cascades, and Siskiyous by Americans. Of this last wave, Cook writes,

It is evident that by 1850 the Indian population of the entire state had been reduced to about 100,000. The decline during the worst decade, 1845 to 1855, was incredible—from approximately 150,000 to 50,000. This desolation was accomplished by a ruthless flood of miners and farmers who annihilated the natives without mercy or compensation. . . . The direct causes of death were disease, the bullet, exposure, and acute starvation. The more remote causes were insane passion for gold, abiding hatred for the Red man, and complete lack of any legal control. (1978, 93)

The last of which is better understood as legal sanction.

The Treaty of Guadalupe Hidalgo, ratified on May 30, 1848, at the end of the Mexican-American War, translated into the U.S. acquisition of New Mexico and Alta California from Mexico—a vast expansion of U.S. territory. This expansion also meant a compounding of "Indian affairs" concerns for the federal government and, considering the hundreds of thousands of Native persons in the annexed territories, the state took steps to extend national Indian policy to address them. A series of surveyors and census takers were sent to investigate their settlement patterns and report back to Washington.

Following these initial investigations, in September of 1850 Congress acted to provide Indian Agents to the new state of California based on the recommendation that the territory's Indian peoples be treated with and then concentrated into districts for effective control. Redick McKee, George W. Barbour, and Dr. Oliver M. Wozencraft were named Federal Indian Commissioners, and they divided the great state into eighteen separate parts with eighteen separate treaties. These men worked under the stated assumption that "as there is *no further west*, to which they *can* be removed, the General Government and the people of California appear to have left but one alternative in relation to these remnants of once numerous and powerful tribes, viz: *Extermination or domestication*" (*San Francisco Alta Californian*, January 14, 1851, quoted in Rawls 1984, 141; italics in the original). The treaties themselves promised tracts of land in return for the relinquishment of the lands signers were currently occupying. It is estimated that this land would have amounted to 7,488,000 acres or 7.5 percent of the state (Rawls 1984, 141). Tribes agreeing to sign and move elsewhere were promised food and other supplies. The basic idea was that it would be cheaper to feed the tribes than to fight them (Ellison 1978, 52).

Yet the logic of this project was quickly worn away. Non-Indian Californians' sentiments toward the possible creation of such reservations grew more and more resentful. By 1852 discussion of whether the state would vote to ratify the eighteen treaties was underway in the California State legislature.

Leaders of the state's representational minority argued for the solemnity of the treaty agreements that had, by this time, already been made with the tribes. Their reasoning, they explained, was that if the Native populations were preserved and "reserved," the Indian could be made useful to whites: "Here philanthropy and charity, hand in hand, might find a field in which to labor" (*Journal of the Senate*, California Legislature, quoted in Rawls 1984, 145). The majority, on the other hand, claimed that action should be taken considering, first and foremost, the Spanish and Mexican precedent in the treatment of Native peoples: under Mexican rule, Indians had been denied the right to own land. Also to be considered was the U.S. precedent of simply removing Indian peoples—relocating their populations farther west. This obviously put a special pressure on California, and the majority argued that the situation demanded a novel solution. Furthermore, the majority claimed that despite continuing experimentation with "reservationing" huge portions of the state, reserving lands for Indian peoples would not do justice to the rights of the white citizenry. At the end of the debate, the differential weights of majority and minority arguments meant one certain course of action: rejection of the treaties by nonratification.

On the national level, in the U.S. Senate, the treaties were also rejected, largely because of the California delegation's opinion. Sidetracking the issue of justice, disgust and blame were generally heaped upon commissioners Wozencraft, Barbour, and McKee, who were thought to have wasted the government's money and made themselves rich prospecting and selling rights to land, all the while offending the logic of human nature with their assumption that the reservation boundaries could be protected from fortune seekers. Fifty-two years would go by before the information about the U.S. Senate's rejection of the treaties would be made public because of an injunction of secrecy; meanwhile the treaties were disregarded with no explanation, lands were taken, and any payment to the signatory tribes or any others was stopped. In the end, the peoples who had entered the treaty process in good faith were not compensated for the land that was taken until more than one hundred years had passed, and after decades of litigation. However, the recovery of their sovereign relationship to the government as Native peoples was a separate issue, and not always possible to recoup.

The ominous backdrop of this transparent politics of racism was furnished by the first California legislature's Act for the Government and Protection of Indians (1850). This act laid bare the legal sanction for genocide as it clarified the California Indian's legal (and social) status. James J. Rawls has made an excellent study of this law and its context, which he suggests revealed "a continuing concern with subordinating the Indians and facilitating white access to their labor" (1984, 86) which had deep roots in the Spanish system of peonage. Indeed, what the "government and protection of Indians" meant in 1850 is horrifyingly elucidating. Rawls explains that the act prohibited whites from compelling Indians to work or to perform any service against their will, yet able-bodied Indians were liable to arrest "on the complaint of any resident" if they could not support themselves or were found loitering or "strolling about" or were "leading an immoral or profligate course of life." If it was determined by proper authority that an Indian was a "vagrant," he or she could be hired out within twenty-four hours for the highest price for any term not exceeding four months. In effect, any Indian not employed could be bought from a county or municipal official at public auction (ibid.).

Furthermore, any jailed Indians bailed out by a white "benefactor" would "be compelled to work for the person so bailing, until he has discharged or cancelled the fine assessed against him" (Rawls 1984, 86). Finally, and most distressingly, the 1850 act established a system of "Indian apprenticeship" by which a white citizen could appear before a justice of the peace with an "orphaned" minor, and, if the justice was convinced that the child was indeed an orphan taken on in good conscience, the white citizen could be said to legally own that Indian child until the age of eighteen years, as long as he or she was fed, clothed, and sheltered. If the latter part of the contract was breached, the master would receive a ten-dollar fine and the minor would be passed to another master.

Thus, in practice, the law condoned kidnapping and encouraged the sale of Indian children and the slaughter of their parents, making possible the enslavement of California Indians. The Act for the Government and Protection of Indians was not repealed until 1863, and even then this was in word only: a special investigator from the Office of the Commissioner of Indian Affairs visiting California reported that, three years after the Emancipation Proclamation, Indian slavery was still not uncommon in California (Rawls 1984, 86).[4]

Meanwhile, the state government had long been subsidizing a California Volunteer Militia, which justified the murder of Indian people in the name of protecting settlers. Vigilante bands also terrorized Indian peoples across the state, supported by subscriptions to pay bounties for Native scalps. Cook estimates that, of the 80 percent population decline between 1845 and 1870, 60 percent was due to disease and 40 percent to extermination practices (Slagle and Davis 1995, 12).

MAIDU CENSUS FIGURES:
THE CONTOURS OF GENODCIDE

Of the Maidu peoples, the Konkow (or Northwestern) and the Nisenan (or Southern) Maidus bore the brunt of the terrors of those early years.[5] Nisenan and Konkow people were ripped from their lands and forced to march to reservations at Nome Lackee and Nome Cult, outside of the present town of Tehama, where they were corralled and later marched again to Round Valley Reservation in Mendocino County. The Mountain (or Northeastern) Maidu peoples, who occupied the high valleys in the drainages of the northern Sierra, were sheltered from the Spanish and Mexican penetration into the Sacramento Valley, and the Americans did not reach their territory until the Lassen Trail was created in 1849. The Honey Lake Maidus are a Mountain Maidu people, and I will focus next on what the censuses tell us about the Mountain Maidu experience of culture contact. These details, though certainly different than those of any other tribe, bear the same general contours of the experience of deterritorialization and genocide in California, and, to a lesser extent, the nation as a whole.

The Mountain Maidus still occupy the high-elevation valleys between Lassen Peak and the Nevada border: American Valley, Indian Valley, and Honey Lake Valley. Mountain Meadows and Big Meadows are aboriginal territories no longer occupied— the former was partially flooded, and the latter was entirely converted to a reservoir for Pacific Gas and Electric's hydro-electric power generation system, beginning in 1902 when the area was secured from homesteading ranchers.[6] From a late prehistoric period, Mountain Maidu population established at about three thousand (Dixon 1983 [1905], 132; Kroeber 1925, 394; Riddell 1978b, 386), the turn of the century figure was, shockingly, near three hundred (see Kelsey 1971 [1906]). Today, Simmons et al. note, "Perhaps 500 to 600 persons of partial Maidu ancestry live today in the Plumas and Lassen County homelands. Only a few of these can speak or understand the language (Shipley 1963, 1–2; 1964, 1)" (1997, 4).[7]

Permanent white occupation of the Honey Lake Valley, on the dry, eastern side of the Sierra, the last of the Mountain Maidu territories to be settled by Europeans, began in 1854, but by then, Mountain Maidu populations were already plummeting due to disease and abuse. C. E. Kelsey's 1905 census indicated eighty-five Maidus in Lassen County, only thirty-one of whom are identified by today's tribal members as indigenous to the Honey Lake Valley. Yet the Honey Lake Valley's chapter of the California genocide can only be partially introduced by census figures: oral historical accounting places at least five villages in the Honey Lake Valley in the late nineteenth century, indicating upward toward five hundred Honey Lake Maidus. Significant for puzzling out the early brutalities in Honey Lake Valley, to which these rough numbers bear a kind of witness, is the fact that Stephen Powers, who was one of the first non-Indians to depict the Honey Lake Maidus, considered them extinct: "There are only a few Indians around this town, and all these belong to Big Meadows and Indian Valley, the aboriginal inhabitants of Honey Lake Valley being now extinct" (1975 [1876]: 26–27). A year later, however, Powers retracted this pronouncement (1976 [1877]: 107). Compelling information apropos to his retraction remains: Ron Morales and Viola Williams remember their grandmother, Roxie Peconom, talking about being visited by an anthropologist at Wetajam, her village, in the 1870s. They believe this must have been Stephen Powers.

THE COLONIZATION OF HONEY LAKE VALLEY

Peter Lassen, a native of Denmark and an over-and-again failed businessman, was one of the first Europeans to trespass and settle in Mountain Maidu territory. Lassen led a train of twelve wagons from Missouri through Nevada to California and his Mexican land grant near today's town of Vina (Tehama County), with almost-disastrous results. His dangerously lengthy route through the desert is today known as the Lassen Trail, but it was known at the time as the Cape Horn Route or even the Green Horn Route, and was abandoned after 1850. After the collapse of the community he hoped to build and then profit from, Benton City, Lassen sold his ranch and left to prospect for gold in the Sierra. Though he never found the storied Gold Lake he sought, Lassen and his party, which included his business partner Isadore Meyerowitz, came upon what is today known as Indian Valley. Lassen and Meyerowitz built a cabin near Greenville, in the year 1851. They are considered to have been the first white settlers. For several years they ran a trading post, as quartz mining built the frontier community into a small but busy town. From Greenville, Lassen and his partner explored Honey Lake Valley. They both settled there for the rest of their lives—which would, in the end, not mean settling for very long.[8]

The population of white interlopers in Mountain Maidu territories was, by 1860 (according to the first U.S. Census), 362 in Indian Valley and 476 in Honey Lake Valley. Lassen built a house near what is today Richard Bass's land, in what is known as Elysian Valley, just north of Janesville. He was murdered on a prospecting trip in 1859. Meyerowitz lived in present-day Buntingville, southeast of Janesville, on the edge of Honey Lake. Meyerowitz and his Indian wife are said to have drowned there—in a few feet of muddy water—on a boating excursion in July 1856.

Here, again, the history books and Honey Lake Maidu memories coincide. Viola Williams and Ron Morales recall that May Charley, their grandmother Roxie Peconom's sister, took up with/was taken up by a white man, and that she drowned in Honey Lake, having fallen out of a boat. Whether or not May Charley was this woman, the possibility of (similar) unions between Indian women and white men is one axis along which we might fill out the picture of relations between the Maidus and whites in the Honey Lake Valley in this early period.

Honey Lake Maidu tribal member Dilly Frow, for example, was taught that Maidu women were stolen by white settlers quite frequently in the late 1800s, and "they'd just make the best of it." Speaking with empathy across generations as we sat by the pool at her home in Santa Rosa, she told me, "Maybe she would decide that that was the best way to protect her siblings, her parents, her children."

Separately, Ron Morales, her cousin, spoke of the flip side of this kind of compromise when he showed me the grave marker of "the first white man killed in Honey Lake Valley," Charles H. Crawford, in 1858. The official story of Crawford's death has it that he died of an arrow wound sustained during the pursuit of Manley Thompson's stolen oxen.[9] Ron's version of Crawford's death, however, has nothing to do with stolen oxen; he claims, instead, that "the Indians didn't like how he treated their women."

In general, Honey Lake Maidu informants describe the Contact period as a time when the Maidus tried to hide themselves as much as possible. Dilly Frow explained that the first Maidu words her mother thought to teach her meant, "Hurry and hide, the white people are coming." She was careful to emphasize the significance of this to me, in a context of genocide and Indian hatred in Honey Lake Valley. Besides physically hiding small children and others, hiding meant aligning themselves with ranching families and distinguishing themselves from the Paiutes, with whom the United States would wage war in the 1860s.[10] An outcome of such "affiliation" with non-Indians, however small, though, is that while histories and revisionist histories have been written considering the relationships of the whites and the Paiutes, both are significantly lacking for the Maidu side.

Today's Honey Lake Maidus are descendants of three of at least six or more original Honey Lake Maidu lineages. Of the Dicks, Stressleys, Browns, Jacks, Peconoms, and Jacksons, only the last three families remain as far as the tribe has been able to establish. The Jacksons, however, are signed onto the Pit River rolls, and have no interest in joining with the Honey Lake Maidus. Thus, today it is only the Jack and Peconom lineages—212 members—that make up the tribe.

As lineages, lines, and populations were forcibly reduced, so too were the memories and stories of Honey Lake Maidu genocide reduced, particularly the oldest stories.[11] Single stories, as above, when combined with others, give a sense of the particularities of the larger genocide, as well as the atmosphere of violence in the Honey Lake Valley. In what follows, the reader will find excerpts of some of the stories of early violence experienced by Honey Lake Maidus that are recalled to this day.

The Jack family line can be traced back to Old Tom, who was born in the early 1800s. Asa Fairfield's 1916 collection of William Dow and Fred Hines' narrative of the 1866 event he calls "'Old Tom' Killed" sheds light upon the erasure of Maidu history in the valley, demonstrating how racist notions shaped the way Maidus from the Honey Lake Valley were discussed. Dow and Hines set the scene the following way.

[Old Tom] was here in 1857, when Mr. Dow came into the valley, and for some time after that he and the other Indians spoken of were the only Indian valley Indians who lived here. He had long been suspected of selling ammunition to the wild Indians living in northeastern Nevada. For some time previous to his death whenever he went to a house in the nighborhood [sic] of his camp and found no men there, he would demand ammunition from the women in a threatening manner. He generally wanted powder and caps, and he picked up all the tea lead he could find. Another thing that looked suspicious was the fact that he had the skins of animals which he could not get in this part of the country. Added to all this, just about this time a large band of Indian valley Indians came into Susanville and told that Old Tom was selling ammunition to the wild Indians. (1998 [1916], 399)

The reader will notice that Old Tom is grouped with the "Indian valley Indians" from the Greenville area, rather than the "wild" Indians. The latter description refers to the Northern Paiutes, a tribe that consistently counterbalances contemporary glosses of "Maidu" with associations of unpredictability and a propensity for violence. Today, tribe members would say that the way Old Tom's tribal identity is not truly revealed reflects the fact that the warlike Paiute presence in the valley eclipsed the more quiet, Honey Lake Maidu presence. Indeed, it is Old Tom's business with the Paiutes—a departure from the rules of tolerable Indianness—that was apparently used as justification for his murder. Dow and Hines continue, explaining that the white pioneers had just come back from massacring an encampment of Paiute people at Eagle Lake. Back in town, Perkins and some other men decided to punish Old Tom for his collusions with the Paiutes—an idea that again confirms the childlike position of the Maidus in non-Indian eyes.

After killing the Indians in Papoose valley the whites went into Susanville and told what they had done. That same day Old Tom's case was discussed and six or seven men went out to his camp, which was then on Gold Run near the old Lanigar place, then owned by John R. Perkins. Perkins went along with them, and after going a short distance south from his house they scattered out and went through the timber. Finally Perkins ran across him. Evidently [Tom] had heard something of what was going on, for when he saw Perkins he started off as fast as he could. Perkins followed and caught up with him, and told him they wanted him to come in and make some explanation about selling the ammunition. He refused to come and started away, but was headed off. The same thing was done two or three times, and at last Tom threatened to yell to some other Indians who were camped near by if he was stopped again. He started off once more and then Perkins shot him several times with his pistol. He ran a short distance and fell down dead. (Fairfield 1998 [1916], 399)

It is in this context of histories of wild versus domesticated Indians that Ron's nickname Comanche is also significant— we might understand his work driving the Federal Recognition of his people as running counter to their predominant silence over the course of history. He is a "renegade," then, in this special sense.

Another place where historical violence manifests itself is in the many stories told by Peconom lineage descendants of Roxie Peconom's life, which spanned from approximately 1850 (pre-Contact) to 1956, well into the lifetimes of the older generations of Honey Lake Maidu tribal members. To the Honey Lake Maidus today, she is, understandably, a touchstone for a pre-Contact world in transition. Fabulous tales are told of her, which I believe reveal kernels of truth about Maidu life on the violent frontier where the Indian world intersected with the non-Indian. I was told, for instance, despite contrary evidence, that Roxie Peconom was kidnapped by whites and indentured as a small child, but that "she swam the Feather River and made it back to this country." More plausibly, I was also told that as a child she had had to hide from first the Spanish, then the Americans, "because they'd make our people do slave work building fences." Other stories of Roxie Peconom's life are better documented: for example, it is said that when she was an infant, the army rounded up Pit River "renegades" in Dixie Valley to march them to the Bay Area, some six hundred miles away.[12] The soldiers came through Susanville and forced Roxie and her mother and father to come along, mistakenly recognizing them as Pit River people. "She left when she had to be carried, and when she came back, she was walking," explained Viola Williams. Her family was gone for two years or more, and had found only starvation, exploitation, and abuse on the forced march, which ended with their permission to return to Honey Lake Valley, their identity as Mountain Maidus clarified. The family carried a white flag and federal documents so their way would be cleared for their return, but they spent much time working for ranchers who demanded their labor along their route home.

The tribe's violent history continues with the story of Bob Junior, Roxie Peconom's brother, who was murdered in 1908, in front of his wife and children, by game wardens who claimed he was fishing out of season. Relatives speculate that the wardens either wanted access to his allotment land for themselves or were sent out by Pacific Gas and Electric.

Bob Junior had left the Honey Lake Valley, in perhaps the late 1870s, to find work. He started a business building fences for ranchers in the Manton/Red Bluff vicinity: Junior and other Honey Lake Maidu tribal members would cut wood in the Sierra, and then he would haul it to the foothills to lay fence. He relocated his family to Manton (eighty miles from Susanville) and received allotment land with coveted river access. His murderer was later convicted of manslaughter. An unnamed, undated contemporary newspaper article in Ron's possession reported that the verdict came as a great surprise to nearly everybody, as it was generally expected that the trial would result in a disagreement, as the jury had been evenly divided in the first trial.

[The game wardens] Bond and Carpenter swore that Bob grappled with Carpenter at the wagon, grabbing Carpenter's pistol which was drawn on him to prevent him from securing a gun under the wagon, and after quite a struggle Carpenter threw Bob away from him when Bond fired the fatal shot. The Indian's wife swore that there was no fight and no struggle, and that Bond shot her husband while Bob was tightening a nut on the wagon.

Family members note that the guilty verdict did not stop a PG&E hydroelectric power plant from being erected on Junior's widow and children's land between the date of his murder and the date of his murder's arraignment. The corporation also built a large irrigation ditch surrounded by an electric fence that both dried up the Junior family's well and killed one of their horses. The Juniors were not compensated for the lands PG&E took from them until 1913, after much clamor.

Still other memories of the early violence remain: Walter Peconom is said to have bludgeoned Henry Vanetti, a white immigrant, to death with a shovel at the dairy they worked at in Mountain Meadows. His nieces and nephews living today say that he was provoked because of Vanetti's unrelenting racist provocations.

Ten years later, in 1910, Peconom was shot by a sheriff at a Bear Dance celebration. Witnesses say that Sheriff Leavitt unjustly accused the victim of taking aim at him; Leavitt later claimed that he killed Peconom in self-defense.[13]

Also recalled and passed down are memories of the waves of disease that swept through the Honey Lake Valley. One victim, rather late in the period of these epidemics, was Walter Peconom's father, John Peconom, who died of smallpox in 1902 at the ancient village site of Wetajam, where the Rousche family had built their ranch in the 1860s. After his illness and death, the village, tenuously shared with the Rousches, was abandoned, and family members never lived together at the site again because their fear of contagion was so strong.

THE LASSEN LEGACY AND FEDERAL RECOGNITION IN THE CONTEXT OF GENOCIDE

I have mentioned that Peter Lassen was murdered in April of 1859 while prospecting in the Black Rock Desert. His death provides a sense of the larger impact of the settlement of the Honey Lake Valley on the Indian people indigenous to those lands. As one historian explains, "Indians were blamed by most people for the shooting, but some suspected whites who believed Lassen had in his possession the map of a silver mine at Black Rock" (Levenson 1994, 40). Though yet another possibility is that disgruntled travelers from the days of the Lassen Trail travails finally got their revenge, unfortunately, "Killed by Indians" (as the twelve-foot monument at his gravesite reads) is still the most popular version. As recently as the year

2000, the *Lassen County Times* ran an article repeating the theory (Morgan 2000). Indeed, I found that the legacy of genocide remains alive in the practice of history in Honey Lake Valley today: non-Indian attitudes in the valley today are continuous with those of the pioneers when it comes to Indian people.

The non-Recognition of two-thirds of California's Indian peoples indicates that the legacy of genocide is alive and well on a national level too. Today's institutionalized expectations are that Indians be inflexibly pure—not adaptable, complicated, strategic, or able to talk back. Because of such expectations, and their implications in the Federal Acknowledgement proceedings, any discussions of non-Recognition need to be linked back to their discursive beginnings: genocide and treaty non-ratification. Allogan Slagle, the founding director of California Indian Legal Services (CILS) and the project director for the Special Association of American Indian Affairs' Federal Acknowledgment Project in California, did much to establish these connections.[14] He and anthropologist Lee Davis wrote, "This refusal to ratify the treaties was a death sentence for the Indians of California" (1989, 329). Slagle and Davis believed this "death sentence" was such at legal and bureaucratic levels only—for instance, Honey Lake Maidu cultural practices did not entirely die out, but the government's (and many anthropologists', historians', and non-Indians') recognition and protection of them did. The power of "the Last of the (fill in the blank)" myth in the American psyche equates cultural transformation in periods of particular stress with cultural extinction.

Many tribes have defied the government's attempt at eradication and its work toward assimilation-to-the-point-of-nothingness. The Honey Lake Maidus are one such tribe, and they should be Recognized today. Yet their chances seem slim, in part because "The Last of" is a myth entrenched not only by social romanticism but also by social logic: the devastation wrought upon California Indian communities was tremendous! How could the softness of culture have survived such hardship?

I have come to understand that it survived *because* of its softness. As an illustration, I am drawn to anthropologist Lowell Bean's keen description of culture change as reflected in California Indian notions of supernatural power. He wrote, "A very rapid loss of power is believed to have occurred after the European contact as knowledge concerning the means of regulating power was lost. Nevertheless, power is always partially retrievable as new rules are established for obtaining and maintaining it" (1975, 25). Particularly, ritual action can restore, shore up, and maintain the cultural dynamics of the "traditional" world and worldview. In chapter four, a description of the Mountain Maidu Bear Dance makes this ritual power clear. For now, suffice to say that across California this power has always been evidenced: in the 1870s, Paiutes brought the Ghost Dance to California, where it was adopted by Nisenan Maidus, Southern Valley Yokuts, and others as a means of explaining the incredible changes in community life and the drastic population crashes tribes were experiencing. This and other movements had transformative spiritual as well as material effects. The Bole Maru religion, a variation on the Ghost Dance, for instance, spread among California's Pomo peoples in this period. It inspired hope, for some tribe members, in a period of spiritual and cultural demoralization. Furthermore, with the coming of the Bole Maru dreamers, Pomo people organized and began to try to get back some of their lands by way of trading ranchers their labor for small parcels, as well as by selling their extremely intricate and beautiful baskets.

BEHIND THE MONOLITH OF TRIBE

I would like to close this chapter with a description of the contours of the vibrant Honey Lake Maidu community to emphasize that the "death sentence" image—the bureaucratic death knell that has sounded more than once throughout the twentieth century but has not yet had any lasting effect— though perhaps evocative of the tortuous waiting at the state's mercy, does not evince the strategic positioning, the hope, and the pride that petitioning also evokes from a tribe like the Honey Lake Maidus. The Honey Lake Maidus are not victims: they conceive of themselves as coming from a place steeped in cultural power to match the state's social and political power. This introduces the way that the tribe's petition for Acknowledgment is as much their own documentation of their fierce survival despite genocide as it is a capitulation to the government's definition of Indianness. For though this book begins with the tribe's despair in the face of genocide, it is ultimately about how they are, indeed, a tribe even given the failings of the government's definition of that concept. Appropriately, then, their petition for Federal Recognition begins with a confident statement that

the Honey Lake Maidu have, since the pre-Contact period, continuously resided within their traditional, ancestral territory, continuously practiced their traditional culture, continuously maintained their community through social/political interaction and cultural practices, and have continuously been identified by external authorities, communities and other entities as an authentic, autonomous, historic Indian tribe. Further, the federal government has taken a number of actions recognizing this specific community as a tribal entity. (Honey Lake Maidu Tribe 2001, 6)

The petition follows with discussion of their distinct dialect, territories, and land use patterns, brief narratives of the Honey Lake Maidu lineages in the past and present, and the history of their interactions with the federal government in the form of treaties and Indian allotments. The introductory section closes with a discussion of "Today's Honey Lake Maidu Tribe." It reads, in part,

Today the Peconom and Jack family lines of the Honey Lake Maidu Tribe are geographically scattered, although a core lives in the Susanville area. Of the 136 membership applications filed at the Honey Lake Maidu office,[15] only 19 are from out of state, not including the Reno/Sparks area of Nevada, which is less than an hour and a half from Susanville and the Honey Lake Valley. Of the remaining 117 applications, 114 members reside in Northern California, with 28 applications from within 2 hours of Susanville. (Honey Lake Maidu Tribe 2001, 11)

One can see how the geographic dispersal of tribe members is spun to emphasize closeness. The petition thus reflects the government's version of tribe such that geographic cohesion is equated with cultural, social, and political cohesion. Balancing the government's interest in such a position—which reflects, in strange combination, a commitment to justice and a need to move with the political winds—is the interest the tribe has in convincingly depicting itself cohesively, itself bordering, at times, upon unsustainable essentialism. There are injustices in the spaces of both postures: the government's unrealistic implementation of its vision of Indianness and the compromises the Honey Lake Maidus have to make in their attempt to meet it. And so, while the Honey Lake Maidus describe themselves, proudly, as a tribe that resides closely in the huge expanse of northern California, another reality, that of tribal members' differences, shows through. Similarly, it will become clear in the following chapters that the realities of the tribal divisions of the Honey Lake Valley have less to do with geographically solid notions than with multiple histories of displacement.

"THE LEGEND," FROM FRANZ KAFKA'S *THE TRIAL*

Before the law stands a doorkeeper. To this doorkeeper there comes a man from the country who begs for admittance to the Law. But the doorkeeper says that he cannot admit the man at the moment. The man, on reflection, asks if he will be allowed, then, to enter later. "It is possible," answers the doorkeeper, "but not at this moment." Since the door leading into the Law stands open as usual and the doorkeeper steps to one side, the man bends down to peer through the entrance. When the doorkeeper sees that, he laughs and says: "If you are so strongly tempted, try to get in without my permission. But note that I am powerful. And I am only the lowest doorkeeper. From hall to hall, keepers stand at every door, one more powerful than the other. And the sight of the third man is already more than even I can stand." These are difficulties which the man from the country has not expected to meet, the law, he thinks, should be accessible to every man and at all times, but when he looks more closely at the doorkeeper in his furred robe, with his huge, pointed nose and long, thin Tartar beard, he decides that he had better wait until he gets permission to enter. The doorkeeper gives him a stool and lets him sit down at the side of the door. There he sits waiting for days and years. (1992 [1937], 213–15)[1]

CALIFORNIA'S NON-RECOGNIZED TRIBES, WAITING BEFORE THE LAW

THE BRANCH OF ACKNOWLEDGMENT AND RESEARCH'S CRITERIA for Federal Acknowledgment (please see appendix A), and "The Legend," a parable nested within Kafka's novel *The Trial*,— one fact, one fiction—represent experiences of uneasy entanglement with the Law: Joseph K., to whom "The Legend" is told, is plagued by summons for crimes he never committed and the nature of which he never learns. Horrifyingly, over the course of the novel, he comes to live the life of one guilty of such accusations, fearfully awaiting his final sentencing. The Honey Lake Maidus are similarly burdened with a "crime" not their own—in their case it is, in fact, the state's. Yet they choose to engage the state through the Federal Acknowledgment process, and in so doing they learn to live the life of a petitioner; they learn to understand themselves as non-Recognized. They search out tribal members long distanced from the Honey Lake Valley, search out histories that comply with their criteria-A-through-G-driven needs, and learn, like the man from the country, to wait in the long corridor before the door of the Law.

The Kafkan sensibility is well suited to the experience of petitioning.[2] As we've seen in the last chapter, yesterday's genocide has given way to ethnocide. After the government's sanction of murder, hangings, and rape after the forced marches, forced indentures, and then the neglect and bureaucratic "extinctification" of California's tribes, it now asks them, by way of the Federal Acknowledgment process, to prove to the state that they *are* Indian peoples. With the blank stare, the supposed nonbias, of the bureaucracy, it asks them to justify why their tribes are descended from so few individuals, and why so few families remain. It asks them to bare their scars, and summon and explain their traumas for government inspection. Meanwhile, their status as "non-tribes" itself works to slowly disenfranchise them, and, as many Honey Lake Maidus told me, more and more is lost every year as the elders get older and eventually pass on.

If one considers deeply and seriously such a trajectory of state policy then it is stunning to read how the Branch of Acknowledgment and Research explains—in checklist format—that

generally, the following [types of petitioners] cannot be acknowledged [as tribes] under the 25 CFR Part 83 regulations because they would not meet all seven mandatory criteria:

✓ Individual Indian descendants;
✓ The descendants of one Indian ancestor (a "lineage") who became separated from his or her tribe and now has many descendants;
✓ Groups of "Indian descendants" of one historic tribe who are no longer in tribal relations;
✓ "Reconstructed" Indian groups who have gathered together scattered remnants of colonial Indian tribes that ceased to exist for long intervals;
✓ Recently created Indian groups that gather together Indians of many tribal origins, either locally or nationally; and
✓ Newly organized groups of off-reservation Indian descendants who no longer meet the membership requirements of the recognized tribe from which they descend. (Branch of Acknowledgment and Research 1997, 38)

Yet the Branch of Acknowledgment and Research's fundamentally negative, bureaucratic definition of what a tribe is *not* belies the reality of Native California history and contemporary life, which California Indian peoples have worked hard to establish for the state. In the 1990s, Congress created the Advisory Council on California Indian Policy (ACCIP), and gave it a mandate, among others, to investigate Federal Recognition. The council was headed by Indians and allies and operated through committee hearings held throughout the state to solicit Indian peoples' input. In 1997 it concluded that the Federal Acknowledgment process does not work in California. The council's Final Report offered the simple numerical evidence (among many others) that since the formulation of the Acknowledgement criteria in 1978, only one tribe had been Recognized through the Branch of Acknowledgment and Research, the Timbisha Shoshones of Death Valley—and that was in 1983. Sixty-four Letters of Intent to Petition have been submitted from California alone (though four of these sixty-four were withdrawn by the senders), with only two Final Determinations completed via the BAR process—the Muwekma Ohlones (2002), a negative, and the Timbisha Shoshones of Death Valley (1983), a positive Final Determination.[3] The Advisory Council's report argues that the state's unfinished justice, its duty to its Indian citizens as mandated statutorily, is rectifying tribal non-Recognition. It asserts that the government has not made good on its legal responsibilities to these California Indian groups. It has never rectified its refusal to ratify the treaties of 1850–1851, and today the injustice continues in its hostility toward Recognizing the tribes it has either long sought to destroy or actively neglected. Such tribes have weathered many changes, and, while focusing on the need for their Acknowledgment, the ACCIP explicitly refutes the government's ability to stand in judgment over them.

Tribal existence and identity do not depend on federal recognition or acknowledgment of the tribe. Federal recognition does not create tribes, rather it recognizes social/political entities that predate the United States. It acknowledges a trust relationship between the tribe and the federal government, and entitles tribes and their members to certain federal benefits and protections of their culture and sovereignty. In practical terms, federal acknowledgment triggers the operation of the whole body of federal Indian law. (ACCIP 1997c, 7)

The Advisory Council report on Recognition thus highlights a way of revising the system that initiates redress: California Indians want the federal government to *recognize* their responsibilities to them. Understanding the double meaning of Federal Recognition/federal recognition is very important. It challenges the state's ability to categorize Indian peoples, even as it remains wedded to those categorizations.

SOVEREIGNTY AND A LEGAL RELATIONSHIP WITH THE UNITED STATES

The famous phrase that defined the Indian nations as "domestic and dependent" quasi sovereigns comes out of Supreme Court Justice Marshall's decision in *Cherokee Nation v. Georgia* (1831), a case in which the Cherokees requested the Court's protection from the predations visited upon their lands by the state of Georgia. The Supreme Court ruled against the state because it recognized the tribe's claim to its territories, yet the favorable ruling was predicated upon the Cherokee tribe's existence as a "domestic dependent nation." Marshall wrote:

They look to our government for protection; rely upon its kindness and its power; appeal to it for relief of their wants; and address the president as their great father. They and their country are considered by foreign nations, as well as by ourselves, as being so completely under the sovereignty of the United States, that any attempt to acquire their lands, or to form a political connection with them, would be considered by all as an invasion of our territory, and an act of hostility. (30 U.S. [5 Pet.] I, 16 [1831])

In other words, the act of appealing to the Supreme Court for redress was understood by the Court as a submission to its superior sovereignty.

The fact that Andrew Jackson and the state of Georgia defied the Supreme Court's ruling—forcing Cherokee families from their homes and homelands—with no repercussion adds another layer of meaning to this case and the way it draws together national understandings of Indianness. The Cherokee case demonstrates ably the violence of inclusion (their partial surrender of sovereignty), but also the violence of exclusion (the kind of violence that the state should not, in all justice, ignore).

This pattern of inclusion alongside exclusion is driven by economic violence, grounded in power struggles over land and its resources. In California, as I have described in chapter one, these issues were enunciated as the problem of where to remove the tribes once the edge of the continent was manifest. The answer was the creation of the nation's first modern reservation system. Unlike the seventeenth-century English colonists' reservations on the eastern seaboard, or the idea of "Indian Country,"—the ill-supervised Oklahoma frontier—in California, Edward Beale's "military reservations" were established on the model of the Spanish missions and "for the convenience and protection of the Indians." More specifically, Beale had planned "a system of discipline and instruction to be adopted by the agent who is to live at the post. [And further,] [e]ach reservation is to contain a military establishment, the number of troops being in proportion to the population of the tribes there assembled" (Rawls 1984, 148).

California's reservations (at various times between 1853 and 1864, Téjon, Nome Lackee, Nome Cult, Mendocino, Fresno, King's River, and Klamath; from 1864 to present, Hoopa, Round Valley, and Tule River) amalgamated many peoples and cultures, with no consideration of the locations of their aboriginal territories. The Advisory Council on California Indian Policy's critical history notes that the United States "failed to provide adequate lands or sufficient resources to make the reservations sustainable, and they became pockets of human poverty, despair and abuse. California Indian survivors of the eradication and removal campaigns found uneasy refuge at these places" (ACCIP 1997b, 7). In fact, reservations were easy targets of California Voluntary Militia members, and other state-supported vigilante groups paid bounties for Indian scalps.

Both humanitarian motives and those of land lust had their role in a growing public outrage against the system, which eventually led to the closing of most of California's reservations. Once closed, the tribes were left to fend for themselves. This often meant squatting on land informally—and temporarily—allowed them by a rancher. Many of these peoples became the "homeless" Indians for whom the Rancheria Act would be intended to aid.

The reservation system introduced the irony that has haunted all successive Indian policy. It generated a need to define and distinguish the Indians from the non-Indians, a parsing that was not always easily accomplished—recall that Roxie Peconom and her parents were mistaken for Pit River people in the 1850s, rounded up, and then marched to a non-specified military reservation until their identities were clarified.

ALLOTMENTS

The General Allotment Act of 1887 (also called the Dawes Severalty Act) authorized the breakup of any remaining reservations into individual allotments, typically 160 acres per household. "Extra" land from such divisions of tribal holdings was made available for sale to non-Indians. Meanwhile, the government kept its hand on the allotted Indian lands by requiring that they be held in trust for twenty-five years before they could be legally transferred to Indian ownership. The avowed purpose of these measures was Indian freedom: freeing Indians from tradition-bound land holding practices and indigenous forms of self-government so that they might enter into mainstream non-Indian America as small-scale farmers. Combined with the end of treaty making (1871), the General Allotment Act signaled the state's desire to end its dealings with sovereign tribal entities and the beginning of the government's intended posture of service to displaced, nontribal Indian persons. The practical result of this policy reorientation was that, within fifty years, almost two-thirds of the land under tribal control was lost throughout the nation. In California, approximately one-fourth of all tribal land was taken out of trust by the allotment process. Yet the ACCIP report concludes, ironically, with the positive effect of this act of theft: "Still, much of the allotted land was retained by Indian owners. By 1893, there were 2,300 Indian allotments in California" (ACCIP 1997b, 7)—more, in fact, than would have been in their hands had the General Allotment Act not been passed.

Indeed, by 1887 the Maidus living in the Honey Lake Valley no longer possessed tribal land to divide. Under Section Four of the Allotment Act, Indians "practicing tribal relations" were actually awarded land—parcels from the public domain. It was not sufficient to simply possess Indian blood in order to be eligible for a Section Four allotment; it was necessary to be a member or have the right to membership in a culturally active tribe (Roth 1996, 40). Today, such allotments, therefore, offer evidence of Federal Recognition for petitioners seeking Federal Acknowledgment. In this way, we can understand that an enduring effect of the Allotment Act has been to bring the burden of bureaucracy into what it means to be part of an Indian tribe. In receiving allotment lands, the Honey Lake Maidus entered into a legal life: Honey Lake Maidu allotment files at the National Archives are filled with letters from Indian persons to the various Indian superintendents in regard to property law, trespass, and probate materials. All reflect the bureaucratic tangle that was Indian land ownership.

Looking, as an example of the legal life, to the documents in the BIA's file on James Sylvanus (Ron Morales and Viola Williams's great-uncle), I found his allotment land depreciating and disappearing before my eyes. On February 25, 1914, the agency clerk at Susanville wrote the agency supervisor at Greenville, H. G. Wilson, the following note on accepting bids on the sale of Sylvanus's land:

While I have not spoken to James Sylvanus recently concerning the sale of his homestead, . . . he has [previously] stated that he would not accept less than $450 for the sale of this land. While I know that this is ridiculous [that is, high], yet I anticipate considerable difficulty and probably not a little delay in having this form completed.

By October 11, 1922, William Rousche, the rancher whose family had assumed occupation of the lands (including the ancient village site of Wetajam, where Sylvanus's family had lived for generations), had sent the Greenville superintendent a letter on behalf of Sylvanus, regarding whether he could sell his land to cover his medical bills. The superintendent wrote Sylvanus back, telling him that he had a credit of $24.62, and noting, "As to selling your land, you refused once to sell for $1000. And the appraisement was less than that. Before it could be offered for sale again it should be appraised to know its value at this late day" (October 14, 1922). Perhaps not satisfied with this answer or able to wait for reappraisal, on October 21, 1922, Mrs. Laney Rousche wrote Superintendent Miller,

Dear Sir: I would like to buy the forty acres of James Sylvanus or Jim Rousche. He tells me he will take $250 for the forty acres. Of this land, the records show there are back taxes to be paid. Would these be cancelled? Would like to know by next mail what can be done with the property as Jim needs the money very badly but unless I can get a good title for the land I do not feel that I want to advance him any more on it.

Early the following year, James Sylvanus died and the Rousches absorbed "Uncle Jim's" land. What they paid for it is not on record. The General Allotment Act had brought him into the state's legal and administrative realm in a very visceral way: Sylvanus's fate had been discussed and weighed from a patronizing, administrative distance, and in its understandings of him, the state had changed him from a tribal member to an "Indian individual," alone and out of context—a "man from the country," awaiting his death. Tribe is neither considered nor mentioned in the state's business with the Honey Lake Maidus during this period: in fact, the allotment files are organized, statewide, alphabetically by individuals' last names.

Via the Allotment Act, the Bureau of Indian Affairs had amassed a set of data so large that it can only be thought of as a Foucaultian *savoir*, built and tended for governmental control over Native peoples. Indeed, one should begin to imagine the Honey Lake Maidu situation as one so entangled within U.S. law as to leave little recourse to it. They are *in* the Law but not *of* it: recorded within its files, yet not Recognized as a tribe with sovereign privileges. It is crucial to understand that while the General Allotment Act represented a drastic change in policy, perhaps even "helping" a tribe like the Honey Lake Maidus by giving them a small bit of control over a small bit of land, the United States nonetheless retained the trump card: the judgment of competence to hold individual title was not an Indian decision.

THE RANCHERIA ACT

In 1905, the Indian Appropriations Act authorized an inventory of conditions among the central and northern California tribes.[4] C. E. Kelsey, a member of the Northern California Indian Association and an attorney, was designated Special Agent for the investigation, during which he claimed to have personally visited every Indian settlement between the Oregon and Mexican borders. His inventory resulted in the rancheria project, which, between 1906 and the early 1930s, used congressional appropriations to buy land for "homeless Indians."[5] The word *rancheria* was borrowed from the Spanish, and meant to indicate an Indian "village home." Typically, rancheria lands were parcels of one hundred acres or less, and they were intended to be shared by multiple tribes. As a consequence, Indian persons who live on rancherias today are Federally Recognized only as

rancheria members—*not* as members of any particular tribe—
and only for as long as they continue to reside there.

In 1923, at the urging of Albert Jackson, whose ancestry
links him to the Honey Lake Maidu tribe, the Susanville
Indian Rancheria (SIR) was established. Initially, no Honey
Lake Maidus moved there, for it was explained to me that
even of the tribe members who did not have homes, few were
willing to move to the undeveloped rancheria, at least initially:
it wasn't until the 1930s that electricity was extended to
"Indian Hill," and I have heard that, through the 1950s, there
was no indoor plumbing. Why Albert Jackson lobbied for the
rancheria is thus not entirely clear. There were no structures
built there for several years. What is certain is that the Honey
Lake Maidus were administered by the government agencies
as "Susanville Indians," and that these Susanville Indians,
composed of many tribes, shared, to a large degree, a common
lot in this period. Susanville was a hub where Indians of many
tribes gathered, hoping for work in the ranching or lumbering
industries. The homeless Indian population—by Honey Lake
Maidu accounting—was high in this period.

In 1927, four years after the establishment of the SIR,
Lafayette Dorrington was dispatched from Washington to make
a census of remaining non-reservation Indians, for the purpose
of assuring that they received some kind of rancheria land if
they had not already. Dorrington's censuses are a key component
in the story of the creation of California's un-Acknowledged
tribes. Those tribes Dorrington defined as "needy" but could
not find suitable land for, or those tribes he did not have the
money to purchase land for, as well as those tribes that he
decided were not in need of land, were not Acknowledged by
the government. As for where the Honey Lake Maidus fell in
his classifications, Dorrington noted that "before discussing
these individual bands of Indians, kindly permit the writer to
advise that so far as homes are concerned, the majority of the
Indians of Lassen County have provided homes for themselves

which compare favorably with, if not better than the average home situated on land purchased for homeless Indians" (Dorrington 1927, 10–11). His assessment supports the Honey Lake Maidu assertion that they were not homeless Indians, but people who had always lived and made their homes, one way or another, in the Honey Lake Valley. Yet the fact remains that had they moved to the rancheria—or had they been awarded their own—they would have Federal Recognition today.

THE SUSANVILLE INDIANS
AND THE SUSANVILLE FIELD MATRON

The letters and reports of the Susanville field matron offer us a tantalizing glimpse of how individual tribal identities were lost/mis-recognized by the government in this period, to the end result of their members' non-Recognition today.[6]

The role of the Indian Field Service's matron was to assimilate Indian women as quickly and efficiently as possible.[7] She was part of a hierarchy of bureaucratic order, below the male clerk and doctor, Indian Agency supervisors, and Washington, D.C.'s commissioner of Indian Affairs. The Indian Agencies, the "fields" within which a field matron worked, were shifting geographies of state control: while Edith M. Young was matron for the Susanville area (itself defined only by the abundance of Indian persons), it was aligned with the Greenville, California, Agency, and then, later, the Roseburg, Oregon, Agency.[8] Indian Agents from each location tried to shuffle Susanville back and forth until Young was fired in 1919, her position done away with, and the Susanville Indians, as they were known in the government's tribeless bureaucratese, were left matronless, but thoroughly changed by the experience.

Important to sorting out this history are stories about Young that are still circulated among Honey Lake Maidu members today. Ron Morales told me that his uncle, George Peconom, who was born in 1871, used to "romance" Miss Young. "George told

me he'd bring her flowers and candies." Such a personal connection implies Young's strong alliance to the community.
Similarly, Viola Williams remembers her mother, Leona, and
grandmother, Roxie, mentioning the field matron fondly. "It
was always 'Miss Young did this' or 'Miss Young did that,'" she
told me. Thus it is a distinct possibility that while the government's programs for Indian people inflicted their own kind of
changes, such changes may have been welcomed in the face of
more disruptive transformations such as the loss of the possibilities of traditional freedom. Viola Williams commented, intending
a compliment, "She was a matron, like the matrons I had at
Sherman [Institute, in Riverside, California—an Indian boarding
school]—she looked out for our welfare, and she oversaw us."

Edith Young's first official field report, from April 13, 1900—
submitted to the Greenville superintendent and then forwarded
to Washington, D.C.—notes that she visited twenty-six Indian
families, three of which lived in what she termed "tepees."[9]
But despite this "primitive condition," she made "suggestions
in a few homes, pictures [were] given, etcetera," as per her job
description. By August of the same year, she describes three
"results," the term from the government report sheet:

1. Four funerals conducted with regular Christian services, with the
result that it is now the wish of all the Indian people to have all
funerals conducted in this way. 2. A desire on the part of practically
all parents to send their children to school. 3. An increased respect
for the Sabbath and desire for greater knowledge of the Bible.[10]

Things were "shaping up" in the Indian camps—shaping up
along the government's lines. One might remark upon the
orderliness that Young seemed to be instituting and certainly
emphasizing, and that her three simple results would have
represented tremendous changes in Maidu lives and lifestyles.
By January 1901, Young even reports that "the Indian people
[were] addressed at one 'Big Time.'" By so doing, the matron was

inserting her government's dictates into Maidu ritual and festival. Meanwhile, she got out a "most successful Christmas tree."

Still, questions remain as to whether Young exaggerated her results for her supervisors (who, it must be noted, repeatedly added comments to her reports second-guessing the gravity of the situations she described) and whether she downplayed what remained of Indian tradition—after all, the official field report format asked for results and not recidivism. What is certain is that Maidu traditions endured, for they have been carried on to this day: the Bear Dance, which was perhaps one of the "Big Times" she mentioned, continued to be held throughout her tenure as matron. We know that in the area known to the Honey Lake Maidus as *hannam sewim*, a Bear Dance was held in 1910, previous to which Leigh Ann Hunt notes that Young requested "detectives to try to prevent liquor sales when the Indians have their Big Time in Buntingville May 22" (1996, 27). Notably, it was at this Bear Dance that Walter Peconom was killed by Sheriff Leavitt.

These had been the "big results" years. But by 1915 Young wrote, simply and perhaps fondly, in answer to question fourteen on the report form—"What report can you make with reference to returned [Sunday school] students? What have you been able to do for them?"—"I try to keep them interested in the weekly religious services, encourage them to come to my home in a social way and for singing; and keep them supplied with books for reading and study."

Ron Morales tells me his impression was always that Edith Young was fired because the Susanville Indians complained so much about her inability to make any material changes for them. Yet the Indian community, from what I can gather from statements by Ron and by Viola Williams, and from letters in the Bureau of Indian Affairs' files, had its own job description for Young, one which involved helping the Indians when they needed their allotment money. Ron, for instance, speaks approvingly of how she helped his family access their assets to cover the cost of Walter Peconom's funeral in 1910—despite the confusion over who had opened fire upon whom in the shoot-out with the sheriff. And he once explained the whole Indian Agency system to me as if it were actually just a big bank that didn't pay interest.

One can see how Young's dual alliances—to the Indian people and to the government—would have put her in a position at odds with both. Indeed, control over allotment lands and assets was of utmost importance to the government, as well as to the Honey Lake Maidus. It meant control over the direction of the Indians' development, essential to the whole bureaucratic project, which in this light can be read as one of patronizing, civilizing, and defining them out of existence.

Indeed, despite Indian resistance via the reinterpretation of the role of the field matron and the survival of the Bear Dance and certain cultural values, real changes *were* effected by the Indian Service, and no resistance was complete. Most important, Maidu families indigenous to Susanville and its environs were settled enough—or taught—to not *want* to live on the local reservation set aside for homeless Indians when it came to that. After all, the government had long been working to erase tribal identities—in part by refusing to mention tribal affiliations, in part by encouraging the lumping together of the Indian community—as it tried to turn the Indian in the direction of the Jeffersonian citizen farmer, economic hurdles and racism notwithstanding. For even as they were sending matrons to "save," "transform," and "develop" them, the Indian Bureau was creating washerwomen and ranch hands, bottom rung vocational additions to the white world's economic order.

REORGANIZING, TERMINATING, RELOCATING, AND RECOGNIZING CALIFORNIA INDIAN PEOPLES, IN THE NAME OF "FREEDOM"

In 1934 Congress attempted to reverse the toll taken on tribal structures by the bureaucratic lumping of Indian people during the allotment period with the Indian Reorganization Act (IRA, also known as the Wheeler-Howard Act). This legislation, drafted in large part by attorney Felix Cohen, was inspired by the Commissioner of Indian Affairs John Collier's vision of preserving tribal assets while developing tribal political structures. The IRA encouraged Indian communities to establish themselves as collective corporations to manage their resources and govern themselves communally by tribal councils organized to certain specifications. At its foundation was Collier's romantic, even stereotyped, notion of Indianness, which stretched to the communitarian and depicted the cultural values of the nation's many tribes as antithetical to modern America's urban and capitalist lifestyles.

In the end, however, the tenets of the original bill were compromised in Congress to suit the public's need for restricting Indian claims to resources. Collier's vision that Indian people should learn to live well among their own kind, preserving and managing their tribal resources in tribal collectivities, ironically ended up tying the tribes closer to American politico-economic structures. Indeed, today the IRA is often glossed as having been a convenient structure for allowing state access to tribal mineral and energy resources.[11] Furthermore, because the Indian Reorganization Act sought to protect Indian cultures and political forms as *rights*, it simultaneously bound tribes ever closer to legal-administrative forms of political existence and expression.

In a circular way, the IRA defined tribe as "any Indian tribe, organized band, pueblo, or the Indians residing on one reservation," thus both building its definition upon the idealized image of the land-holding tribes and bureaucratizing a notion of "tribal organization." Having an IRA-organized tribal government (possessed of land) came to define tribe for the U.S. government. But most significantly for my argument in this book, the IRA reinvigorated the government's use of the notions of Federal Recognition and non-Recognition.

William W. Quinn, lawyer and former Branch of Acknowledgment and Research historian, has written about the fluctuations in the meaning of the term *recognition* over time (1990). In particular, Quinn identifies a change from a *cognitive* understanding of recognizing Indian tribes to a *jurisdictional* Recognition of them. This can be dated to 1871, when Congress acted to end the practice of government-to-government treaty making with tribes. Before 1871, recognizing a tribe meant owning up to the existence of that tribe.[12] After 1871, as the term became bureaucratized, it began to carry a sense of the government's dominion. This was firmly entrenched as a kind of bureaucratic dominion by the 1930s and the Indian Reorganization Act.

And so the very opposition raised in 1872 by the commissioner of Indian Affairs to the concept of the federal ability to r/Recognize tribes remains salient today: Commissioner Francis Walker asked, "How are Indians, never yet treated with, but having every way as good and complete rights to portions of our territory as had the Cherokee, Creeks, Choctaw and Chickasaws, for instance, to the soil of Georgia, Alabama, Mississippi, to establish their rights?" (quoted in Quinn 1990, 347). Walker apparently understood that, in its jurisdictional hubris, not only was the government Recognizing certain tribes as legitimate, but it was also "delegitimizing" others.

The threat of delegitimation, or non-Recognition, that looms behind the jurisdictional stance of the Federal Acknowledgment procedures today also has particularly clear ties to the Indian Reorganization Act of 1934. The IRA identified tribes by geographic and social proximity to one another (those "having a common bond of occupation, or association, or residence with a well-defined neighborhood, common unity, or rural district"), blood quantum (first proposed as a 25 percent requirement for individual members but later enacted as a 50 percent requirement), lineage, and a kind of corporate organization based on a formal constitution, bylaws, and a membership list. This definition of tribe uncomfortably melded a cognitive approach to Indianness with a jurisdictional one, suggestive of the compromises that occurred in its transformation from bill to final act. Particularly, lawyer and historian Terry Anderson has noted that the bill "contained no reference to tribes 'now under federal jurisdiction,' and . . . [further,] [t]he word 'recognized' would seem to [have referred] only to the fact of a group's existence" (1978, 9). John Collier himself clarified for members of the congressional committees on Indian Affairs who questioned his intended cognitive notion of recognition: "The object of this definition is to include all Indian persons who, by reason of residence, are definitely members of Indian groups, as well as persons who are Indians by reason of degree of blood" (ibid.). The object, in other words, was lowercase r recognition of existing tribes. Yet the means by which this would occur—particularly, the problems with identification of tribalness "by reason of residence"—led to a kind of jurisdictional stance, and, eventually, the capital R Federal Recognition process.[13]

Indeed, the same requirements of Indianness established by the Indian Reorganization Act are uncritically used today by the Branch of Acknowledgment and Research, and, in the same way as the IRA, the boundaries it sets for Recognized tribes work as doorkeepers of a door that rarely opens for petitioners. Tribalness "by reason of residence" (see the Federal Acknowledgment procedure's Criterion B in appendix A) transparently parallels the interest in resource extraction and domination that has driven U.S. Indian policy from its earliest days: the tribes that matter to the state are those with resources. This is also to say that, from the state's perspective, if tribes exist that have no land and no Acknowledgment, it is better to keep them that way.

THE INDIAN FREEDOM ACT

Continuing in this tradition of battering away at the tribal resources and sociopolitical structures of Indian peoples, Congress proposed an Indian Freedom Act in 1953, House Concurrent Resolution 108. It was a reaction to both the land claims cases (which seemed, threateningly, like Indian people fighting for their sovereignty) and the Indian Reorganization Act (which, in its limited way, was reentrenching *tribe* as a political category). The "freedom" this new act proposed was the end of any and all fiduciary or trust relationships between the federal government and various Indian groups. What it meant was tribal termination. In 1958, after several failed attempts to have the California tribes collaborate in their termination through an insidious tribal consultation process,[14] Congress passed California's Rancheria Termination Act. It listed forty-one rancherias that were to be terminated after the tribes had consented to a plan for the distribution of their assets, and after each rancheria had been provided with certain infrastructural improvements. Thirty-eight of the rancherias on the list eventually consented, "largely because the BIA misrepresented the purpose of the program, and coerced tribal members to approve the distribution plans" (ACCIP 1997b, 14). Bureau "Termination" meant they were now ineligible for federal benefits and no longer Recognized by the government. The Greenville Indian Rancheria, in Indian Valley, a close Mountain Maidu neighbor of the Honey Lake Maidus, was Terminated as a tribe. Termination meant a loss of tribal lands yet again. The Terminated tribes were free of the government's bureaucracy—but were also opened to culture loss as federal protections fell away.

In 1983 California Indian Legal Services filed a class-action suit, *Tillie Hardwick v. United States,* on behalf of twenty-eight California tribes, arguing that the government had turned its back on its trust responsibility and the provisions of the Rancheria Act by not providing the infrastructural improvements to the tribes marked for Termination. The government offered a settlement for seventeen of the tribes, and they were un-Terminated.[15]

While the Honey Lake Maidus could not have been Terminated by the Rancheria Termination Act because they were not party to a rancheria, the act nevertheless had effects on tribes similarly un-Acknowledged. As the ACCIP *Recognition Report* notes,

> In effect, the policy shift from tribal organization and support for tribal self-government to termination of federal status effectively precluded these unacknowledged tribes from obtaining services for the first time from the BIA. The BIA was not about to recognize these tribes as eligible for federal services when it was both eliminating the level of services to existing federally recognized tribes and terminating the trust relationship with some of those previously recognized tribes. (1997c, 14–15)

Had the BIA recognized its responsibility to the off-rancheria Honey Lake Maidus before the dispersal of tribal members in the sixties and seventies, their probability of meeting one of the BIA list's fatal "checks" would have been greatly reduced. Yet the reality is that, for the Honey Lake Maidus, the Great Depression, the experience at Indian boarding schools like Sherman (which trained Indian children for vocational work oriented toward city life), and the World Wars had already dislocated much of the tribe. John Peconom (who is in his eighties and the grandson of Roxie and John Peconom) was sent to the Indian boarding school in Riverside, California, and he notes that this moved him into what he called "non-traditional locales": he went to college, joined the army, and settled at a job in Richmond, California.

Other families moved away from their homelands out of economic necessity. Dilly Frow, whose family moved from Susanville to San Francisco for work in the 1920s, back to Susanville, and then back again to San Francisco in the late 1930s, emphasizes the ties of tribe despite such relocations. "Whenever you had a problem, you could go back to Susanville. You knew someone there would feed you and yours."

Still, in the sixties and seventies, as more of their allotment lands were sold or lost due to mismanagement, the dislocation of the tribe became more complete. Richard Morales, Ron and Viola's brother, for example, was encouraged by the federal Indian Relocation program to move to Cleveland, Ohio, where he worked as a bus driver. The Relocation policy overlapped with Termination, running from the 1950s into the 1970s.[16] Its focus on finding jobs for Indian people—which tended to be in locations far removed from their tribes—extended the geographic scattering of families and transformed the idea of the tribal geographic and cultural core. The core, or tribal heart and homeland, became remote in time and space. For the Peconom descendants, of Roxie Peconom's twelve children, seven bore children of their own, and in this third generation, Relocation or time at an Indian boarding school resulted in parts of at least five of their families living far from the Honey Lake Valley.

FROM RECOGNITION TO ACKNOWLEDGMENT

It was 1978 when the Department of the Interior (DOI) came up with a set of rules for Acknowledging Indian peoples (or "entities," as the government called them) wishing to be recognized as official tribes—the same Indian peoples who had been administratively elbowed out of the official federal relationship by policies aimed at exactly that for over one hundred years. In the 1970s, as today, the government's concerns with definitions of Indianness and tribe were closely tied to the politico-juridical pressures of current events, including two contemporary federal court cases in which the determination of tribal status—and Indian access to non-Indian resources—figured prominently.

In 1975 the Passamaquoddy tribe won its case against the state of Maine, when District Court Justice Grignoux held that the Indian Trade and Non-Intercourse Act of 1790 applied to all tribes, whether formally Recognized or not. An oft-ignored act still on the books, the non-intercourse aspect of the act forbade the alienation of Indian lands without permission of Congress.[17] *Passamaquoddy v. Morton* translated into three hundred thousand acres of "average quality timber lands" for the tribe and an option on two hundred thousand more (Brodeur 1985, 107).

Also in 1975, Ninth Circuit Court of Appeals Justice Boldt ruled that Indian tribes, whether Recognized or non-Recognized, that exercised treaty fishing rights in Washington were entitled to half the commercial fishing catch (*United States v. Washington*). Following *Passamaquoddy* and *United States v. Washington*, the small number of petitions for status adjustment before the BIA ballooned to forty. It was quite suddenly in the government's interest to develop a new means of regulating Indianness. The DOI put a moratorium on evaluating the tribal determination cases before them so that the department could figure out what to do.

At the time, Washington's Stillaguamish tribe's case was up for evaluation. The moratorium sideswiped their petition, putting them on hold indefinitely. The tribe decided to sue the assistant secretary–Indian Affairs in federal court (*Stillaguamish v. Kleppe* [1976]) and the court ruled with the tribe that the BIA's delay was "arbitrary and capricious," ordering an evaluation of the case within thirty days. The outcome was that the Stillaguamish were quickly Recognized and the BIA promised to prioritize the creation of a set of criteria for making tribal determinations.

One option would have been to follow the advice offered by the commission Congress had authorized to advise on the situation of Native peoples, the American Indian Policy Review Commission. The American Indian Policy Review Commission's Task Force Ten delivered a "Report on Terminated and Nonfederally Recognized Indians," concluding that "'federal recognition' and 'non-recognition' are really terms used to arbitrarily exclude Indians from services and that all Indians are included within the plain meaning of the statutes.

It is clear that budgetary considerations have dictated Indian affairs" (U.S. Congress 1976, 1096). It recommended an office *outside* the BIA to establish the existence of federal relations with tribes who supposedly had never had any. "The term 'non-federally recognized,'" reads the report, "need not be used again. Obviously, the statutes do not authorize the distinction." (ibid., 1098).

Tom Tureen, the directing attorney at the Native American Rights Fund, worked out the "obviousness" of this statement in legal terms for the report. Much of Tureen's reading of the statutes relied on the assumption that non-Recognized tribes had signed treaties with the federal government. For the situation of a tribe like the Honey Lake Maidus, which cannot prove decisively that its leaders signed the Wozencraft treaty at Chico,[18] Tureen pointed to 1891's *Tully v. the United States*, which was a case about the U.S. government's liability for certain tribes' roles in frontier violence.

Congress did not intend to limit the liability for depredations simply to those tribes, bands, or nations that sustained treaty relations with the United States. . . .

The policy of the United States in dealing with the Indians has been, as we understand, to accept the subdivision of the Indians into such tribes or bands as the Indians themselves adopted, and to treat with them accordingly. (1976, 1672)

Crucially, what *Tully* means for this context is that tribes possess an original sovereignty that the state should duly recognize. Recognition via treaties or other official U.S. business conclusively proves that a tribe exists, but a lack of such evidence does not mean that a tribe does not.

Yet instead of a radical turn toward *Tully* and an immediate extension of Recognition/Restoration to the non-Recognized and Terminated tribes, the government chose a more restrictive route, for the electorate's stake was in protecting its property from Indian land claims rather than in addressing their social injustices. The government turned to the bureaucracy and what it produced was the Federal Acknowledgment procedures.

THE FEDERAL ACKNOWLEDGMENT PROCESS

The Department of the Interior's 1978 criteria were based loosely on the "Cohen Criteria," named after Felix Cohen, well known for both his work on the Indian Reorganization Act and his *Handbook of Federal Indian Law,* which was published under the auspices of the Department of the Interior in 1942. The Cohen Criteria, stated in the *Handbook,* were "considerations" of tribal determination that had manifested themselves organically in the practice of law and tribe-state relations. Although, as we might imagine, the history of such relations as reflected in the law was often contradictory, Cohen's criteria rationalized Indian policy—the criteria reflect something more than a simple summary of precedence.[19] Significantly, Tureen's analysis had followed the lead established by the Cohen Criteria, and, indeed, the reader will find that the *Tully* ruling looms largely in the background. "The considerations," wrote Cohen,

which singly or jointly, have been relied upon in reaching the conclusion that a group constitutes a "tribe" or "band" have been:

(1) That the group has had treaty relations with the United States.
(2) That the group has been denominated a tribe by act of Congress or Executive order.
(3) That the group has been treated as having collective rights in tribal lands or funds, even though not expressly designated a tribe.
(4) That the group has been treated as a tribe or band by other Indian tribes.
(5) That the group has exercised political authority over its members, through a council or other governmental forms (1982 [1971]: 271).

Other, *less conclusive,* considerations, according to Cohen, are congressional appropriations, the group's "social solidarity," and other ethnological and historical determinations. Even more significantly, according to the Cohen Criteria, *any* of these five main criteria were enough to warrant tribal Recognition for legal purposes.

But Cohen also explained that Indian case law had specified that "it is not enough, however, to show that any of the foregoing elements existed at some time in the remote past" (ibid., 271). To this end, he cited the solicitor's opinion on the status of the Miami and Peori Indians under the Oklahoma Indians Warfare Act (1936):

It is not enough that the ethnographic history of the two groups shows them in the past to have been distinct and well-recognized tribes or bands. A particular tribe or band may well pass out of existence as such in the course of time. The word "recognized" as used in the Oklahoma Indians Welfare Act involves more than past existence as a tribe and its historical recognition as such. There must be a currently existing group distinct and functioning as a group in specific respects and recognition of such activity must have been shown by specific actions of the Indian Office, the Department, or by Congress. (ibid. 271–72)

Nevertheless, Cohen noted the pitfalls of making such a determination: "The question of tribal existence has generally been treated by the courts as a simple yes-or-no question. It remains true, however, that an Indian tribe may 'exist' for certain purposes and not for others" (ibid. 272).

This issue of tribal existence versus extinction is, legally and analytically, an extremely hairy one. Cohen's nod in the direction of the idea that "there must be a currently existing group distinct and functioning as a group in specific respects" was translated, in the political contexts of the creation of the Federal Acknowledgment criteria, to mean that successful petitioners must show "identification as an American Indian entity on a substantially continuous basis since 1900." By "substantially continuous," the Branch of Acknowledgment and Research means to say that "there are no long interruptions in the tribe's members doing things together such as living together, worshipping together or meeting and making decisions on behalf of the group" (1997, 44). And what this means in practice today is that the answer to the question, "Does there have to be some kind of documentation [of social and political continuities] from each decade since 1900?" is "Yes" (ibid.) It is this burden that makes otherwise reasonable criteria practically absurd: what the criteria require is documentary evidence for continuities that are exceptional among dominated peoples, in large part because to find such evidence, one must turn to the dominators' records. And those records reveal a disproportional preoccupation with the "unmaking" of the nation's tribes.

What also becomes clear when comparing the Cohen Criteria with the list of federal criteria (see appendix A) is that the 1978 Criteria for Federal Acknowledgment not only amplified the amount of proof needed to win recognition *seven times*, but they also shifted the emphasis toward a heavy reliance upon anthropological and historical evidences, making treaties and acts of Congress nondeterminative on their own. Anthropology and anthropologists—this one included—have, ever since, been a necessary part of the Federal Acknowledgment Process.

ACKNOWLEDGMENT'S BUREAUCRACY

Jack Campisi, anthropologist and critic of the Federal Acknowledgment process, has written that "the word 'acknowledgment' was a semantic sleight-of-hand, a way to sidestep a challenge that the regulations were an invasion of Congress's plenary power" (n.d., 3). For Campisi, this sleight of hand reveals as much as it conceals: in his reading, only Congress can Recognize the government-to-government relationship between a tribe and the state. *Acknowledgement* was a secretarial designation proffered by the Solicitor's Office of the Department of the

Interior, parent office of the Bureau of Indian Affairs. Attorney
Faith Roessel explains that "accordingly, a tribe named in a
treaty or receiving benefits from an act of Congress has been
recognized, and *acknowledging* that status is an administrative,
perhaps nondiscretionary act" (1989, 2, author's italics).

Yet discretion was precisely the reason for creating a super-
visory role over Recognition, and, predictably, an elaborate set
of regulations and bureaucracies was devised for evaluating
and Acknowledging tribes. Congress's recognition of the BIA
by giving it the crucial power of Acknowledging tribes—
which in effect made Recognition and Acknowledgment synony-
mous—conforms to the historical pattern of injustice toward
Indian peoples: as we saw in the allotment period, Indian futures
would become more and more contingent upon administrative options rather than nationally enforceable law.

The new bureaucratic apparatus imposed on those groups
seeking such "status adjustment" was the Branch of Acknowledgment and Research (BAR). BAR comprised three teams of
three members empowered to review the genealogical,
anthropological, and historical aspects of what came to be
known as a tribe's *petition,* the word itself one of submission.
Next, the procedures were set. A Letter of Intent to Petition
would assign the tribe a number in the ever-growing queue of
petitioners. Petitions received by BAR would be welcomed
with review and then a Letter of Obvious Deficiencies.[20] Then,
after an unspecified amount of time, the revised petition would
go on active status. While active, one of the BAR teams would
review the petition and issue a proposed finding. Next, the
petitioner and "interested parties" would have 120 days to
comment on the proposed finding. Finally, a Final Determination would be stated by the assistant secretary–Indian Affairs.
Petitioners and others might file requests for reconsideration
with the Interior Board of Indian Appeals.

The lived reality of the experience of petitioning will be
discussed fully in chapters four and five, but it is important to

emphasize here the exertion demanded of the process: the queue of petitioners was 188 tribes long as of February 2005, and while the Branch of Acknowledgement and Research does not like to make any promises, it averages about one petition review per year. A sense of this experience might be expressed through analogy to Kafka's "In the Penal Colony" (1971 [1919]). BAR's process is like that story's unstoppable machine of torture, the Harrow, which slowly, literally inscribes (with painful, barbed quills) a prisoner's sentence upon his body.

THE RISKS OF REFORM
IN THE CONTEXT OF A CASINO BACKLASH

I have argued that, for all intents and purposes, 1978's Federal Acknowledgment process created a science of Indianness. Rigidifying post-IRA understandings, this science was based on an idea of the existence of two types of Indians to whom the state should, and should not, administer: the Recognized and the non-Recognized. Task Force Ten's radical and idealistic recommendations were betrayed by the government in its 1978 Federal Acknowledgment regulations, which empowered the administrative branch and made the Cohen Criteria into a tight-fitting noose for the non-Recognized tribes. This history makes painful the reality that, in 2004, the very changes suggested in 1977 are still being requested. The Advisory Council on California Indian Policy's California Tribal Status Act of 1997 brought Task Force Ten's suggestion of an office outside of the BIA to review Recognition cases back before Congress. It also proposed substantial changes to the Acknowledgment criteria in terms of the evidentiary burden. Though it did not meet with success, the vision lives on. Its most recent reincarnations were H.R. 361, and S. 611, both from 1999. Neither was adopted.

The missing piece needed to understand the puzzle of why the Federal Acknowledgment process is so impervious to reform

is Indian gaming. Today the pressure upon the federal government for tightening the aperture for Federal Acknowledgment—
how many peoples get through—is the supposedly economically
aggressive tribal tactic of opening a casino.

In 1987 the U.S. Supreme Court affirmed, via *California v.
Cabazon Band of Mission Indians*, that the laws of the states
only apply to Indian Country when they are prohibitory laws
related to criminal sanctions. This meant that state regulatory
laws do *not* generally apply—and that California was denied
the right to regulate Indian gaming.[21] With the Indian Gaming
Regulatory Act (IGRA) of 1988, Congress extended this ruling
legislatively, even as it diluted its full implications. The act
stated that "Indian tribes have the exclusive right to regulate
gaming activity on Indian lands *if* the gaming activity is not
specifically prohibited by Federal law *and* is conducted within
a state which does not, as a matter of criminal law and public
policy, prohibit such gaming activity" (author's italics). It created
a National Indian Gaming Commission to obviate infiltration
by organized crime, and it required tribes wanting to conduct
Class III gaming (electronic gambling and card games played
against the house) to negotiate a compact with the state in
which the casino will be located.[22] The last provision involves
a clear concession of tribal sovereignty. Meanwhile, the IGRA
requires the state to come to the table for such negotiations
"in good faith," though there is no direct means of enforcing
this provision. (California's tribes found this to be true when
Governor Pete Wilson refused to negotiate with them in the
1990s. They retaliated by running their gaming operations as
they pleased, flouting the state's attempts to shut them down.)
Finally, unlike commercial gaming enterprises in Atlantic
City or Las Vegas, the Indian Gaming Regulatory Act stipulates
that the profits from Indian casinos left after giving the state
its cut be used exclusively for tribal development, social services,
and projects in the larger community (that is, for the surrounding
local governments).[23]

In practice, it has not only been the case that Recognized tribes seeking casinos have to make compacts with the state: the tribes simply seeking Federal Recognition are put under pressure to cut deals regarding gaming prospects with *local* government in order to win its support of their petitions, as well. Graton Rancheria in California, for example, which won Restoration of its tribal status as the Federated Indians of Graton Rancheria in December 2000 through Congress (a clever though difficult way to subvert the Federal Acknowledgment process), was initially only supported by Representative Lynn Woolsey on the condition that the tribe promise not to open a casino. Her Restoration bill was unanimously approved in June 2000, but then-Assistant Secretary–Indian Affairs Kevin Gover objected to the antigaming condition because of its implications for tribal sovereignty nationwide.

In sum, a major effect of the Indian Gaming Regulatory Act has been that making the discursive jump from knowing that a tribe is petitioning for Federal Recognition to thinking that they will open a casino has become a matter of course for local governments. And this means that while reform of Federal Acknowledgment was nearly impossible for over twenty years, it is now beginning to occur—in the direction of making the requirements *harder* for the tribes.

In California, the politics of gaming and the situation of the un-Acknowledged tribes intersect in ways that are elucidating. In November of 1998, in answer to Gov. Pete Wilson, California voters passed Proposition 5, which created a template for state compacts and represented approval for Indian gaming operations. It was later established as unconstitutional by state courts, but was followed up by another popularly supported ballot measure. In March of 2000, 54 percent of California voters showed their support for Proposition 1A and the idea of Indian gaming as a means for economic self-sufficiency for the state's tribes. By 2004, there were fifty-three casinos spread across the Golden State, and the new governor, Arnold Schwarzenegger, was trying to make good on his campaign promise that the gaming tribes would be made to pay their "fair share" to the state. In this context of transformation, California's tribes may gain political clout, especially if their casinos start gapping budget shortfalls. Yet the un-Acknowledged tribes, in particular, may become further marginalized: representatives of the governor's office assert that California does not negotiate with "landless tribes" (Kovner and Mason 2004, B1). And while there was early talk of a program of "revenue sharing" between gaming tribes and Acknowledged peoples who do not run casinos,[24] there is certainly also the tendency to look out for oneself: five tribes negotiated a deal with Gov. Schwarzenegger in June of 2004 that might set a precedent for the rest of the state's tribes, a precedent that 25 percent of the profits from excess slot machines (two thousand machines is the cutoff) would go to the state.[25] The overarching questions are whether a sovereign entity should have to pay a "fair share," what it means if they agree to do so, and, most important for me, whether the state is *due* a fair share when more than two-thirds of its tribes have never been extended the same.

Over the course of this chapter we have seen how Terminations have become de-Terminations, how congressional interventions sometimes make for justice, and how the work of organizations like the American Indian Policy Review Commission and the Advisory Council on California Indian Policy can offer critical resistance. But the message of Kafka's "The Legend," which opened this chapter, is about the lived reality of injustice in the meantime, in the interstices of these interventions. *The Trial's* K. is *never* able to prove he was wronged in having the process applied to him, even though the reader believes he was indeed wronged. Like the man from the country, K. waits before the door to the Law and he is, in fact, only waiting for his death. Kafka's final point is that absurdity only leads to more-horrible absurdity: at the end of the novel, K. is led to his death by twinned and bumbling bureaucrats, one on each of his arms. And the door to the Law is closed both for him and for the man from the country.

Because of this, I close with a sober reminder of the state's power. Georges Pierre Castile has posited that the key to understanding Indian policy is in its *anomaly*, which can only be explained by the rich symbolic place Native peoples hold in the American psyche; he claims, like Slagle, that "the message sent by Indian policy finds its significance in audiences other than the Indians themselves" (1992, 178). While I have worked to make economic and political *sense* of this history of Indian policy, as part of a continuing, systematic oppression for non-Indian economic gain, Castile brings the material and the symbolic perspectives together. He explains that, as a consequence of the national imaginary of Indianness, "the FAP [Federal Acknowledgment process] has . . . been more symbol than substance (only a few petitions have been approved), but it does at least constitute another symbolic commitment to the continued existence of tribal peoples" (ibid., 180–81.) If this is plausible, as I believe it is, we should specify that Federal Recognition appears to be a flimsy, solely symbolic commitment to Indianness, with a list of conditions: as long as gaming is not part of the scenario, as long as state sovereignty and administrative prerogative can remain intact, as long as the "right" determinations are made, and as long as the image of primordial Indianness can be preserved for the United States' legal-foundational myth of the Indian tribe.

CHAPTER THREE

MAPPING THE BOUNDARIES OF ANTHROPOLOGY AND TRIBE

AMERICAN ANTHROPOLOGISTS BEAR A PORTION OF THE RESPONSI-
bility for the myth of primordial Indianness, and, today, they
have a responsibility for reenvisioning it. For the case of Federal
Acknowledgment, the mandate couldn't be clearer because of
anthropology's role in the process. I agree with Jack Campisi's
statement that "if anthropology and history are to be used to
determine tribal status, then those who use it should adhere to
the standards of the disciplines and should be subject to scholarly
review by their peers. That is the burden they should bear"
(n.d., 12).[1] His comments reflect upon the irresponsible employment of anthropological considerations in Recognition decisions
without concomitant academic review. He implies that Federal
Acknowledgment is a system with limited accountability, whose
petitioners have little recourse in the event of a negative determination. That this is effected in the name of anthropology is,
indeed, disturbing.

The synthesis of evidence required for an Acknowledgment
petition puts a heavy anthropological burden upon tribes, neces-
sitating anthropological research, if not the employment of an
anthropologist.[2] Criterion A in 25 CFR Part 83.7 explains that

Evidence to be relied upon in determining the group's substantially
continuous identity shall include one or more of the following:
. . . (5) Identification as an Indian entity by anthropologists,
historians or other scholars.
(6) Repeated identification as an Indian entity in newspapers
and books.

(7) Repeated identification and dealing as an Indian entity with recognized Indian tribes. (Bureau of Indian Affairs 1994, 264)

BAR demands that Indian people assemble anthropological and historical evidences, which means that they carry the burden of, and are marked in a real way by, anthropologists' pronouncements upon them. Self-identification or identification by other Indians only comes last on the list. Anthropology's own complicated and perhaps flawed history of the analysis of culture change is what is emphasized in the tribe's case.

Perhaps the most well-known example of this is furnished by the Mashpee trial, *Mashpee Tribe v. New Seabury et al.* (1978). The Mashpee Wampanoag Indians had received title to their lands in the mid-1700s, yet they slowly lost authority to non-Indians in their town's political structures over the ensuing centuries. In 1978, the tribe sued one of the developers of the land still nominally theirs. The grounds for their case was the 1790 Indian Trade and Non-Intercourse Act, which forbade the sale of Indian lands by individual states without the authorization of Congress. This time around, if the tribe played it right, the occupation of Indian lands by non-Indians might be considered theft, by U.S. law.

Yet *Mashpee Tribe v. New Seabury et al.* also provided the state of Massachusetts an opportunity to respond to the federal extension of Indian sovereignty in the liminal period before the finalization of the Federal Acknowledgment criteria.[3] The trial became focused on the question of whether the Mashpees remained a tribe despite major changes over the course of three centuries of Contact, a tribe that had the right to bring a land claims suit against the state of Massachusetts. Over the course of the unraveling of *Mashpee Tribe v. New Seabury et al.*, the anthropological concepts of tribe and culture were made to carry the burden of their own proof. Eventually, they were casually discredited in favor of a kind of Cape Cod real estate developmental justice.

The juried trial's parallel to and its presaging of the Federal Acknowledgment process (FAP) are clear. The same question that most petitioning tribes face again and again in the Branch of Acknowledgment and Research's Letters of Obvious Deficiency was the question that cost the Mashpees their case with judge and jury: "In what ways are you a tribe?" does not often lend itself to a quantifiable answer when the financial stakes are so high, the historical burden so great, and the adjudicatory position one of skepticism. As the Mashpees' attorney, Lawrence Shubow, commented at the end of the trial, the legal machine seems only to have compounded arbitrary injustices: "We have a mystery. We have a tribe that was in existence [according to the jury] in 1834. What became of it? *Did it go into orbit?*" (quoted in Campisi 1991, 152, author's italics)[4]

Not into orbit, but the way of the dodo—or so the Mashpee outcome seemed to answer. What is clear is that the New Seabury defense attorneys quickly pulled anthropology's "tribe" apart. James Clifford described what anthropology on trial looked like in such a climate:

On the stand it was difficult to explain that the word *tribe* could mean different things to a scholar discussing a range of aboriginal systems, reservation Indians of the nineteenth century, and legally reorganized groups of the 1930s, or that the term was unlikely to mean the same thing for an author of evolutionist theories writing in the 1950s and an expert evaluating the aspirations of eastern Indian communities in the 1970s.

[Anthropologist] William Sturtevant's testimony compared various Native American tribes. Rather than asserting a sharp definition of the institution, he portrayed a field of family resemblances and local histories. He suggested that it would be simplistic and unjust to establish a list of essential "tribal" attributes against which individual cases could then be checked. (Clifford 1988, 322)

Yet these simplistic methods seem to be how the judge and jury decided whether the Mashpee Wampanoags were a tribe by all rights. As Clifford described, the fine line between an "Indian headband" and a bandanna in a teenager's hair was the measure the court believed it could justly tackle, and the slippery work of which the judge and jury made haste (see 1988, 346).

Legal definitions get caught up on the issue of culture change, just as anthropological definitions sometimes still do. And both legal and anthropological definitions of tribe are born of contexts of political and economic struggle. Morton Fried's slim volume, *The Notion of Tribe* (1975), in fact, lays out the case that the only workable definition of tribe is that it is a political artifact of the state's contemporary and historical interactions with Indian peoples. The Boston jury's denial of Mashpee tribal identity after three centuries of the violent creation of one fits here as a case in point.

CREATING CALIFORNIA'S TRIBES

Anthropologists have long been interested in the places where one cultural identity becomes describably distinct from another, and ethnography has long been a tool for either confirming or erasing such boundaries. In California, the scientific delineation of tribal groups by non-Indians began with the Spanish explorer Juan Rodriquez Cabrillo's expedition to Chumash territories (today's Santa Barbara vicinity) in 1542. No general ethnographic outline of the California tribes as a whole, however, was attempted during either the Spanish or Mexican periods of California's history, from 1542 to 1850. Science, it seems, was placed second to the absorbing state programs of domination, conversion, and economic exploitation.

After 1848's Treaty of Guadalupe Hidalgo, when Alta California was taken for the United States, the Californian project was an individualistic one, anchored by notions of Manifest Destiny and expressed through a frontier spirit of personal domination of the wilderness as well as the American dream of the gold rush. It was not until the journalist Stephen

Powers decided to traverse the state in the 1870s that a map of the state's diverse peoples' territories was penned.

After Powers, the mapping of Indian territories occupied Californian anthropology well into the 1960s (Heizer 1966, 2). Alfred Kroeber, in his 1925 *Handbook of the Indians of California*, emphasized the fact that territorial boundaries were a particularly logical place to begin when approaching California's Indian cultures:

There being no written documents, the element of time enters infinitely less than in works which it is customary to designate historical. In the stead of time, the geographical factor looms large. It is not that this dimension is necessarily more important in savage life than that of chronology; but it is a hundred times more readily operated in, and is on the whole the most available means through which some glimpses of time perspective are attainable. (1925, v)

Hand in hand with such mapping was the recording of language distinctions among Indian peoples. Linguistics was perceived to bridge the materialist-idealist chasm between tribal boundaries and tribal culture. As Robert F. Heizer explained it, "The main tribal units are identified on the basis of the languages which they spoke. The tribal map is, therefore, essentially a linguistic map. Within the geographically bounded major-language units, it is possible to establish subdivisions which are based upon speech dialects, or politically separate units" (1966, 9).

Indeed, in the late nineteenth century, John Wesley Powell, director of the Bureau of American Ethnology, had sent a series of linguists—among them Henry W. Henshaw, Jeremiah Curtin, Albert Gatschet, and J. Owen Dorsey—to California to "collect vocabularies" and establish these all-important linguistic/territorial boundaries (Heizer 1966, 19).[5] In 1891, Powell's monumental *Indian Linguistic Families of America, North of Mexico* divided California into twenty-two language families. In 1913, Roland Dixon and Kroeber reduced the number of language families from twenty-two to fifteen; in 1919, Kroeber whittled the number down to seven on the basis of more study and comparison: Penutian, Hokan, Algonkian, Athabascan, Uto-Aztecan, Yukian, and Lutuamian, represented graphically as a map. Today, this linguistic map remains the most popular depiction of Indian California.

How ethnolinguistics connects to the reality of territorial ownership, and how anthropology's pronouncements connect to state practices, are both exemplified by the California land claims cases. California's Land Claims Commission hearings should be regarded as of particular importance to this study of Federal Acknowledgment, for in the hearings we find anthropologists testifying, similarly, for or against Indian interests, and we find a significant instance of the bureaucratic engulfing of California's tribes. In the end, the Land Claims Commission also allows us a glimpse through the aperture of justice afforded the tribes by the state.

LAND CLAIMS IN CALIFORNIA: 1928, 1946

In 1928, the California Indians Jurisdictional Act authorized California's attorney general to sue the federal government on behalf of the tribes whose lands had been stolen following the nonratification of the treaties of 1851–52. The claims of all tribal plaintiffs were consolidated, and the descendants of any Indian living in California on July 1, 1852, were qualified to participate. Although not every claimant knew which treaty their ancestors had signed, they were allowed a part of the settlement, "based," as the ACCIP put it, "on the Congressional and administrative presumption that all Indians of California, given the choice, would have chosen treaty-making to outright annihilation" (ACCIP 1997b, 12). The case was settled, sixteen years later, in 1944. Payments were for the most part distributed during the 1950s, though it should be noted that the last occurred in 1974.

A second land claims case was authorized as 1946's U.S. Indian Claims Commission Act. California's tribes felt that the settlement of the 1928 claims had been unjustly minimized when the government subtracted the Bureau of Indian Affairs' administrative costs from the award. Essentially, the tribes had had 7.5 million acres stolen from them in the 1850s, and their compensation, in the 1940s, had been only $5 million. This second case was only settled in 1963, though some distributions remain outstanding to this day (see ACCIP 1997b, 12). California's Indian people were awarded $29.1 million for sixty-four million acres west of the Sierra. The Honey Lake Maidus, like most California Indians, recall receiving individual checks for $633.00.[6]

The 1946 Indian Claims Commission Act was grounded in anthropological-cum-legal understandings. Claims to aboriginal title were to be founded upon proof of discrete groups occupying discrete pieces of land. Anthropological conceptions of how a tribe legitimately occupied land it owned tended toward economic and ecological understandings of tribe. The anthropologists employed as expert witnesses struggled over these awkward representations of the reality of California Indian land use.

The anthropologists, in fact, were dramatically divided. Some of Kroeber's own students found themselves opposite their mentor, testifying for the government.[7] Kroeber argued for the tribes, advancing a broad, ecologically based understanding of land use. Linguistic evidence—a people's names for local geographic features—was translated to mean that people's "ownership" of that area. The attorneys for the Department of Justice, and anthropologists such as Julian Steward, however, argued for a more limited understanding of aboriginal range and use. Julian Steward's claim, that a typical tribe used only core areas of the larger range at a significant rate, would have reduced the compensation to Native peoples by 80 percent. Although, in the end, the commission's finding was for the tribes, Steward had voiced legitimate concern over the way tribal land use was portrayed by Kroeber and Omer Stewart throughout the hearings, particularly as far as how a tribe's claim to the "broad version" of its territorial boundaries would hold up in practice. As late as 1970, Steward wrote, "O.C. Stewart's own data . . . show that neither band nor tribe members did in fact repel trespassers" at the ostensible edges of their lands (1970, 136).

The reader can imagine how an expansive definition of one tribe's territory might mean a diminished territory for another. Kroeber admitted that, occasionally, there was overlap between two tribes' holdings, but he believed that the more important issue was that of establishing a definite tradition of ownership in California in order to move toward restitution for the Indian peoples living there. Indeed, from one perspective, the individual claims of the tribes—and whether they overlapped or not—did not matter in immediate terms because of the way the Indians of California sued the U.S. government as a single unit. Yet for the tribes and their understandings of their history, it did and does matter. Kroeber's map of California was used in the commission hearings, and it is a map that represents an uneasy compromise of the ethnological evidences as to which tribe claims, for example, the Honey Lake Valley. For the Lassen County region, it depicts Maidu, Paiute, and Washoe peoples all meeting at Honey Lake. Because of this compromise, the Northern Paiute claim on Honey Lake Valley was subtracted from the acreage considered in the California settlement. Ron Morales cannot forget that this means that the government has validated Paiute claims on Honey Lake Valley. Having established a definite tradition of ownership among California's peoples, Kroeber's case seems, to Ron, to have proceeded to give away the land the Honey Lake Maidus claimed, and still claim, is theirs and theirs alone.

The lasting ill effect of Kroeber's map on the relationships between the Maidus and Paiutes in Honey Lake Valley, as well as Julian Steward's dissent with the legally upheld econo-ecological definition of tribe, serve as reminders of the political nature of such defining. This was not entirely lost on Kroeber, who, though comfortable testifying for a broad definition of tribal territory and submitting a map full of compromise, questioned the use of tribe as a descriptive at all. After the Claims Commission hearings, he wrote,

> It is impossible fully to examine continental conditions in the present compass. There were tribes that fitted our conventional image of the tribe: in the Plains, perhaps also in the East; there were more groups that did not fit it. The ethnic nationality is sure, as having been usual in most of the United States and Canada. So is the band-village-community-tribelet group. "The tribe" [however] is a minority phenomenon. It might yet prove to be wholly a phenomenon of Caucasian contact, construal, pressure, or administrative convenience. This is at least a problem to be kept in mind. (1955, 312)

Kroeber had applied the term *tribelet* to California groups since the 1920s, describing it through analogy to the preunification German or Italian states. *Tribe*, as used in the East and on the Plains, reflected much larger populations with concomitantly elaborated political institutions and hierarchies. *Tribe* as such simply did not exist in the same model in California, Kroeber claimed, where a few hundred members, representing linked kin groups, filled the organizational capacity for social cohesion. Kroeber argued that, for California, the state did not deal with the fundamental sovereign political unit, the tribelet; it dealt, for its own convenience, only with the larger unit, the tribe. Nonetheless, he worked to adapt the term *tribe* to the California situation, perhaps because he recognized the unsupportable insult contained in the diminutive term. Kroeber explained that

> in any strict usage, the word "tribe" denotes a group of people that act together, feel themselves to be a unit, and are sovereign in a defined territory. Now, in California, these traits attached to the

Masut Pomo, again to the Elem Pomo, and the Yokaia Pomo, and to the 30 other Pomo tribelets. They did not attach to the Pomo as a whole, because the Pomo as a whole did not act or govern themselves, or hold land as a unit. In other words, there was strictly no such tribal entity as "the Pomo"; there were 34 Pomo miniature tribes. (ibid., 100)

In so stating the state of Native California, Kroeber's words critically undermine the meaning of *tribe* emphasized by the Federal Acknowledgment process in its dealings with California's Indian peoples.

The 1946 Land Claims Commission's decision was appealed, and the final case was not decided until 1963.[8] After the appeal, hearings were held to determine whether the "Indians of California" was an identifiable group with the right to present a claim in the first place. The Indian Claims Commission found that the Indians of California was indeed an identifiable group, as defined by the California Indian rolls (*Thompson et al. v. United States* [1964]). Yet the unfortunate result of such a large grouping with a singular verb, as well as the manner in which the California Indian rolls, beginning in 1928, had asked for an applicant's tribe by way of descent from Indian individuals, was that participants were conceived of as persons with Indian blood instead of as members of particular tribes. This means that today, participation in the land claims suits is not considered evidence of any value in the Federal Acknowledgment proceedings. That the result of the hearings denied "tribe" to the claimants in the end indicates a larger denial and might be understood as part of a long-term effort aimed at cultural erasure. Lumping the tribes' land claims cases together as a single case on behalf of the Indians of California versus the United States,[9] state and anthropological testimony served to reinforce the idea that most of California's Native peoples were unnamed—tribally nondescript and even nonexistent.

ANTHROPOLOGICAL SHORTCOMINGS AT THE
BRANCH OF ACKNOWLEDGMENT AND RESEARCH

In the fall of 1992, at a hearing on Federal Recognition before
the House of Representative's Committee of the Interior and
Insular Affairs, Eni Faleomaveaga, the congressional representative from American Samoa, asked George Roth, BAR anthropologist, whether there was a consensus on the validity of the
government's definition of Indianness. Roth answered, "I would
say that our comments from anthropologists under the regulations
indicate a definite lack of agreement as to what this criteria
should be" (1992, 37). There is, indeed, a great deal of disagreement, which itself reveals the extent to which the criteria of tribe
do not work—and that means that there is something for anthropologists to agree upon.[10] The agreement to disagree coalesces
around a single idea: that via the Federal Acknowledgment
process, a discipline whose strengths lie in methodological
subjectivity, comparative evaluation and cultural relativism
are used to make hard and fast determinations. The disaster
that is determining Federal Acknowledgment, in other words,
has much to do with the application of anthropological expertise
to such an inflexible format as that of the tightly circumscribed
tribe the government is willing to Recognize. While anthropology
as a discipline has turned away from a conception of tribe as
an evolutionary stage in primitive humanity's progression toward
statehood, it has retained tribe's usefulness as an ethnographic
concept. Today, the anthropological definition of tribe could be
said to differ from one such entity to the next, based on a combination of self-identification and history. Yet this relativism
was not helpful to the Mashpees in the mid-70s, nor is it helpful
to today's petitioners: when faced with binding judgments—the
possibility of administrative Termination—lengthy, subjective,
case-by-case analysis of each petition amounts to its own kind
of injustice.

When I consider anthropology's general contribution to the Acknowledgment proceedings, as well as the critique of so many anthropologists, nothing is more alarming to me than the testimony of the architect of the Federal Acknowledgment process, Bud Shapard. Shapard, former BAR chief, has worked, since retirement, on the Acknowledgment petitions of many un-Recognized tribes. He told those present at the 1992 congressional hearing on the Federal Acknowledgment process that "after fourteen years of trying to make the regulations which I drafted in 1978 work, I must conclude that they are fatally flawed and unworkable. They take too long to produce results. They are administratively too complicated. The decisions are subjective and are not necessarily accurate. The criteria are limited in scope and are not applicable to many of the petitioning groups which are in fact, viable Indian tribes" (U.S. House 1992b, 66).

Shapard explains that too much input became the regulations' curse. "There were, if I recall correctly, something on the order of 400 meetings, conversations and that sort of thing prior to the final drafting of the regulations. That was a blessing in one way because we really didn't know what we were doing. It was the first time anybody [had] tried to do this sort of thing. But it, in fact, proved to be the curse of the regulations" (ibid., 154). The parallels between the compromises involved in the creation of the Federal Acknowledgement process and the congressional compromises of the original IRA bill submitted by Collier and others in the early 1930s are striking.[11] But even more than the dilution of the original intent that occurred in both cases, I am interested in how the shortcomings of the IRA were *built into* the Federal Acknowledgment process.

In particular, I have found that peoples who possessed land bases were those approached for establishing IRA governments, and that these peoples modeled *tribe* for the 1978 codification of the definition.[12] It's a fact proven through the failure of the

Federal Acknowledgment criteria to reflect the experience of California's non-Recognized tribes. For a tribe like the Honey Lake Maidus, who never owned land communally under the U.S. legal system, proving a political relationship among members since 1900 (as per Criterion C) is extremely hard because there were few resources for leaders to allocate or over which tribal members could interact politically. The kind of political history of tribe that a people like the Honey Lake Maidus can tell, then, is typically one of family leaders or figures who were of personal inclination or means, who acted in political capacities for particular issues. Yet a typical critique BAR supplies when drawing Negative Determinations is that such leaders do not reflect a tribewide authority.[13] Nonetheless, the kind of leadership I described in the Honey Lake Maidu petition is how leadership in California tribelets was apparently organized, according to Kroeber: "In daily life and dress, the chief might not appear perceptibly different from other members of the tribelet. He functioned on occasion, rather than professionally or full time" (1963 [1955], 107).

Similarly reflecting a model that does not fit the historical, social, or political experience of California's Native peoples, when Criterion B asks for proof of social continuity, the burden on landless tribes is significantly greater than for those with land. Tribes that do not own significant pieces of their aboriginal territories have been buffeted much more strongly by economic winds that have pushed and pulled them in many directions, often away from the lands of their ancestors. Nonetheless, BAR expects to see a "significant" amount of social cohesion among tribe members, whose friends, close relatives, and workmates are expected to come, predominantly, from within the tribe. All these things make putting together a strong case for BAR less likely to be possible for one of California's non-Recognized tribes.

Nonetheless, connections to the land are what non-Indians and Indians alike come back to as a definition of Indianness.

Indeed, according to their own definitions, Honey Lake Maidu religious, emotional, and historical ties to places in the Honey Lake Valley are what truly make them who they are. But though this might make it seem that the two share a definition of Indianness, 25 CFR Part 83.5's inflexible demands of documentary evidence of ideational orientations steamroll the facts about what it has been like to be a landless, non-Recognized California tribe in a frontier milieu of legally sanctioned violence and domination. Such a focus on geography or territory (tacit in the government's case, loudly emphasized in the Honey Lake Maidus') easily comes to mean a focus on a geologic rather than social scale—that is, it easily comes to equate authentic Indianness with timeless cultural stasis. The result is that the government looks for static Indians, and the tribes do their best to present themselves as such, despite, in both instances, the obvious contradictions.

HONEY LAKE MAIDU ANTHROPOLOGY

Ron Morales and I talk extensively about borders. It's fairly his obsession. What Federal Recognition is about for both Ron and his sister, Viola, is making a claim for being the aboriginal people of this valley so that the archaeologists who consult for commercial interests, state museum NAGPRA representatives, anthropologists from California's university system, the BIA, the Forest Service, and the local journalists and community members will (lowercase r) recognize the borders that establish Honey Lake Maidu cultural precedence and Honey Lake Maidu identity in the Susanville area. Official tribalness, for the Honey Lake Maidus, seems at least in part to mean the ability to define and control their boundaries. Key to this sovereign control of boundaries is a fluency in local ethnography.

Though he never finished high school, Ron knows the anthropological works on the Mountain Maidus forward and backward. He knows that anthropologists' concern with mapping language and culture areas has helped lead to the modern-day antagonisms felt between Recognized and non-Recognized groups in Susanville. And he knows that scholarly opinions have an important role to play in the creation of a petition to win Federal Recognition. Both Ron and Viola understand that their Federal Acknowledgement petition can be a response to the BIA's definition of tribe. In this way, the essentialist approach the Honey Lake Maidus take to tribe should be thought of as a kind of radical essentialism that is part of a larger historical and scholarly conversation with, but also against, domination.

Ron and I talk, for instance, about Francis (Fritz) Riddell's archaeological work for California's Parks and Recreation Department: how, from Ron's perspective, Riddell must have had to work rather hard at ignoring the Maidu experience and Maidu history in the area to have written much of what he did about Honey Lake Valley belonging to the Northern Paiutes. "Something is better than nothing, he's told me that before, Riddell," said Ron. "But I don't know about that."

Nothing was what the Honey Lake Maidus insisted on for years: the older generation was particularly adamant that the important places and cultural information not be shared with untrustworthy folk. Leona Morales explained on audiotape that she never even showed her children certain sites because she was afraid they would tell their teachers or another outsider. Today, Ron, her son, carefully guards his knowledge of such sites. For instance, Ron told me a story about how "Ronnie Ree-gan," when he was governor of California, sent him a letter asking where the Maker's Footprint was located "so they could put up a plaque or something." As he went on, the story became a kind of X-Files conspiracy drama: government officials tried to track him down and force him to tell his secrets, but he outwitted and escaped them. Leona's concerns about school-teachers, and Ron's about the California-governor-turned-U.S.-president, are both stories about hiding Honey Lake Maiduness from the state.

This orientation to secrecy is key to understanding Honey Lake Maiduness, and key to understanding how Honey Lake Maiduness contradicts BAR's expectations of culture, Indianness, and tribe. For the tribe, part of what it means to identify culturally as a people is an orientation to protecting what is *not* shared—a fundamentally agonistic orientation that also works, at times, against cultural cohesion, as in the case of the hidden/lost Maker's Footprint.

Another way to think about this is that BAR looks for Indian cemeteries, Indian potlucks, Indian churches, Indian organizations, and Indian gatherings, but doesn't give a second glance at Indian silences.

Ron and I would also spend a great deal of time talking about the history of the Honey Lake Maidus in the valley and the article he, Viola, Steve Camacho,[14] and William S. Simmons published in *The Journal of California and Great Basin Anthropology* (1997). It offers the Honey Lake Maidu perspective on the anthropological debates of the last century, very much in conversation with Riddell's "Honey Lake Paiute Ethnography" (1978a), which did the same for the Paiutes. Elsewhere, Riddell explains that he attributed Honey Lake Valley to the Paiutes because of ethnolinguistic evidence: his Paiute informants had names for important locations in the valley, but he said his Maidu informants did not. "Honey Lake Maidu Ethnogeography" is the Honey Lake Maidu reply after a long silence: "Based mainly upon the testimonies of nineteenth and twentieth century Maidu inhabitants of the Honey Lake Valley in Lassen County, California, we present a Maidu perspective on local knowledge, such as where they lived, hunted, gathered, and buried their dead in the prehistoric and early historical periods" (Simmons et al. 1997, 2).

In practical terms, how this was accomplished was by providing Maidu place-names for locations in the valley. (See map 2). The introduction explains that

drawing on family tape recordings and interview notes in the possession of the authors, as well as a range of other sources, this article is
intended as a contribution to Maidu ethnogeography in the Honey
Lake Valley region. While acknowledging that several ethnic groups
lived in or near this region in the early historical period, and that
boundaries are social constructs that may overlap and about which
groups may hold different interpretations, we document a cross-gen-
erational Maidu perspective on their territorial range in the remembered past. (ibid.)

   In most of this introduction, one hears the anthropologist,
Simmons—his tact, his carefulness. Ron and Viola are more
confrontational in their anthropology. In fact, anyone who
talked with them would understand their project as that of
ousting the other "ethnic groups." They also envision their
work as remedying the anthropological situation created by
Riddell. The siblings maintained a strained relationship with
the otherwise well-respected archaeologist, who passed away
in 2002. Over the course of my residence in Susanville, some
of the rough places in their relationship with Riddell have
become smoother, but the fact remains that anthropology has
an effect on people's lives, and neither Ron nor Viola is happy
with Riddell's anthropology nor with its effect on their lives.[15]
Ron in particular has been known to blame Riddell for the
Honey Lake Maidu tribe's non-Recognition. In this way, Honey
Lake Maidu self-understandings bring anthropology to trial as
well as any Massachusetts court.
   In the *Handbook of North American Indians* (Riddell 1978b),
Riddell wrote that the Maidus had only migrated into Honey
Lake Valley at around 1700. But the day I met with him, Fritz
Riddell explained, "I don't know, still, if that was right." Ron
will not easily forgive him for what he considers this published,
thus public, disrespect for the Maidus. He particularly will not
forgive him his map of Honey Lake Valley, which erases much
of the Maidu presence (see map 3). Ron likes to point out that
Riddell spent some of his youth living next door to Kitty

CALIFORNIA

Eagle Lake

Honey Lake

1. Tommy Tucker Cave
2. Hot Springs Mountain
3. *Wollolok'om*
4. Buntingville
5. Janesville
6. Rice Canyon
7. Fox Mountain
8. Honey Lake
9. Elysian Valley
10. Sand Slough
11. Diamond Mountain
12. Gold Run Creek
13. Susanville
14. *K'asim Jamanim*
15. Worley Mountain
16. Antelope Mountain
17. Porcupine Hill
18. *Supom*
19. Susan River
20. Smith Creek
21. Eagle Lake
22. Thompson Peak
23. Hot Springs
24. Fredonyer Mountain
25. Lone Pine
26. Maidu Burial Area
27. Long Valley
28. *Sumbilim*
29. *Kojo*
30. *Wetajam*
31. Charley Brown's Burial Ground
32. Servilicn Burial Area
33. Willow Creek Valley
34. Maidu Burial Site
35. Shaffer Mountain
36. Maidu Village Site

N

Hills & Mountains

Maidu Boundary

0   5   10 miles

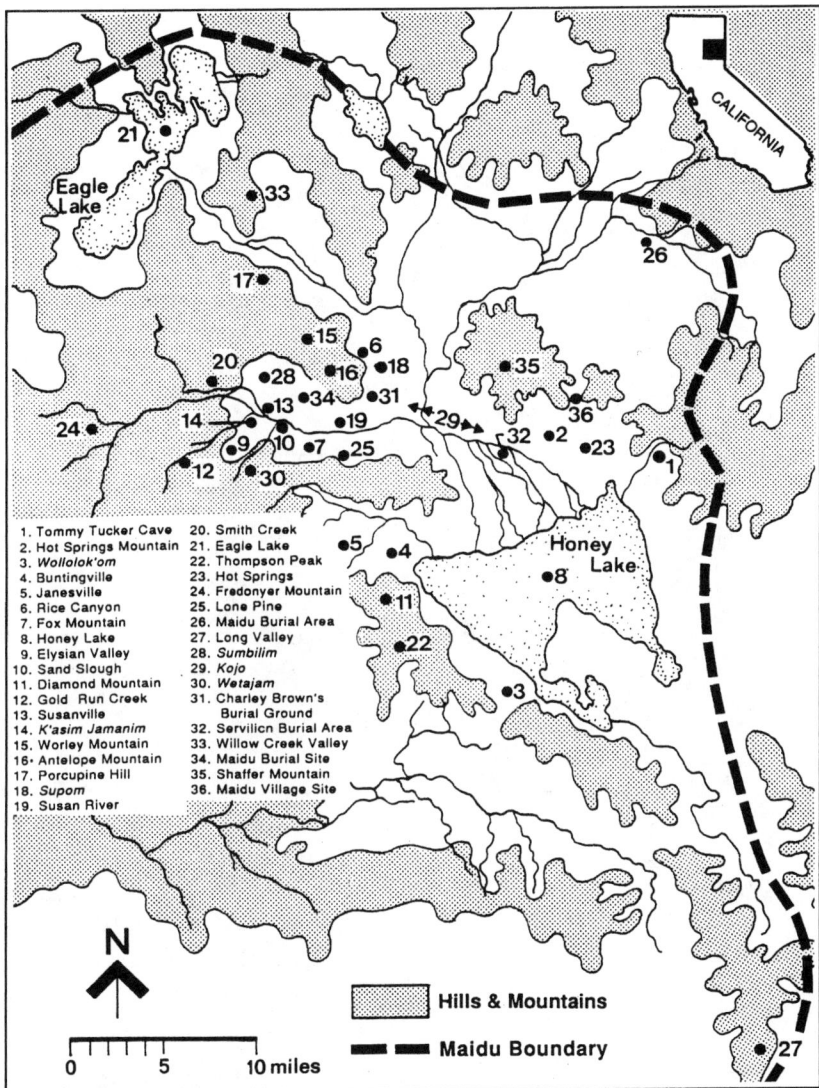

Numbered site locations and territorial range of the Honey Lake Maidus. William S. Simmons et. al., *Journal of California and Great Basin Anthropology*, © 1997, by permission of Malki Press, P.O. Box 578, Banning, Calif., 92220, (951) 849-7289.

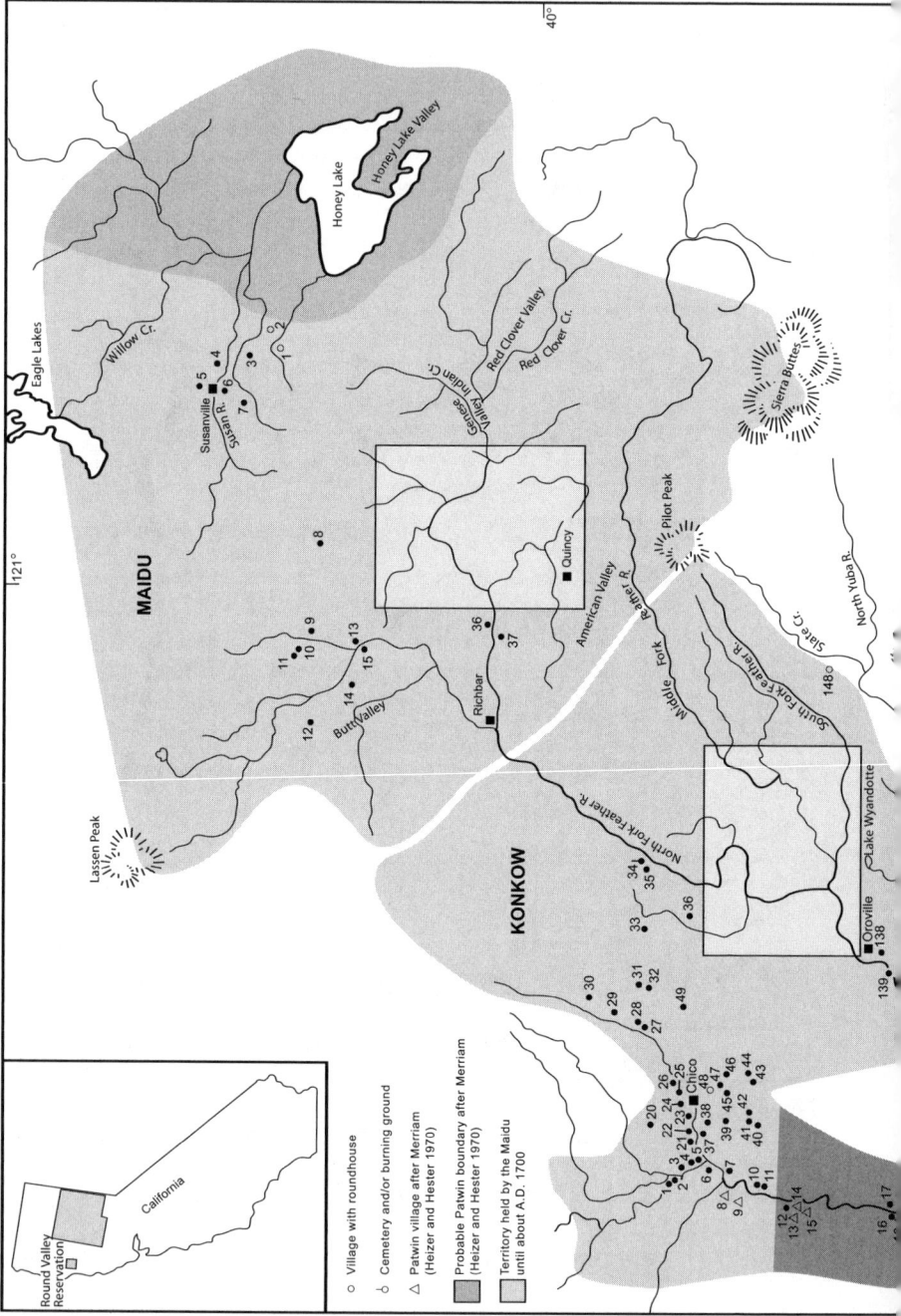

Legend:

○ Village with roundhouse

⬙ Cemetery and/or burning ground

△ Patwin village after Merriam (Heizer and Hester 1970)

■ Probable Patwin boundary after Merriam (Heizer and Hester 1970)

Territory held by the Maidu until about A.D. 1700

Round Valley Reservation

California

MAIDU

KONKOW

Lassen Peak

Eagle Lakes

Willow Cr.

Honey Lake

Honey Lake Valley

Susanville

Susan R.

Red Clover Valley

Red Clover Cr.

Genesee Valley

Indian Cr.

Quincy

American Valley

Feather R.

Pilot Peak

Sierra Buttes

North Yuba R.

Slate Cr.

South Fork Feather R.

Middle Fork

Richbar

Butt Valley

North Fork Feather R.

Oroville

Lake Wyandotte

Chico

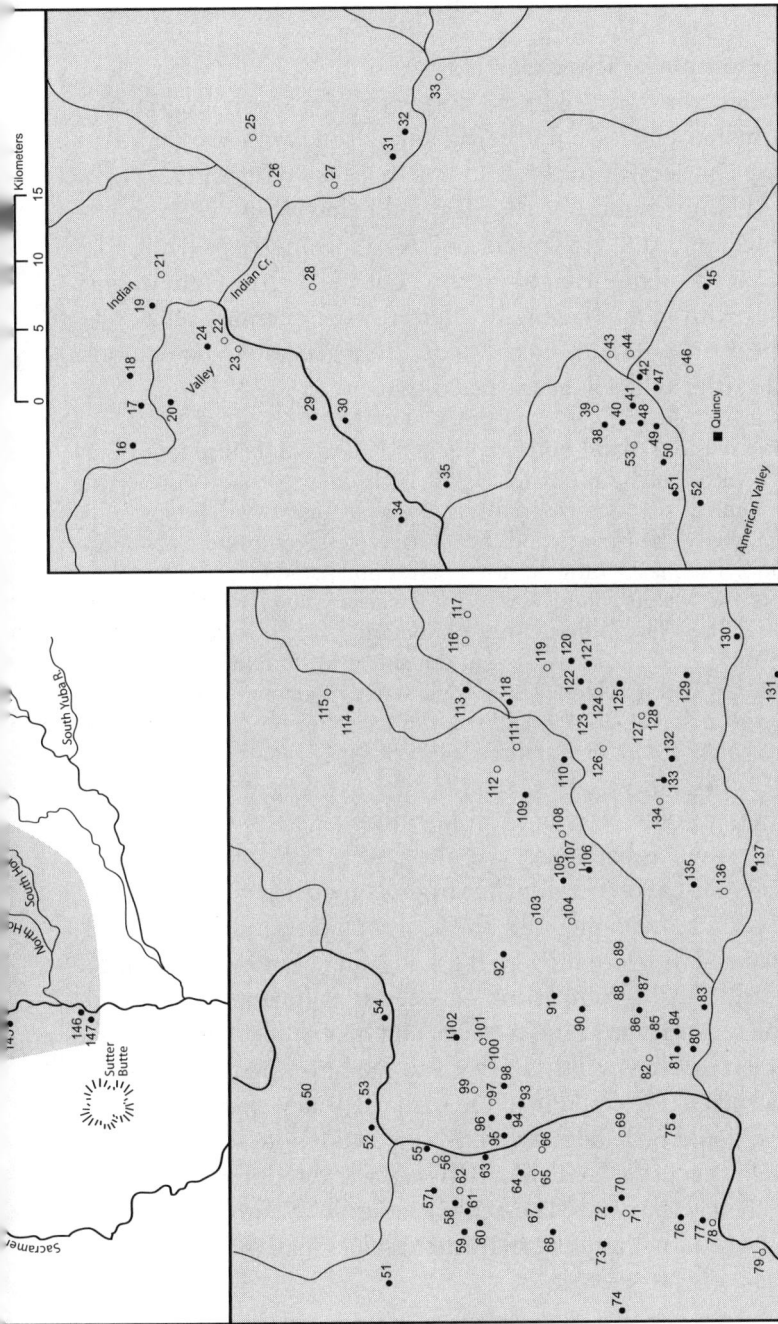

Maidu and Konkow tribal territory and village locations. Frances Riddell, "Maidu and Konkow," © 1978, *Handbook of North American Indians*, Vol. 8, "California," 370–86, by permission of the Smithsonian Institute.

Joaquin's place. Kitty married and raised a child with Dave Servilicn, son of the old-time "head of all the Mountain Maidu," but she herself was a Northern Paiute. Ron says it was Riddell's strong connection to the Joaquins that biased his work.

My impression was that Riddell believed sincerely in his science, and that he understood Ron's wrangling with it. He himself was committed to puzzling out the map of Honey Lake Valley with more digging. In a letter of commentary on a draft of the article, "Honey Lake Maidu Ethnogeography" (Simmons et al.), the archaeologist insisted that

> some day the Indians, both Maidu and Paiute will realize that their only link with the prehistoric past is through archaeology. Until such time as they realize that fact their patrimony will be lost and squandered. The Indians and the archaeologists must find a common ground. Time is running out for a better understanding of the native past of the Maidu/Paiute/Washo/Pit River meeting ground of Honey Lake Valley. The Indians should demand that the archaeologists carry out extensive excavation at the site at Milford [Mata, which is claimed by both the Honey Lake Maidus and the Honey Lake Paiutes]. And the archaeologists should see to it that the crew excavating the site is composed of local Indians. (1995)

His letter points to a larger antagonism between many Indian peoples and archaeologists. It also points to Riddell's belief in archaeological objectivity. Yet from Ron's perspective, anthropologists are fundamentally the tools of larger, Indian, political projects. Thus, when Riddell asked him about the possibility of doing a DNA comparison between the ancient bones found in the seventies at Karlo, Nevada, and his own genetic material, Ron did not have to think twice to see how science is socially constructed. He could imagine the potential power of what he knew would be Riddell's DNA-bolstered Paiute science, even though accepting Riddell's challenge was tempting.[16]

The Honey Lake Maidu tribe's radically essentialist counter-point to Riddell's theory that the Maidus came into the Valley in the 1700s is their story of the migration of the Paiute people into Maidu country. I have heard it told numerous times: In the late 1860s, Chief Winnemucca realized that the Pyramid Lake peoples could not win their war against the whites, realized that they would be hunted down until they were all killed. And so he told his warriors to settle down on the edges of the Honey Lake Valley with the Maidu people and in that way hide their identity until a safer time. The last line is always something to the effect of the Maidus watching a long train of slim, dark-skinned people, the Paiutes, crossing into Honey Lake Valley.

Once the rancheria system and the anthropologists, with their maps and monographs, had finished the work of dividing it up, the valley was never big enough to share. Today, the status of tribe and tribe's claims to territory are resources over which the Honey Lake Maidus and Wadakut Paiutes fight. The main stage for these antagonisms over boundaries is the home turf of BAR's Federal Recognition review team, that mysterious but powerful office on the East Coast where petitions get sent to wait.

WASHINGTON'S TAKE

In December 2000 I visited the Branch of Acknowledgment and Research in Washington, D.C. Historian John Dibbern and anthropologist George Roth[17] both recognized that the idea that Federal Acknowledgment will erase boundary-dispute problems with other tribes is a common one for petitioners. But they insisted, as Dibbern put it, that "petitioners can include their boundaries [in their petitions] but they mean nothing. The BAR doesn't have a determination on them. *We're not setting tribal boundaries*" (author's italics). In fact, Dibbern and Roth implied that they already knew about the tensions between the Maidus and the Paiutes in the valley because of letters they had received from the Wadakut Paiutes. In surprisingly avuncular fashion, Roth told me (without being explicit about any of the details they may have known), "It all gets very political." He told me that he got himself embroiled in Indian politics when he was doing field work, noting, "The echoes of past mistakes carry down for generations." My feeling at the time was that he meant that the echoes of governmental mistakes carry down for generations. In retrospect, perhaps he meant anthropological mistakes. I cannot be sure.

And so, despite how intelligent and personable these two BAR members were, their understanding of tribal boundary setting seemed to be informed by their patronizing conception of Indian feuding. For certain, Dibbern and Roth represent a bureau that denies the politics and power of its Final Determinations by ignoring its own role in intertribal feuding and the way Indian people like the Honey Lake Maidus are oriented to the Acknowledgment process, in part by boundary setting.

In fact, BAR's vision of geography—as reflected in its latest guide to petitioning, "The Official Guide to the FAP Regulations, 25 CFR 83"—is like a darkened set that only the actors bring to light. This deemphasis of geography deserves careful attention. Indeed, although BAR encourages tribes to focus upon providing evidence of the actors' "tribal community," I have argued that strict requirements of tribal community are just another way of validating a model of Indianness based on the continued possession of land. At heart, the Federal Acknowledgment regulations deemphasize indigenous claims to certain land holdings and boundary making. Simultaneously, they focus on evidences of social community, particularly as documented by anthropologists, rather than by a people's oral histories or myths concerning local geography. I believe that the logic of such requirements and ways of approaching tribe is that this is a way of excluding those peoples likely to make land claims of the state.

The Honey Lake Maidu vision of geography upsets BAR's order of evidence completely: the scenery comes first, the actors are secondary. In approaching Acknowledgment, the tribe began with place—they were, they asserted, the *Honey Lake Maidus*—and they brought the appropriate families to the project only later. They, unlike BAR, are at ease with the idea of Federal Recognition as overtly political (though they hate its injustices), because they know the marginalized politics of non-Recognition; the explicit politics of the Federal Acknowledgment process are liberatory in comparison. And so, even as primordial connections to the land were the basis for their petition, so, too, were place's instrumental assertions contemplated—exactly what the Federal Acknowledgment process tacitly discourages. They chose to put Honey Lake Valley first because of their dispute with the Paiutes, their commitment to recognition in their ancestors' lands, and their orientation to protecting its sacred attributes and loci from developers and other Indian peoples who seek to claim them. Later, they began the process of deciding which unit worked most cohesively for the petition, and they turned to outside experts whose claims supported their own. Quite authentically, what was at stake for them organized their answer to BAR's question, "What is the Honey Lake Maidu Tribe?"

When I returned from Washington and told Ron Morales that Federal Recognition would not eject the Paiutes for him, he said that he wanted the boundaries written up in the petition nonetheless. He believed that getting them down on paper would be one step toward making them real—and exclusive. The Honey Lake Maidu tribe's vision for the boundaries of the Honey Lake Maidu territory are represented in map 4. In the petition, we wrote:

Honey Lake Maidu tribal members have recently summarized oral history to outline the traditional areas used by their ancestors. Traditional territorial boundaries spanned from Clear Creek to Homer Lake, down along the Diamond Mountain Range to Long Valley, across Honey Lake Valley to Five Springs, around Horse, Eagle and Poison lakes, over to Butte Lake and back to Clear Creek.

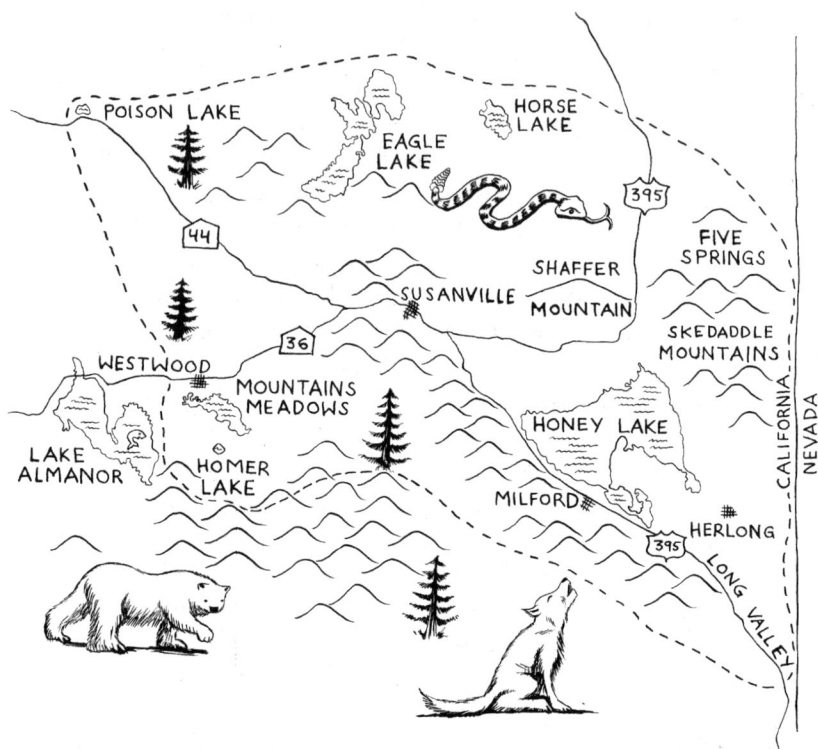

Aboriginal territory of the Honey Lake Maidu Tribe. Honey Lake Maidu Tribe, 2000. Illustrated by John Isaacson, © 2005.

One cannot help but notice how incongruously comprehensive the Honey Lake Maidu boundaries are. Honey Lake Maidu bleeds far beyond the Honey Lake Valley and comes to signify the (expansive) sovereignty the tribe expects to come with Recognition. Their point is: regardless of what BAR's rules are, our rules are that when we are Recognized, those are the places to which our sovereignty will extend. Their essentialist borders are an agonistic way of taking the power of tribe back from the state.

THE CRUSH OF OVERLAPPING BOUNDARIES

Ron told me that "what really got me involved in reading and learning an awful lot was when Tuscarora was putting a gas line clear up through [to] Canada . . . in 1994 or 1995." Clyde Woods, an archaeologist consulting for Tuscarora, "was the coordinator for the Indian part of it. He wanted to meet with local Indians."[18] Held at Denny's in Susanville, the meeting was to be a discussion between Woods and any local Indian people who knew of burials or village sites in the vicinity of the proposed pipeline route. Woods mentioned that he had already met with the Federally Recognized group on the rancheria. Ron explained, "He said he had a 'boundaries map,' and he had 'Paiute' stamped all over this Valley." Ron knew better, though, because of what his grandmother, mother, aunties, and uncle had told him. Ron asked Woods where he got his information: "'We went to Fritz Riddell [and William Evans—the two articles are reprinted together by the Lassen County Historical Society],' he said." Ron was surprised—he'd been listening in, as a small boy, when Riddell and Evans interviewed his mother and grandmother, interviews that resulted in Evans's "Ethnographic Notes on the Honey Lake Maidu" (1978), which Ron had never read. Ron asked, incredulous, "*Evans* is the one who said that this was Paiute land?"[19]

Ron promised Woods that he'd show him some evidence to the contrary. He went to the public library: "First time I ever been in a library." He read Riddell's work. When he could not find any other researcher's work on the Mountain Maidus—partially because of the near-complete hegemony of Riddell's ideas in town—he called Bill Simmons, who had been in contact with Ron's sister Yvonne Morales. Ron asked Bill to send copies of books and articles from the UC Berkeley collections, and he asked Woods to send him books from Colorado. His goal was to change the Tuscarora map, to get Maidu territory drawn onto it, in its rightful place.

His disgust at having to do this at all was expressed to me through an analogy to the popular *Ishi, Last of His Tribe* mindset: "It's like people saying there are no more Yahi—it's just not true![20] We're [their] neighbors in the Hum Bug area, we should know. It seems like, how could people [anthropologists] *be* so damn wrong?" Unmentioned but understood here—because it was the topic of another conversation Ron and I had been having—was a recrimination of the anthropologist(s) who watched Ishi die over the years of his "captivity" and then pickled his brain and sent it to the Smithsonian.[21] As with the grave-digging archaeologists, racial violence undergirds his understanding of cultural anthropologists and their discipline.

KROEBER

After Riddell and Evans, Ron said he read Kroeber. He has no kind words for the man. As I have described, he doesn't like that Kroeber left any room at all for the possibility of Paiutes in the Honey Lake region.

My own opinion of Kroeber's writing on the Maidus, however, would make Kroeber's the most honest disclosure of the complications of mapping boundaries. In the *Handbook of the Indians of California* (1925), Kroeber claims that Northeastern Maidu territory extends to the *crest* of the Sierra Nevada. "Beyond," he writes,

it becomes uncertain. Eagle Lake, Susan Creek or River, Honey Lake, and Long Valley Creek—an inferior system behind the end of the Sierras—drain a tract the ownership of which is doubtful. Susan Creek and the Susanville region have usually been ascribed to the Maidu, but there are Atsugewi claims. Eagle Lake has been variously attributed to the Atsugewi, the Achomawi, and the Northern Paiute. Atsugewi ownership seems the most likely.[22] Honey Lake was not far from where Maidu, Paiute, and Washo met. It seems not to have had permanent villages, and may have been visited by all three of the tribes in question. On the map the problem has been compromised by extending all their territories to its shores. (1925, 391)

He later mentions, "On the other hand, the lack of permanent villages makes the question seem more important on the map than it was in native life" (ibid.)—and in the end, he severely restricts the Mountain Maidu presence on his map of Honey Lake Valley.

Because of this, Ron is of the opinion that "Kroeber never even set foot in Lassen County." Although I believe that Kroeber may simply have been trying to say all that he felt he could reasonably say in the case of the Honey Lake Maidus, he certainly had some inkling of the impact of these mappings.[23] Ron, however, has no time for this kind of "reason," and considers Kroeber's compromises betrayals. For Ron's purposes, and for the purposes of the rest of the Honey Lake Maidu petitioners, as they face BAR, just the opposite is necessary: constancy, commitment—and blackness or whiteness.

A third problem with Kroeber, according to Ron, is that Riddell's intellectual lineage can be traced back to him. Ron claims that Riddell followed Kroeber's lead in putting the Paiutes in the valley. But he does not stop there: Ron's summary of a body of literature on the Northern Paiutes is astute in the manner that it picks up on the inbred lineage of informants that anthropologists like Riddell, Isabel Kelly, Omer Stewart, and Julian Steward relied upon. First off, "Kelly didn't know if she was talking to a Maidu or a Pit River [let alone a Paiute]," says Ron. Then we have Omer Stewart, who interviewed Susie Buster (Pit River/Paiute), who was a half sister to Old Man Joaquin, Julian Steward's informant; in turn, Joaquin's daughter Kitty was Riddell's informant. No wonder they were all told the same thing. According to Ron, Paiutes from any other family would tell it differently—what they would tell would be the story of how the Paiutes trespassed into Honey Lake Valley in order to hide among the Maidus and escape Nevada's violent frontier.

I include this here not because I agree with Ron's depiction of the Northern Paiutes as interlopers, but because I agree that part of the injustice of the Federal Acknowledgment process comes from the anthropological layers that are tangled around the history of the valley and, therefore, the Honey Lake Maidu petition. And I have found that there are even more layers to Ron's theory about anthropological inbreeding: namely, the fact that anthropologists are hired to put together petitions for tribes using ethnographic evidence from other anthropologists, only to be evaluated, at BAR, by anthropologists. Petition-writing anthropologists do their best to bridge social scientific ethics and their personal alliances with the at-times racist/sexist/colonialist writings of earlier ethnographers; but then the anthropologists at BAR are asked to read such petitions with black-and-white lenses—because all the information submitted is limited by the criteria themselves. One way to understand this is to think of the BAR anthropologists as truly reduced to the status of technicians of the Federal Acknowledgment criteria. Indeed, while the BAR anthropologists appear to have made field visits to petitioners (if only for two-week periods) before 1994, this aspect of their anthropological investigations is no longer being performed. Anthropology without field work means that petitions are evaluated without any degree of the holism—the attempt at deep connection—that is what makes cross-cultural communication possible.

CULTURAL ECOLOGY, POLITICAL ECONOMY

Considering the California Indian land claims cases and the position that Kroeber took toward territorial ownership, Kroeber and Ron might be closer to one another than Ron is willing to consider. Kroeber's understandings of tribe and its boundary lines based on linguistic evidence of land use match the Honey Lake Maidus' own expansive way of mapping their world in the terms of the Maker's creation of it, and the visiting, hunting, gathering, and traveling that occurred there.

Such ecological-economic definitions of tribe, however, are double-edged swords when it comes to Federal Acknowledgment.

In Kroeber's case, while he recognized a Maidu presence in the Honey Lake Valley, he also questioned it. Later, Fritz Riddell and his student Evans, like Kroeber, reasoned that a Sierra *Mountain* Maidu people in the Great Basin ecological zone that is Honey Lake Valley would have been anomalous. Evans, for example, emphasized that the Honey Lake Maidus only utilized the valley seasonally. From a similarly critical angle, the work of Honey Lake Maidu tribal members to protect Mountain Meadows—an area outside of Honey Lake Valley—from tourist development seems, at first, to simply point out the essentialist absurdity of calling themselves "Honey Lake" people.

Viewed plainly, cultural ecology relates to the Branch of Acknowledgment and Research's economic expectations for tribes. BAR's petitioning guidelines explain that, if possible, it is beneficial to demonstrate continuous economic connection among current members and the historic tribal community, thus tying primordial economic activities to current ones. Specifically, BAR says that proof of identification as a tribe since 1900 can come in the form of "a significant degree of shared or cooperative labor or other economic activity among the membership." BAR has no illusions that this will be possible for all tribes, yet the connection is an important one considering the larger political framing of the Federal Acknowledgement process as a gatekeeper for tribal gaming, as I have argued in chapter two. In other words, we might see how, for BAR, primordial economic activity—defined and constrained, traditionally, by a group's cultural ecology—is considered outstanding proof of tribalness, but that overtly instrumental economic motivations toward tribalness create a situation to which skepticism is the most appropriate response.

This assumption is contradicted by the reality that, for most non-Recognized tribes, appending themselves to the state's roll of the Recognized is to a large and often primary degree about economic opportunity: for the Honey Lake Maidus, Recognition offers the possibility of access to monies for housing, health care, education, land, and business ventures. The way the Honey Lake Maidus approach the Federal Acknowledgment process is with these economic possibilities in mind. Their focus upon territorial boundaries defined by use, oral history, and myth thus repositions the stakes that tether the Federal Acknowledgment process in a quadrant of political neutrality, despite bureaucratic intentions.

In a war over territory-read-as-resources, and resources understood as money and R/recognition, the tribes attempt one thing and the states attempt the opposite, and the Federal Acknowledgment process is battered at from both sides. In whose favor the trenches will give way is the abiding interest. We can see, for instance, that Evans and Riddell's work could be used against the Honey Lake Maidus by those with other interests (non-Indians, the Nevada casino lobby, or the Northern Paiutes, to name a few), but this itself does not mean the Honey Lake Maidus are left powerless: in the petition, for example, we worked to use Evans's "seasonal use of the Honey Lake Valley" to the tribe's advantage, explaining that this seasonal occupation was evidence of land use patterns that were distinct from those of other Mountain Maidu tribes. Satisfyingly, seasonal use of Honey Lake Valley also makes sense of the Honey Lake Maidu claim to Mountain Meadows: the tribe used the latter in the spring and summer months.

ROLAND B. DIXON

It was either Clyde Woods or Bill Simmons who first sent Ron Roland B. Dixon's work on the Mountain Maidus. In *The Northern Maidu* (1905), Dixon writes that

the entire Honey Lake Valley is said to have been permanently occupied in early times by the Maidu; and it is declared emphatically that no Paiutes were settled there until after the coming of the first white immigrants, or just before. Whether the Maidu occupied any part of upper Long Valley [which is connected to Honey Lake

Valley, to the south] is very uncertain. From the fact, however, that Reno and the region thereabouts are mentioned in the creation myth, it is possible that the Maidu at one time extended farther in this direction. (1983 [1905], 125)

Dixon's work supports the existence of a Honey Lake Maidu tribe by pointing to specific medicinal plants used by Maidus that were gathered from the Honey Lake Valley, including what he called "wild pea," or what is known as *subilim* by Honey Lake Maidus (see Simmons et al. 1997, 34).[24] Dixon also writes that "tobacco grew plentifully in the region about Honey Lake, and was traded from there quite extensively" (1983 [1905], 202).

Furthermore, Dixon is specific about the provenance of the distinctions that exist among the different Maidu linguistic groups:

From the comparison of the myth cycles of the Northeastern and Northwestern Maidu, I have already pointed out that we might suppose there had been a movement of the former section eastwards from the area of the Sacramento Valley. . . . As has been already pointed out, there is a complete absence, apparently, of any sort of a migration legend, all portions of the stock declaring emphatically that they originated precisely in their present homes. While placing the creation of the world uniformly in the vicinity of Durham, in the Sacramento Valley, the Northeastern Maidu [Mountain Maidu], for example, declare they are the descendants of the pairs of human germs planted by the Creator in the lands which they now occupy, and that from that day to this day they have continued to live in the region where their ancestors came into being. (1983 [1905], 344).

Significantly, then, according to Maidu mythology, the last place the Creator was seen on this earth was at the edge of the Skedaddle Mountains, which is to say, leaving the "far side" of Honey Lake Valley (Morales, Williams, Camacho, and Simmons, forthcoming). In short, Honey Lake Maidu conceptions coincide, even today, with Dixon's: the Honey Lake Valley has always been their home, from creation.

BACK TO TUSCARORA

The long and the short of Ron's run-in with the Tuscarora company's pipeline and contingent of consultants—now that its anthropological impact on Ron's life has been told—was that

Clyde Woods had to work with us, had to put us in his book. Trenching it, they had Maidu monitors there, paid as much as Susanville Indian Rancheria folks. They found bones, right by Five Springs where I'd said they'd be. Shut the job down. They hit a village! But because we're non-federally Recognized we never had a chance. The Rancheria claimed the bones and Clyde did it all behind our backs—took them to Davis and then let the Rancheria rebury them.

Meanwhile the Honey Lake Maidus had involved the Pit River Nation for support, as well as the California Heritage Commission (hence the meeting I attended with Bill described in the introduction) and the Advisory Council on California Indian Policy, which included comments on the situation in its report to Congress in 1997. And, in the end, the Honey Lake Maidus, Ron told me with a devilish look, made Tuscarora reroute the pipeline at great cost.

Ron Morales is hoping to use anthropology to turn the Honey Lake Maidu case around, to re-create his people as an officially Recognized tribe. Dealing with anthropologists is an old story for the Honey Lake Maidus. Ron's grandmother is supposed to have commented (having spoken, in her time, with Stephen Powers in the 1870s, Riddell and Evans in the 1940s, and Shipley in the 1950s, among others), "Anthropologists! An anthropologist will stick his nose up the ass of a wild hog just to see why it makes a noise." I might add that today BAR asks the tribes to do that work themselves, and to have eyewitnesses report back to them with what tribe members may or may not have heard.

CHAPTER FOUR

THE BEAR DANCE
DIGESTS THE STATE

THE DESCENDANTS OF LEONA MORALES HOST THE MOUNTAIN
Maidu Bear Dance at the Roxie Peconom Campground in the
Lassen National Forest every June. Over the weekend, non-
Indians and Indian people of many tribes camp together, eat
communally, and just spend time with one another. The Bear
Dance is not a powwow—there are only a few local venders
present and there are no dance competitions. Its dates are not
posted or advertised. Nonetheless, people start moving into the
campground named after the Honey Lake Maidu matriarch
starting the Wednesday before the weekend of the event. By
Friday, the grounds are filling up with people from as far away as
Alaska, New York, and the Czech Republic, and they sometimes
stay through Monday morning.

Ron Morales describes coming to the Bear Dance as similar
to "white people going to church." His niece Wanda Brown
likens it to the celebration of a new year for your spirit. Spirituality is at the heart of the Bear Dance, whether it is interpreted
as kindness and openness toward other people, the medicine
of the sweat lodge, the ritual cleansing at the stream, or the
playing of handgame late into the night.

My study of non-Recognition, however, brings me to the
question of how the Federal non-Recognition of the Honey
Lake Maidu tribe complicates their role in "Lassen County's
oldest existing Native American cultur[al]" event, as a Forest
Service sign announces. As I unravel its political aspects, I ask
that the reader bear in mind the paramount spiritual focus of

the celebration. The Bear Dance is an event at which political strains become evident, first because it is a valuable cultural resource over which many separate Recognized and non-Recognized peoples stake claims, and second because it requires extensive behind-the-scenes work between federal agencies and non-Recognized people for its staging. At the same time, because the event is fundamentally a ritual of renewal and a rite of community means, too, that it is a good place to find healing—and proof of the strong roots of cultural survival. There are similar stories to be told across California, stories, for instance, of Kumeyaay and Mojave bird singing; Hupa, Karuk, and Yurok summer dance cycles; Konkow handgame championships; and the Coast Miwok Strawberry Festival at Kule Loklo.

COYOTE STORY

Wooly Maidem,[1] Ron's daughter Lauri's rottweiler, is digging in frustrated response to his capture and leashing after a visit from the Forest Service. The huge fire lit in the meat pit to dry it out is going strong, and it makes Ron, Pano, and me sleepy as we think about the day and the Bear Dance to come. Ron and I talk about how we do not want to go back to town, how it is much more agreeable out here in the woods. The dry-nostrilled sensation of breathing ponderosa pine smoke reminds me of peanut husks, vanilla, and green apples; Wooly's ditch throws off the clean smell of fresh dirt. I plan to pitch my tent. Ron says he'll go back, though—he never sleeps out, says he would miss his bed too much.

But as the afternoon heads toward evening, we linger by the fire in Ron's lawn chairs, thinking and talking. We consider the employee of the Lassen National Forest who had raced in earlier in the day, in the midst of the practical preparation for the weekend's three days of dancing and purification, eating and visiting, when the world will be renewed and the bear and rattlesnake are placated with fronds of *munmunim*.[2] As the dust from her truck settled, she told Ron and Mike McCourt, a non-Indian friend who does quite a bit of volunteer construction work for the Bear Dance Foundation, that their dogs had to be on leashes on Forest Service land. She said that Allen Lowry had just been into the office to report "two rottweilers scaring old people out at Roxie Peconom." (Lowry hadn't mentioned Mike's similarly unleashed Lab and border collie.) Allen Lowry is a Greenville Maidu who lives on the Susanville Indian Rancheria and who used to be chair of the Bear Dance Foundation in its early years, before his resignation under a cloud of suspicion and a hail of accusations that he was stealing from it. Our unnamed Lassen National Forest employee had driven out—"as a friend," she'd said—to warn Ron that the Forest Service would eventually be forced to come down on him if he did not stick to the forest's rules.

Reflecting on why the satisfying work of hauling out the larger-than-life cauldrons for the venison stew, building the cookstove out of cinderblocks, and drying the meat pit had been interrupted, Ron said to me, "Yep, you look out and there are sometimes coyotes walking on the edges of this camp." "Really?" I asked, not catching his drift. "Oh, yeah. It's the Forest Service, always checking up on us. And then it's Stan Lowry [Allen's father] camped at the end of the parking lot"— I had not missed his camp; it was marked by an enormous California bear flag—"and so Allen comes by to check us out." It's just *like* Coyote, the devil, he said, to want to be a part of things, but unwittingly destroy them too.

I told him that I should have known something was afoot because yesterday, when I was driving in from Milford, a coyote was running alongside my pickup. Ron looked down at the cinder-filled logs and told me, in response, "One time I look up and there was a big old guy sitting up on top of the hill there. I said, 'Don't look over there,' to them that was with me, but I glance a little out of my eyes at him like this. I don't look over for a long while. We ignore him. And pretty soon I see him start to be lying down, and soon he falls asleep." His voice faded out, and the story finished itself in silence. The rest had been told to me many times before in another form, as a variation on the story of Coyote at Wepum Mountain, which lies in the middle of Mountain Meadows, where Roxie Peconom's husband, John, was born.[3] Please see appendix B, where the story appears in Ron's own words. My own telling of the story follows.

In ancient times, the people, after much anguish, succeeded in catching and caging the father of all coyotes, the Trouble-Maker himself, and they too "ignored him" until he fell asleep. Then they fell upon him and killed him. They left his carcass in a covered pit atop Wepum Mountain to waste away, and they celebrated because they thought that they would be done with Coyote forever. Still, they were very careful: they waited until many months had passed before they finally thought it safe to open the cage and clear his bleached bones away. Yet as soon as the door to the cage on the hilltop was opened, they heard his yipping and howling as Coyote rambled off, faster than their eyes could see.

I could sense the importance of Ron's story for the situations with both the Forest Service and the Lowrys. Coyote wants attention, wants you to react, and waits until it looks like you've forgotten him to make his move. Also: he's never completely erased from the picture. "But it feels too good out here," Ron said, rebutting our silence. "You leave all that bad stuff out at the highway."

This is the oft-repeated prescription for the ceremony that one hears from many mouths over the weekend—from someone in the sweat lodge, from the cook, from the prayer leader at Sunday's sunrise ceremony. The two-mile dirt road to the Roxie Peconom Campground is for slowing down: you wave at the oncoming cars, you stop for the cattle you may see coming down the way, and you change out of your everyday mind. You quiet yourself, and you leave your bad feelings out on the tarmac. At the campground, the fifty-foot circle edged with varnished halves of logs has been blessed, and you should approach it with a good heart. But not everyone realizes this, and some forget. For Ron, the ceremony is too important to risk by giving the Forest Service or any angry Maidu Coyotes a reason to crack down on him or his family and friends who help stage it every year. Ron decides to take no chances with his dogs at the ceremony; he'll keep them leashed.

WHOSE BEAR DANCE?

The old-time Bear Dances in Honey Lake Valley are spoken of in terms of both host and place: the Lone Pine, Sand Slough, or Janesville Bear Dances—or as, respectively, Lamb Samson's, Bob Tail's, or Kitty Joaquin's Bear Dances. I found the association of a place with a host to be an important indicator, in everyday speech, of the area's localized family/tribal identities. Yet this manner of describing place-as-host, host-as-place in a sacred and politically specific geography known to all has been disrupted by loss of territory and the administrative imposition of the fiction of *tribe*. For instance, the particular Bear Dance of which I write in this chapter is sometimes called the Susanville Bear Dance, yet because it isn't associated with the Susanville Indian Rancheria, the label is at times confusing and contentious. It invokes the history of the Bear Dance Foundation—Allen Lowry and then the Morales descendants' co-option of the foundation in the mid-1990s—as well as the nonspecific "Susanville Indian" period of the BIA administration at the beginning of the twentieth century.

Meanwhile, the Honey Lake Maidu petition for Federal Recognition I drafted highlights that this event is the "Morales descendents'"—even though it is also a Honey Lake Maidu event, a Mountain Maidu event, a Susanville event, and "Lassen County's oldest existing Native American cultur[al] event." Though there are, for instance, pots, utensils, and bear hides that belong not to its hosts, but to the Bear Dance itself, for the Morales descendants the Bear Dance is "theirs" in part because it is crucial to making the case of their people's continuous cultural and political association in the Honey Lake Valley/Lassen County region.

Other factors, too, undermine these autonomous namings and self-envisionings—namely, the Forest Service's administrative circumscription of this Bear Dance. By the end of this chapter, I will have shown why, when the celebration is sometimes referred to as the Lassen National Forest Bear Dance, the response is made that it is, rather, the Roxie Peconom Campground Bear Dance, the matriarch's name invoked to soften the claim of the state.

A HONEY LAKE MAIDU HISTORY OF THE BEAR DANCE

The tradition of the Bear Dance has a history longer than memory. As early as the 1870s, Bear Dances were documented by white emigrants to the Honey Lake Valley. A Susanville *Lassen Advocate* article from 1887, for example, reads, "A grand Indian dance was given at the Digger Camp near [William Rousches's] ranch last Saturday night. Quite a large delegation of 'pale faces' from Susanville attended." This "camp" was Wetajam, the site of a large village where Honey Lake Maidus had lived for centuries upon centuries, and where Roxie Peconom's grandfather, Wetajam, was the headman.[4]

The Honey Lake Maidus, as I've mentioned, remember Lamb Samson and Bob Tail (also known as Bob Taylor) as important leaders of the old-time Bear Dances in the valley. Their Bear Dances were held, respectively, at Sand Slough (a separate corner of the area known as Wetajam) and Lone Pine (also known as "the Bass Ranch"), through the 1930s. Lamb Samson was Wetajam's grandson, and Bob Tail was Old Tom's son. Tribe members also know that Bear Dances were held at

Stressley's Ranch, before it was ever known as such, but was instead called *Supom*—a place that is today marked by twenty-eight roundhouse depressions surrounded by ever-encroaching subdivisions.

As I probed Honey Lake Maidu peoples' memories further, with the goal of documenting a "Honey Lake Maidu" Bear Dance in every decade of the twentieth century for their Acknowledgment petition, it became clear that there were multiple celebrations going on in some years, and that there were certain reliable hosts. I focused on Honey Lake Maidu hosts, but sometimes distinguishing the Honey Lake Bear Dances from those of other Mountain Maidu peoples who had moved to the Susanville area was difficult. My informants agreed that any Maidu or even Paiute person could and would attend any Bear Dance: for instance, Big Rosie George's Bear Dances could be described as Susanville Indian Rancheria Bear Dances because they were held in that vicinity. Yet Rosie was the daughter of Roxie Peconom's brother, George Davis.

Kitty Joaquin, a Northern Paiute whose first marriage was to the grandson of Servilicn, a well-known Mountain Maidu leader, began to sponsor Bear Dances in 1926 in Janesville, just outside of Susanville. She continued to do so until her death, in 1953. This period, between the late 1920s and the late 1940s, was one of transition, emblemized by the sponsorship and the alliance of all Lassen County Maidu individuals and tribes, and even the Paiutes and non-Indians, in the celebration of the Bear Dance. During this period, until Gladys Joaquin Mankins's assumption of her mother's role, Honey Lake Maidus attended many Bear Dances in the area, including one held in the 1920s (at what today is Susanville's Memorial Park) at which Roxie Peconom sang.[5] I have already introduced the longstanding animosities between the Joaquins and the Peconoms, but in the 1930s and 1940s, many Honey Lake Maidu elders alive today remember attending Kitty Joaquin's Bear Dances, and Peconoms are amply documented in photographs at Bear Dances on her ranch in this era. In 1949, for instance, Ron Morales and Viola Williams's brother, Shine Morales, was the bear—he was caught on film with their young siblings, Yvonne and Earl, watching with big smiles and wormwood fronds.

Gladys Joaquin Mankins's sponsorship of the Bear Dance (1953–1988) began at a low point in the population density of Indians living in Honey Lake Valley, and it opened a new era. Local tribes were greatly reduced in numbers because of the young adult generation's attendance at federal Indian boarding schools and because of economic pressures that forced members to move away. Hosting the Bear Dance communally, as Lassen County Indians, was probably the only practical option. And Mankins's Bear Dance—or the Janesville Bear Dance, as it was also commonly called—became even more of an intertribal, interracial affair than her mother's.

Not unrelated, Mankins's tenure as host coincided with a period of Indian activism across the nation. In Maidu country in the 1960s and 1970s, California Indian dance groups were formed, and the Janesville Bear Dance became a well-known locus of California Indian and Maidu traditionalism. Anthropologist Leigh Ann Hunt explains that

many Indian people pooled their resources and energy to work together, and cultural events of one group became the "property" of all tribes alike as they supported one another. This may partly explain the growth of the Janesville Bear Dance, as it became a Big Time symbolizing cultural heritage for all California Indians rather than being "just an old habit" as Kitty Joaquin [once said]. (1996, 34)

Cultural preservation and identification were becoming recognized as political statements. In fact, in 1977 the Janesville/ Mountain Maidu Bear Dance was named one of the state of California's heritage treasures by then-Governor Jerry Brown, who dropped in on the Bear Dance via helicopter.

During the Kitty Joaquin and Gladys Mankins eras, as Shine Morales's role as the bear shows, Honey Lake Maidu ceremonial leadership continued within the larger transformations of the event. Viola and Ron tell a story about how Dan Williams, Kitty Joaquin's second husband, a famous Maidu doctor and spiritual leader, went to Roxie Peconom in the early 1950s, when she was approximately one hundred years old, and asked for her blessing for Gladys's sponsorship of the Janesville celebration. Roxie gave him a bear hide to use and told him that she would give her blessing as long as there was no drinking at the celebration.[6] Aside from (but contingent upon) the tradition of sociopolitical leaders being the only ones to possess bear hides, the Honey Lake Maidus consider this an act important because it binds the Mankins's celebration to their own long family history of sponsorship.

The Mankins era came to an end when Gladys died and her land was inherited by her unsympathetic step-children. The 1988 Bear Dance, which followed her death, is described by the Honey Lake Maidus as a transition-period Bear Dance, when divisions over which direction to turn arose. One route led to the Bear Dance held at Roxie Peconom Campground for the last fifteen years, another to a kind of dead-end—a separate Bear Dance, held once, outside Honey Lake Valley.

In 1989, in an attempt at cooperation, the Lassen Yah-Monee Maidu Bear Dance Foundation[7] was incorporated as a state nonprofit with Allen Lowry as its chair, and Ron, Marvina Harris, Charles and Everett Smith, and Connie Pimentail as members.[8] The Bear Dance Foundation worked with the Lassen National Forest to found a campsite at which to hold the 1989 celebration. It was named the Roxie Peconom Campground.

The staging of the Bear Dance in the Lassen National Forest has opened a new can of worms: no longer facing the loss of land in the Honey Lake Valley, the Morales family now lives with the hard reality of hosting the Bear Dance on the only site open to it anymore—Forest Service land, which is bound up in bureaucracy. As Ron once told me, out at the new site, "You have to go to Congress to get a tree cut down." Alternatives to this frustrating relationship, as the Bear Dance Foundation generally sees it, will only come through Federal Recognition. In essence, the struggles over land and hosting that followed from the loss of the Mankins's land and roundhouse remain the important struggles today.

There is also another point to consider: how this history of celebrating the Bear Dance intersects with the Honey Lake Maidu petitioning project.

HOSTING THE BEAR DANCE

In the tribe's petition for Federal Acknowledgment, we placed the work of hosting the Bear Dance in the context of a kind of "ceremonial political authority": Honey Lake Maidu tribal leadership is exercised through organizing and hosting the Bear Dance. This complemented another argument we made about general, tribewide "family-based political authority" in answer to Criterion C, which asks for political continuity over the course of the twentieth century. The petition read:

Family is the engine for the cultural work of staging the Bear Dance every second weekend in June, as Leona Morales' descendents have since 1989.

It begins with the salmon cleaning that takes place in the fall. Ron and Viola's cousin Mona and her son David usually bring up the salmon from Oroville.[9] Together (and with about seven interested neighborhood cats), the family cleans and freezes the salmon, storing it up at Indian Heights Full Gospel Church.[10]

Next is the Lassen County Children's Fair in the beginning of May, where the family raises the money it costs to buy all the food and other items for the Bear Dance. Viola's daughters make a trip to Reno, where they stock up on tomatoes, onions, flour, baking soda, and paper plates, etcetera. The work proceeds to Viola's kitchen, and ends up at the Lassen Yah-Monee Maidu Bear Dance Foundation's ever popular fry bread stand, staffed, for example, in 2000 by Viola's children and their families: Nonie, Misha, Ramie, and Tom Crosno, Wanda Brown, Amy Metcham, Season Brown, and Linda Hutt. Wanda's son Maitland made the sign that adorned the stand, which usually pulls in about $1,300, ready to be spent the next month.

There are still many, many preparations to make. Ron Morales needs to oversee the work of the prison crew, arrange the kitchen (with its two stoves and two large cooking pots), string the lights, bring the cleaned salmon to Susanville Supermarket to be filleted, dry the meat pit, order the toilets and dumpsters, arrange for a refrigerator truck, pick up the raffle tickets at the printers, and do the two to three days of work it takes to prepare the Bear Dance flag the traditional way. On the Thursday before the Bear Dance weekend, Ron Morales helps the men running the sweat (Radley Davis and his crew; Davis is Roxie Peconom's brother George Davis' grandson, and a member of the Pit River Tribe) find willow and rocks. Ron also delegates the task of picking a large quantity of wormwood for the Bear Dance itself. Meanwhile, he gives the tobacco he made last fall to Radley as a present for use at the sweats. Mona [Ron's cousin] brings the acorn Ron and his family collected in the fall up from her house, leeched, cooked and ready to thaw and eat on the day of the actual bear's dance, Sunday.

Amidst these exciting preparations come certain problems, predictable after ten years of hosting. These usually involve last minute negotiations with the Forest Service (on whose land the event is held) for parking arrangements, clean-up, and other site management issues.

Throughout these preparations and in the running of the event itself (when anyone can lend a hand), certain orders and practices are evident. First, old-time understandings of gendered work organize labor: men handle meat, pancakes, stew, salmon—any food that requires cooking. Women sit together and make salads on the picnic benches, and it is always a woman who brings in the acorn soup that she has prepared at home. Men do the hauling and chopping of wood. Women organize the serving of food, the raffle and the concession stand. Second, there are certain understandings of community put into practice that are different than those of the dominant, non-Indian culture. For example, all are welcome at this event, and everyone is fed, at no cost. At Bear Dances described by Roland B. Dixon at the beginning of the 20th Century, a clown brought food to the poorest families at the end of the celebration (1905: 320). Today, families leave laden with tin-foil packages of salmon. Third and finally, the understanding of what it means to host the Bear Dance is also culturally encoded: contrary to dominant norms which encourage attention-garnering, hosting the Bear Dance means quietly stepping back so that the guests can enjoy themselves. (Honey Lake Maidus 2001, 62–63)

Perhaps the most important insight into Honey Lake Maidu ritual practice and its relation to sociopolitical order at the Bear Dance, unmentioned above, is that participants use it as a means of linking contemporary change to the old-time practices. According to tribal members—who often expressed this by ignoring my questions or insisting that the Bear Dance is as it always has been—the Bear Dance transcends history and is always traditional because of its ability to ingest change.

The BIA's Branch of Acknowledgment and Research is not so flexibly able to integrate change. Because of this, as petition drafter I worked to bring tribe members' primordialist understandings of the Bear Dance together with the constructivist project of creating a compelling narrative of tribal political and social practices across the decades; I realized that it would serve the people I knew were a tribe to downplay their ritual's own flexibility. In writing the history of the Mankins period, for instance, I tried to carefully wrap the contemporary Honey Lake Maidu celebration of the Bear Dance in the cloak of its long history and convey the Honey Lake Maidu understanding of the continuity of their tribal participation in the event. I emphasized that Roxie Peconom blessed and donated the bear hide that enabled the Mankins Bear Dance and stated that it was thus natural for the Honey Lake Maidu to take the lead in keeping the tradition going in a new locale. My translations of the Branch of Acknowledgment and Research's criteria and the Honey Lake Maidu perspective told a story that downplayed those aspects of Bear Dance history that would indicate changes in family sponsorship, subtly avoiding the complications of the Susanville Indian period and the way that the Bear Dance Foundation began as a multitribal entity.

The Honey Lake Maidu Recognition strategy, and my own, in response—a posture of impatience with the details of Criterion C and distrust of the state's demands of disclosure—amount to a kind of discursive conservativism. To me, this seems quite an appropriate response to the government that administratively lumped all the tribes and now demands, for Acknowledgment, that each has "maintained political influence or authority over its members as an *autonomous entity* from historical times until the present" (italics in original; see Appendix A).

CELEBRATING THE BEAR DANCE

The Dancers—and Spring—Arrive

The Maidu Dancers and Traditionalists have come to the Bear Dance every year since its relocation to the Lassen National Forest, and they dress in their regalia and begin dancing Saturday afternoon. Gorgeous songs—made by mingled voices, whistles, clappersticks, and the tireless drumming of a log pounded on a board-covered earthen pit—spread across the campgrounds, down the stream, among the alders. The dancers, by their cocking, rhythmic body movements, are transformed before one's eyes into quail and other birds, even *sumi,* the deer, with long canes for front legs, dancing with halting steps. Women dancers frame the men's performance, adding their focused energy as they rock softened and beaded strips of animal hide between their hands, lifting one foot then another from the soft, dusty earth. They are bejeweled with flowers. It is finally spring in Mountain Maidu country—penstemon and dwarf waterleaf peek up through the Jeffrey and ponderosa needles.

Sustenance

By the time the dancing's begun, the cooking crew has already fed the assembled guests two meals. The main cook is a Choctaw/Cajun/African American man from Oroville who feeds about three hundred people six meals over three days. On Saturday and Sunday, he wakes up before dawn and adds more grounds and water to the cowboy coffee that's been cooking all night, and he starts frying salmon, salmony pancakes, eggs, and potatoes.

Another crew oversees the cooking of Sunday's dinner: beef knuckle, and sometimes venison, slow-cooked over fifteen hours in a rock-lined pit and made into stew.

The cook tells me, "I come here to feel human again." His work exemplifies the seamlessness of the ritual and the reversals it enacts—the food he serves represents the cooperative, easy nourishment that sets this space apart from the day-to-day struggles. I believe that "feeling human" and eating together move us all beyond the everyday differences that divide us. It makes *me* think far beyond race and tribal status, beyond to how all of us are alike in our need for contribution, and in our stomachs.

Praying for Washington

Ron Morales and Viola Williams's cousin, Radley Davis, and his crew have also long since pulled up, and have already gone out with Ron to collect willow and rocks from the Honey Lake Valley. They have set up a sweat lodge, upstream from the ceremonial dancing circle, near a pool in the stream. They must get the fire started well before dawn to have the rocks ready for the first of the sweats that will run throughout the weekend.

Radley is a gentle man when he runs a sweat. A boy speaks out of turn, a woman steps between the sacred fire and the mound in front of the willow structure, but Radley only reminds them of the right way to do things—ask first to speak, never step between the lodge and the fire—saying, "It's okay. Next time you'll know." He teaches his crew of teenage boys[11] how to handle the tarps to keep out the light, making learning an integral aspect of the sweat.

Learning and healing. He listens to the people in his sweat, the sound of their breathing, maybe even the opening of their pores, and although we're all from different backgrounds and experiences, he fits us in. I silently pray for strength in facing bureaucracy, and later, Radley mentions this aloud, and prays for Federal Recognition, and for his cousin's tribe's endurance and my own. He buoys me. And I remember that if I go step by step I can make it, at the same time that I realize that you don't feel the heat as much when you are singing, following the vocables. The way he describes Federal Recognition to All Our Relations is as a trial. He says, "It's confusing for our old people to have to prove themselves," and his voice is full of feeling for these elders. Then he prays for the persons who make up the Branch of Acknowledgment and Research, he prays for Washington, D.C., and he prays for reconciliation between Federally Recognized and non-Recognized tribes.

He tells us that by sweating we rid ourselves of weakness and fear. I drop into the mountain-born stream, seal it all out, and am renewed.

Handgaming

He sto your moneyyy
He sto wiilli-wee-to willi-wee-to
He sto your money
He sto wiilli-wee-to willi-wee-to
Your moneyyy your moneyyy
He sto winnike-to winnike-to
Your money your money
He sto winnike-to winnike-to

—Top power song, Bear Dance
celebrations, Janesville, 1979[12]

The handgame team from Berkeley, which includes (mostly) non-Indians from the Bay Area and Los Angeles who began attending Bear Dances in Janesville thirty years ago, has been playing the Tyme Maidu from Berry Creek Rancheria.[13] More or less playfully they taunt one another, "Hey, you just sang that song, don't you know any others?" The game goes on for three hours, not including the break that respectfully takes place during the dancers' performance. It finally ends with Berry Creek taking the pot. There will be a rematch later that night.

Handgame is a game of chance about guessing how the opposite team has hidden two sets of marked (also called black or dark) bones. It is also a game of spiritual power—good players have the ability to call or read the hiding team's bones/minds with the aid of their spiritual helpers. Handgame players often also win prizes serially at the raffle because of this gift. Meanwhile, in the Maidu and sometimes Paiute style I've seen played, the hiding team may be able to block the other team's guesses by singing power songs, making certain hand motions, or jeering at/distracting the guessing team. As the game heats up, the jeers get tougher.

Tradition is referenced, toyed with, joked about, then reinvented in these games. Teams try to "out-Indian" one another with their knowledge of songs and their clever manipulations of terms to confuse the team they are playing. They might, for instance, call for the white/unmarked bone instead of the black bone as is usual with the clever *"tep yos!"* which means "dark reversed," or they might call *"sewim!"* to mean that the black bones are lying toward the creek. These tactics sometimes catch the hiding team during moments of distraction, and, confused, they hand over the bones even though the calls may have been wrong. There are also traditions of luck or power: smoking a cigarette is said to help your team, and sticking the counting sticks in the sand helps to secure them, so the other team can't win them. Taylorsville Maidu Farrell Cunningham told me that his father and his buddies created some powerful handgame songs based on Korean folk songs they learned when they were stationed in that country with the army, and that when they sang them when a game was close, they had a long string of wins.

Handgame is a teasing conflict, a way of reflecting real conflict back in the form of mockery: now a member of the Konkow Berry Creek Rancheria is playing handgame with some Mountain Maidus, who comment, "Oooooh, you're all Recognized and have that biiig casino. . . . Let's play for some real money!" Someone from Berry Creek responds, "Naw, we're playing for vouchers today!"

Powerful handgame players have preternatural endurance. This is a game that is known to have gone on for over twenty-four hours straight. Players have bet their cars or homes and have even lost mates (both in gambles and because of them). Because of its requisite tenacity and focus, handgaming is the natural companion of petitioning for Federal Recognition. I believe that part of the cultural logic of the Honey Lake Maidu petitioning effort taps into the energy of handgame. At the very least, handgame lends the Honey Lake Maidu Tribe the understanding that they can outlast the government at its own game.

Ritual Power versus the Government

The Bear Dance accords with old-time orders of power and its acquisition in the same way that handgame does. On a grander scale, however, it works as an annual rebalancing of the forces at work in the world. As such, the Bear Dance requires a submission to universal power for all those involved, for it is only by submission that one is strengthened. Meanwhile, throughout the weekend there are contestatory, restorative, and social events that rebalance personal and tribal powers, such as handgames, sweats, and gatherings with tribal members and friends. This accords with the cultural ideas that, one, power is excreted throughout the natural world and is sentient—it is anyone's to possess if he or she plays the bones right and if power itself so desires it—and, two, constant struggles exist between those who accumulate power. Anthropologist Lowell John Bean has written that, in Native California generally,

man is viewed as the central figure in an interacting system of power holders. As the articulating link between all expression of power, man has been provided with guidelines for acquiring, keeping, and wielding power. Since power is sentient and personalized, man can interact with power or conduits of power much as he would with humans. Power can be dealt with rationally through a system of reciprocal rules (expectations), which were established or handed down to man in early cosmic times. Without individual or community action by man through such rituals as world renewal ceremonies, the balance of power in the universe would be upset, and one side of the system might be disproportionately favored over another. Individually acquired power (knowledge) and traditionally acquired power (held by priests or shamans) must continually be employed by man to maintain the dynamic equilibrium or harmony of the universe. (1975, 26–27)

Working within this general cultural framework, I suggest that the Bear Dance can be seen as a ritual manner of harnessing universal power to face Federal Acknowledgment. Another way to think of this is that the Bear Dance provides the cultural juices that digest the Federal Acknowledgment process, and it is this digestion of the state's power into Maidu terms that is perhaps the most empowering/powerful of any of the Honey Lake Maidu petitioning practices.

In fact, the tribe's petition was brought to the June 2000 Bear Dance, and it was there that the Tribal Council signed off on it. Mailed from Susanville to Washington the next day, the petition's presence reflected, on yet another level, the ritual's intention of world renewal through the rebalancing and realignment of power.

The Anger of the World Maker

At dawn on Sunday, when the dance leader blesses the circle in preparation for the Bear Dance that will take place that afternoon, people stagger from their tents still wrapped in blankets and sleeping bags to take part. One of the dancers tells us the story of the Bear Dance, and offers prayers for the new year.

He says that the World Maker, *Kodojapen*, called a Big Time for all the animals at the beginning of time, to try to get them to work together because he was going to create humankind. All the animals showed up except Bear and Rattlesnake, thus demonstrating their refusal to cooperate. The World Maker, growing angry, called to them by name, and when they finally showed themselves, He threw acorn bread at them. The blows whacked off Bear's tail and flattened Rattlesnake's head.[14] Kodojapen told them that, because of their unwillingness to cooperate when He asked them to, they'd have to lend their spirits to the Bear Dance, which became humankind's chance to supplicate and control the unpredictability of these two creatures in the year to come.

Prayers are then offered by anyone wishing to offer them. Often, they are prayers for a new year of community, family, and "coming together instead of coming apart," as someone puts it. They are prayers for strength, and, in the context of the ritual, they mean personal as well as cultural renewal. The fire lit in the sacred circle remains burning all day.

Before everyone goes back to bed or to the sweat, the rattlesnake, or "flag,"[15] is hung outside the circle, and the bear hide is hung on a post beside it. The rattlesnake has been painstakingly made of tassels from big leaf maple sapling bark and dyed with alder in the traditional pattern of the hosting family. The two wait at the edge of the circle, and no one may photograph them, or any aspect of the ceremony, without Ron's explicit permission, though even then one risks offending any number of participants. Nonetheless, this morning Ron asks me to take a photo "for our petition," he says. "If they get mad at you. Send them to me." I back out and get someone more foolhardy—my boyfriend!—to do the deed.

Dancing the Bear

During the dance, I watch as bear and man fuse. Another man carries the rattlesnake flag and helps guide the weak-sighted bear through the circles of the community. Sometimes the bear will grab a small child or a pretty woman—he is a libidinous, cranky animal, just awakened from hibernation, and he is awesome even as he is clumsy. Two to three hundred people in four or five concentric circles of clasped hands—little children in the middle—dance in alternating directions with munmunim in their hands, up their noses, and/or tucked behind their ears. The dancers sing, "Weda weda wulunai, ho-o wulunai": *weda* means a "big time" (or "big feed," as Viola calls it), *wulunai* means "dancing."[16] There is tremendous unity of community in these circles. A dancer may not know everyone there, but there is something all present have shared, and so there is a knowing togetherness and an opening of spirit between people. In the dust and the hot sun, the dancers' arms are nearly pulled out of their sockets, but all of this is rewarded with a pass of the bear nearby. Then, one breaks the hand clasp and brushes the bear with a frond of munmunim. After some time of passing through the circles, the rattlesnake flag leads the bear toward the stream, and the bear in turn opens the circle from the outside: the hand-holders are thus drawn to the creek, where they ritually wash.

The Maidu Dancers and Traditionalism

Frank LaPena (Nomtipom Wintu) is the leader of the well-respected dance group known as the Maidu Dancers and Traditionalists. His dancers hail from a number of tribes. He has written about the creation of the group in 1973, under Frank Day. Day, a Konkow Maidu, was a religious leader and painter who taught dance to "a group of neophytes to the Maidu dance tradition" (1997, 27). LaPena describes how Frank Day re-created the dances from the songs. Anthropologist Rebecca Dobkins notes that

Day himself had never seen the dances he described, since, in his words, among "the Konkow Maidu people, Konkow tribal dances were extinct in 1900. Now remember that." Since the Konkow

Maidu did not have an active dance tradition, creating the Maidu dancers in 1973 was not a matter of reinvigorating an existing tradition, but of forging a new tradition based upon understandings of the past. Day's memories of what he had been told, and the dance songs he sang, interplayed with the more recent experiences of the younger dancers. (1997, 19)

The Maidu Dancers and Traditionalists' performances on Saturday and Sunday at the Bear Dance are an extremely important part of the celebration. What is more, Frank LaPena and his son Vince, who also sings and dances, are two important spiritual leaders of the event.[17] They often lead the sunrise prayer on Sunday, and they help coordinate the community's dancing of the Bear Dance proper. Thus, the history of Frank Day's amalgamation of the traditional with the modern is necessarily a part of the celebration of "the oldest existing Native American culture" in Lassen County. What I posit is that unlike BAR's skeptical understanding of historical tribal change, such mixtures are evidence of the vitality of Honey Lake Maidu, Mountain Maidu, and Maidu tradition, despite disruptions over time. Just as Frank Day has been described as "an example of an Indian person who chose not to be forced to choose between two worlds" (Dobkins 1997, 19)—which is to say, "He used what worked to make his world whole" (George Longfish and Joan Randall quoted in Dobkins 1997, 19)— making the world whole by integrating the modern community with the past is exactly what the Bear Dance is about. Physically, the modern community dances or performs the traditional community during the event: members, some of whom live far away from their traditional lands, some of whom attend for the first time in decades, join hands and concentrically dance themselves complete, in an old way.

The layers of understandings attached to the community that is danced are also like concentric circles. As Radley Davis explains, on the deepest level the spiritual work of the Bear

Dance has to do with humans coming together on the basis of their common biology. On the next level out from this "center," it's about Indianness generally (perhaps best exemplified by the Maidu Dancers and Traditionalists, who perform Maidu tradition but are assembled from a number of tribes and traditions). Further still, it's about Mountain Maiduness in particular; it is a celebration of Mountain Maidu cultural tradition and cultural survival. And finally, for Federal Recognition and for the Forest Service, the Bear Dance is also positioned as a *Honey Lake Maidu* event. As such, the Bear Dance's cultural and political functions are sometimes at odds with one another.

POLITICS

Over at the Jack descendants' camp there is some shouting. Apparently Marvin Benner, Viola's son as well as Tribal Relations Officer for the Forest Service, told some of his fellow members they would have to move their cars from one side of the creek; the Forest Service had approved only seven cars on "the sensitive north bank" and there were twelve parked there. With Ron's approval, Gina Garcia, the tribal secretary, and her sister Yvonne quickly write up a petition against the Forest Service—and against Marvin, for his role as parking monitor, which is understood by many as work on behalf of the Forest Service. I hear indignation rise in people's voices: "How dare they tell us what to do at our ceremony!" Ron puts the petition up at the concession stand—a board between two trees—and he asks the old-timers who come in off the highway to sign it, too, when they reach for the guest book.

Later, the trouble long brewing between Ron and his nephew Marvin flares up when the petition is sent to the Lassen National Forest. Viola, Linda Hutt, and Wanda Brown write a letter countering the petition and the Honey Lake Maidu tribe on behalf of the Lassen Yah-Monee Maidu Bear Dance Foundation, in opposition to their (double) chair, Comanche.

Their conflict points to nascent tensions between the Bear Dance Foundation and the Honey Lake Maidu Tribe. Furthermore, it reveals the family fissures built into the Bear Dance Foundation, composed as it is of a sister and a brother and two of the sister's children. It also hints at the male power struggle—between an uncle and a nephew roughly the same age—along which the females align themselves by closeness of blood. That Marvin figures as an agent of the state as well as a Native person aggravates each position, and it's clear that the Forest Service is used as an arena for exerting dominance in these relationships. That this drama, part and parcel of old tensions with the Forest Service rearing a many-mouthed head, would arise at the most sacred of Maidu ceremonies is a great misfortune.[18]

I interviewed Marvin in November 1999, hoping to explore some of the tensions between his job and his family and to get his perspective on this tribe's Federal Acknowledgment.

MARVIN BENNER AND THE FOREST SERVICE

The way Marvin describes himself, and the way he talks, is in expanding digressions and returns. It's similar to how he describes his passion for playing steel guitar: he might start with "Old Danny Boy" and end up playing ragtime. It's also similar to the way his mind wanders when he's at meetings with the Forest Service, his employer.

He spoke about the difference between the bureaucratic "mission statements," "time allocations," "cost benefit analyses" and how the people he cares about, Indian people, talk; he also spoke about the differences within himself—fifteen credits away from a B.A., he says, he can play their game, be one of them, but still have flashes of something else sometimes when he is talking to other Forest Service employees. "I can be sitting in a meeting and in a flash I am thinking, instead, of my family"— sometimes he thinks of the story of the Pit Rivers who attacked an encampment of Maidus, brutally killing everyone but one young boy whose mother hid him under a burden basket. When the Maidu men who had been away returned and found their dead they were intent on revenge, but the Pit River chief responded with an offering of peace and regret: three Pit River girls. One of the girls, Nellie Thomas, was Marvin's great-grandmother on his father's side. The little boy who survived was his great-grandfather on his mother's side, John Peconom. That these things happened in what is now the Lassen National Forest is mind-blowing, he told me. Non-Indian members of the Forest Service can talk all day about the forest, but he thinks of it in a much different way. His family history—events from long before he was born—have defined who he is and have left indelible marks upon his daily consciousness. Marvin frames his discussion of the creation of the Lassen National Forest's Roxie Peconom Campground in terms of these familial, historical connections.

The story of the development of the new Bear Dance site is miraculous to Marvin. In 1988, Charles and Everett Smith, who were expected to take over sponsorship of the Bear Dance, decided not to take it on. Then, at a Forest Service Civil Rights meeting, Marvin heard that there was ten thousand dollars available for a worthy project. While his family, tribe, and community were anxious that there might be no Bear Dance in the coming year, Marvin realized that funding the creation of a site on Forest Service land might make it possible. It did.

Ron, Viola, and Marvin speak of coming upon the land where the Roxie Peconom campsite would eventually be developed, and finding it to be a mirror of their ideals: the land had a creek and a flat, spacious area covered in pine needles for camping and dancing. "We went out there, checked it over, and I even brought a picnic lunch for us," explained Marvin. It was like coming upon a relatively intact piece of the spiritual homeland, preserved as part of Lassen National Forest. Marvin wrote, in *News from Native California*,

My great grandmother [Roxie Peconom] spoke of the times, before the coming of the white man, when the Washo, Paiute, and Maidu met near the north base of Diamond Mountain in Lassen County and traveled up to *papykodt* (the Willard Creek area) and camped. There they would trade and have a good time and my grandmother, Leona Morales, suggested that it was a good site for a wedam. It occurred to me that the idea could be taken one step further. If a campground were developed on the site, it could be used by the Native American community for traditional activities and by the general public. It was a win/win proposition. . . . The site gives one a certain gladness to be there, a goodness surrounds you. It's no wonder that the tribes in times past gathered there. (1989, 19)

Sanctioned even by the matriarch Roxie Peconom, the site was a perfect fit.

Still, the tribe's narrative of constancy ignores the fact of Forest Service conscription—and it ignores the idea that there was a negotiation through which a win-win situation was reached. I now realize that *ignores* is the key word here, for ignoring the state (to whatever degree possible) is one way that the Honey Lake Maidus have coped with its impositions over time. With their backs deliberately turned to it, the Honey Lake Maidu posture is one of sovereign "ignore-ance": the purity and ancientness of the Bear Dance ritual become successful answers to the Forest Service's encroachments and the prying eyes of BAR. This kind of Coyote sovereignty creates obstacles for Forest Service attempts to dominate Maidu ritual practice. Turning the tables to "acknowledge the state" through this lens of Honey Lake Maidu sovereignty, we can ask, What is the Forest Service's interest in the wedam? What did it win by funding the creation of Roxie Peconom? How is the relationship between the two groups complicated by the non-Recognized status of the Honey Lake Maidus? What leverage does this offer the Forest Service, and what leverage does this offer the Honey Lake Maidus?

Marvin, meanwhile, remains positioned between the Honey Lake Maidu and Forest Service postures. And he admits that despite the success of the creation of the Roxie Peconom Campground, his job with the Forest Service is a hard one. He has to remain impartial—"mutual," he says—when concerns about his own tribe come up in his dealings with other tribes and the Forest Service. I have heard Marvin and Ron butt heads over Marvin's "mutuality" again and again. But while Marvin's situation is complicated, it is also certainly unique, and he believes he is in a position to get the non-Recognized "recognized." This may not be in the sense of having complete sovereignty, but by way of the kind of recognition the Forest Service can offer, which in turn can hopefully be used as a crowbar for prying open the capital R kind of recognition. He explained that although non-Recognized tribes do not fit Congress's, the executive's, or the BIA's bill for a government-to-government relationship, the Forest Service has made room for consulting with non-Recognized peoples. "At the Forest Service," says Marvin, "we *know* we can't turn our backs on local Maidu people." "Working together" is both a legal reality and a practical one for the Lassen National Forest.

His confidence in Forest Service R/recognition, however, is betrayed by his contingency plan for Federal Recognition: that the eleven autonomous bands of the Pit River Nation place the Honey Lake Maidus "under their umbrella of sovereignty," so that Ron will have sovereign status behind him when he speaks to the Forest Service and makes his demands. This sovereign attachment would be based on tribal ties such as those with the Pit River peoples through Nellie Thomas. Although this is a practical solution—Marvin knows how the Forest Service works—it is simply not satisfying to Honey Lake Maidus like Ron or Gina Garcia, a young Old Tom descendant who involved herself deeply with the Honey Lake Maidu petitioning effort. Marvin's alternative vision of Recognition itself parallels the eclecticism of Forest Service policy toward non-Recognized tribes, which seems to acknowledge them even as it marginalizes them in practice.

WORKING TOGETHER

Tribal Relations Program Manager Linda Reynolds's 1995 report, "Tribal Governments and Communities in the Sierra Nevada Ecoregion: A Sierra Nevada Ecosystem Project Assessment," reveals some of the legal reasons why the appearance of working together, even with non-Recognized peoples, is so important to the Forest Service.

Reynolds's report is meant, in part, as a how-to for tribal relations managers like Marvin for making it through the complex of legislation with bearing upon the Forest Service's relationship with local Native peoples. It states, "Although not recognized tribes, these communities along with individual Indian people must still be considered under a suite of federal and state laws dealing with environmental analysis, religious freedom, archaeological sites, and protection of Native American human remains" (1995, 7). Statutes the Forest Service must comply with include: the American Indian Religious Freedom Act of 1978; the Religious Freedom Restoration Act of 1993; the National Indian Forest Resources Management Act (which directs the secretary of the interior in consultation with the tribes to assess the status of Indian forest resources and their management); the Native American Graves Protections and Repatriation Act of 1990; the National Environmental Policy Act of 1969 (which includes, with environmental protection, considerations of "cultural values and diversity"); the Federal Land Policy and Management Act of 1976 (which asks for coordination of land policy with tribal agendas); the National Historic Preservation Act of 1996; and the Archaeological Resources Protection Act of 1979.

These statutes apply to the non-Recognized, but whether they *get applied* to the non-Recognized is the real question. Reynolds told me that there is no codified interpretation of this relationship between the Forest Service and the non-Recognized tribes. Instead, the answer is found in regional interpretations of what removing "obstacles to developing a working govern-ment-to-government relationship" with Indian people means. In one national forest, it could imply that the Forest Service has a role in bringing Recognition to the non-Recognized. But in another it might mean defining *tribe* in strict ways, thus removing the "obstacle" of factionalism among non-Recognized Indian communities in places such as Susanville. Local Forest Service districts are given leeway to interpret these ambiguities in their daily practices.

Yet Reynolds's report—its physical existence, even—suggests that Indian peoples (and the body of law that shadows them) reshape understandings of the Sierran ecosystem by their presence, concerns, and demands. This reshaping of the orientations and responsibilities of the Forest Service involves a crucial reshaping of federal manners of "handling" Indian peoples. Indeed, an alternative to thinking of the Bear Dance as the last cultural gasp of the Mountain Maidu peoples, as much of the non-Indian public would assume, is to understand it as the working legacy, negotiated with the state, between two effectual sovereigns, the U.S. government and the Honey Lake Maidus. Here, again, the Bear Dance defies expectations because of its flexible articulation between change and cultural stasis.

A LETTER FROM RON MORALES TO THE FOREST SERVICE

The way Ron Morales figures it, the Forest Service is part of the government and so they have to be suspicious of the non-Recognized tribes. It is his experience that Forest Service officials can always hold non-Recognition against the Honey Lake Maidus and capriciously enforce the laws of their own making, despite the idealism of Reynolds's report. Nonetheless, he asked me to help draft a letter to the Lassen National Forest that summa-rized his complaints against it. Evidently, he retains some hope for the relationship, if only because of his attachment to the Roxie Peconom Campground. In what follows, I include his main points within the larger contexts in which he understands them.

From his perspective as chair of the Bear Dance Foundation, the Forest Service makes holding the Bear Dance very complicated. Ron has trouble getting the Forest Service to allow dead wood on or near the site to be cut, and for the past few years he has gone to great physical lengths to haul the wood needed for the ceremony from elsewhere. The basic pattern that he sees is that the Forest Service's multiuse approach to the nation's forests means that it validates things like cattle grazing over ceremonial use of the land by Native people. One year, to his great gall, the regional office gave permits for the Roxie Peconom Campground (for the entire week before the Bear Dance) to a group calling themselves the Paiute Renegades, black-powder shooters and practitioners of the frontier arts. Ron and his tribe have contributed a lot of work to the site named for his grandmother, and they feel a great deal of propriety over it. They want the spiritual power that they know resides there to be protected. And the way they understand it, the Forest Service bureaucracy does its best to constrain their activities, despite their statutory right to host their event in the forest.

For instance, for many years the Forest Service would threaten the cancellation of their ceremony if the Bear Dance Foundation did not pay permit fees and carry insurance. Yet when Ron attended the Forest Service's 1999 California-wide Tribal Summit, other tribes informed him that they never have to pay permit fees and that insurance requirements are waived because of the religious nature of their ceremonies. Ron and Viola had been struggling for years to buy insurance, estimated to cost eight hundred dollars. And only in 2000 did the Lassen National Forest concede that the Bear Dance Foundation should not have to pay its thirty-dollar use permits. Despite this (small) concession, it was hard for Ron to forgive and forget. Probably because it was so hard-won, and probably because the Forest Service still pressures the Bear Dance Foundation to purchase insurance, to the point of refusing to discuss long-term development of the Bear Dance site because of what the forest supervisor says is the tribe's unwillingness to work with him and his agency.

Added to this, but left unsaid in the letter, is the personal tension between Ron and District Ranger Bob Andrews, who Ron says once told him in exasperation, "If you don't like our rules, find yourself another place to hold your ceremony." Their relationship is another example of the way that the Bear Dance entails an annual rebalancing among power holders.

THE DISTRICT RANGER:
A BUREAUCRAT AND HIS BUREAUCRACY

Bob Andrews told me that at meetings and in mandates about American Indians from the U.S. Forest Service in Washington, D.C., there is an assumption of similar tribal backgrounds and family ties in a National Forest region or on a reservation. Mention is rarely made of rancherias. He was not aware that the Susanville Indian Rancheria is considered a single, bureaucratically Recognized tribe even though there are members of a number of ethnological tribes who live on it. Nonetheless, he is beginning to realize that there are tensions between the rancheria and the nonrancheria groups in Susanville—the Susanville Indian Rancheria's Paiutes lining up against the Honey Lake Maidus—and some of the rancheria's Maidus aligning against them as well. The latter is perhaps the most confusing fact of all: the situation can be Maidu versus Maidu when it comes to the Bear Dance.

It became clear to me that the Bear Dance Foundation's status as a state-of-California-registered nonprofit organization was the reason he dealt with it at all. When I pressed him, and mentioned the Reynolds report, he told me, "I have greater responsibility to work with Recognized tribes in government-to-government relationships. At Roxie [Peconom Campground], though, I work with un-Recognized the same as the Recognized." He also made it clear that he talks quite a bit with Allen Lowry, and that between Lowry and Ron, he "gets it from both sides." This position—in between interested parties, pulled in multiple directions (and awaiting direction from above for how to deal with it)—is a classic one from the origins and history of the Forest Service and its national forest system, which describes itself on its brown and yellow signs as "the land of many uses."[19]

At this point Bob Andrews put away his papers and told me about why he thinks he and Ron do not get along, do not work together like the Forest Service brochures might suggest: it all has to do with the Bear Dance Foundation's unwillingness to follow Forest Service procedures in its celebration of the Bear Dance. "I won't be rushing to formalize a longer term agreement with the Bear Dance Foundation when its members don't even obey the rules set for the yearly permit renewal." For instance: purchasing insurance and having dogs on leashes— "What if that big dog of Ron's knocked someone over and *I* had to go to court?" One of these days he said he is going to have to fine Ron "and think of the drama!" Drama, because he said he really thinks he understands Ron's position. He gave Ron's side of the story as he imagined it: "'My people lived here for centuries and died here and I have to go to the U.S. Forest Service and sign an *agreement?*'" But Bob Andrews cannot stop thinking about accountability and liability, bureaucracy and law, and his responsibility to them.

Throughout the interview, he expressed the feeling that having to deal with Native peoples because of the Roxie Peconom Campground only makes his job more irritating. This is surely because he does not think that dealing with Indian people should be such a large part of his job, if a part at all. But his irritation at having to deal with Indian people might also be considered an important impact that the Honey Lake Maidus have upon the state: involvement with Indian people triggers a kind of bureaucratic backfiring upon the state's own bureaucrats, especially when the Indians do not behave/are not organized as the policy reports expect or predict they should be.

We should consider, too, that while hosting the Bear Dance on Forest Service land is an imposition in many ways for the Bear Dance Foundation (and for Ron Morales, in particular), the Bear Dance Foundation also gets something for its troubles: not only money for site development that it would not otherwise have, but also certain advantages that come of the Forest Service's trepidation in the face of its necessary walk through the tangle of federal Indian law. Indeed, though the Forest Service causes Ron significant irritation, it must be noted that the Bear Dance Foundation is not the powerless victim of the Forest Service. In their posture of guerilla sovereignty, foundation members have built extensive structures at Roxie Peconom Campground without Forest Service permission: for instance, the kitchen retaining wall that the organization now wants Forest Service monies to finish. And I must admit that I heard someone make a joke (?) about ringing tree trunks in the fall so there will be dead wood on-site that might be claimed and used for the Bear Dance.

Meanwhile, in the extremely tense meetings with the Lassen Yah-Monee Maidu Bear Dance Foundation, at which the Forest Service tries to "administer" the event and the Honey Lake Maidus try to "host" it (reflecting their separate understandings of the Bear Dance's malleability versus its constancy), the Lassen National Forest's monolithic understanding of Maiduness rears its head as a threat.

SPLITTING ROOT HAIRS: MEETINGS, CLASHES, AND DIFFERENT "FACILITATIONS" OF HONEY LAKE MAIDU AND FOREST SERVICE RELATIONS

There were three important meetings between the Forest Service and the Bear Dance Foundation while I lived in

Susanville and immediately thereafter (March 2000, October 2000, and May 2001). The Forest Service's spin on these meetings is that they were mildly successful, and that the two groups are slowly beginning to work together—with the help of a costly, professionally trained facilitator from the Sacramento Valley. Ron's take on the meetings was expressed as an understanding he said he'd come to: "White people lie with their words and faces." Though he was raised not to smile and shake hands with people he doesn't like or doesn't trust—raised not to sit at the table with enemies—that's what he sees Forest Service officials doing again and again. And thus, while the Forest Service might like to position itself as the beneficent protagonist in the drama, the Honey Lake Maidus reposition it as the antagonist.

Meetings between the Forest Service and the Bear Dance Foundation, I should add, are organized through Marvin Benner, who calls his mother and asks her when his sisters and uncle can meet. The result is that most foundation members are not really sure what a meeting is about or how long it will last, and what is more, Marvin's call usually comes only a day before the scheduled meeting. This Forest Service "shuttle diplomacy," founded in bureaucratic notions of communication, is most indicative of the breakdown in communication: the Tribal Relations guy has to get the tribes and the bureaucrats to relate, and, in the local Indian world, Marvin's job is next to impossible, partly because of his affiliations with both tribe and state. Understandably, tribal members find the fact that they rarely deal directly with those who wield the power in the Forest Service insulting.

The March 10, 2000 meeting—in response to the letter I'd helped Ron write—included the new forest supervisor, Ed Cole, District Ranger Bob Andrews, and Cindy Diaz, who works on event planning and permitting. Also present were Ron, Viola, Wanda Brown, Marvin Benner, myself, Mike McCourt, and a third non-Indian ally, Steve Camacho. The two most important topics of discussion at this meeting were topics that bore upon each party's conflicting ideas of Indianness.

First, there was a serious conflict about understandings of ecology and land use. Toward the end of the long and frustrating meeting, Cindy Diaz explained that she needed to see fewer cars parked within the boundaries of the campsite, because the weight of the cars might damage the root hairs of the trees. This seemed compelling to me at first, but Ron and Viola were convincingly adamant that two days out of the whole year was not going to kill any trees. Ron argued, "What about the cattle—don't they damage root hairs?" Viola's clincher was, "You've got environment concerns, well, *we're Indians, we know* about taking care of the environment!" This resort to the primordial signaled a complete breakdown in the discussions. What the Forest Service representatives did not seem to understand was that the Roxie Peconom Campground is a power spot in the old tradition, and *only good can happen there*—not even harm to root hairs. And to Ron and Viola, bureaucratization of the sacred was pure affront.

This cultural communication gap was also related to the issue that would eventually land Marvin into hot water at the Bear Dance, the issue that everyone present referred to as "controlling the Indians": who would do the work at the Bear Dance of keeping Indians from hundreds of miles away from parking their cars wherever they wanted (that is, in spots not approved by the Forest Service's biologists)? Everyone looked to Ron, the main organizer, who flatly said he would not do it. He said, "This is *their* event!" What it means, culturally, to host a Bear Dance does not include administering what guests can or cannot do, though this is certainly part of the Forest Service culture. Clearly, the two viewpoints were at odds.

Dorothea Theodoratus and Frank LaPena have written about power spots and spaces sacred to California's Native peoples, and their words speak to the impasse of perspective we came upon at this meeting:

Federal land management policies and their burdensome, often ethnocentric, interpretations and distortions sometimes serve to polarize the assessment of Indian claims as unusual and illogical. In other words, the qualities of a place or a region that make them sacred—as well as the concomitant reverence and spiritual activities of the native practitioners—are profoundly different from mainstream perceptions of these places, attitudes and activities. This is, of course, the problem of converting Native American site realities into "understandable" non-Indian categories. (1992, 212)

I believe that it is the Forest Service's perception of Honey Lake Maidu "illogic" that translates into its patronizing tone and approach.[20] And I found that conflict over understandings of appropriate land use led directly into conflict about who the Forest Service believes should be hosting the Bear Dance.

Indeed, the meeting's second conflict of perspective came fully to a head at its close, when talk turned to the future of the Roxie Peconom Campground "collaboration." Part of the long-term plan of the Bear Dance Foundation is the construction of a roundhouse for ceremonial use.[21] To summarize the conversation that surrounds the following excerpt, the foundation is frustrated because, although roundhouse plans were submitted in 1990, there has been no progress to date on approving them. And even smaller projects like roofing the arbor where dinner is served on Bear Dance Sunday have been stalled. The Forest Service, however, does not believe it can support the (further) development of the Roxie Peconom Campground if the cultural endeavors there might exclude other Indian people or tribes who want to be involved.

> *Viola Williams*: Before we can build a roundhouse *who* has to be included?
> *Bob Andrews*: Other Maidus—on the rancheria.
> *Viola*: We have gone to them!
> *Bob*: If lots of groups come to us and say, "We want to be involved," I can't exclude them. They *have* shown an interest. They have said they'd like to be involved with events that happen at Roxie Peconom.

Viola: I'm sorry that we weren't included at that meeting. We could sit down with any of them. I don't want to see no trouble with them, though.

Bob: But hopefully they'd all be willing to sit down together—

Ron [growling]: The Susanville Indian Rancheria has nothing to do with the Bear Dance!

Bob: I thought they sponsored the Bear Dance insurance.

Ron: That was only one year—

Bob [smugly]: The original signers of the early permits were Maidus from the rancheria.

Here, the Forest Service had finally laid its program bare. Despite the strenuous protests of the Honey Lake Maidus, it was threatening them with steamrolling their hosting of the Bear Dance in the name of what it deemed was the most convenient condensation of their Nativeness: the Forest Service wanted happy, cooperative "Susanville Indians." It was an attempt to harmonize Maiduness and Maidu-Maidu conflict. Consistently, the Forest Service turned what were political discussions toward racial concerns in order to sideswipe a specifically Honey Lake Maidu sovereignty—the Forest Service's confrontations with the Bear Dance hosts were subverted by arguments focused on their "larger responsibility to all Indians," as well as an instrumental retreat to legal-administrative categories such as Federal Recognition.

This issue was carried on, months later, in another Forest Service–facilitated meeting that neither Ron nor Bob chose to attend. With these two players out of the picture momentarily, and with Marvin Benner, Wanda Brown, and Cindy Diaz in the driver's seat, talk moved toward the possibility of sharing the site with other Maidus, keeping in mind the greater goal of building a roundhouse for the Forest Service's "public," as well as for ceremonial use.

As she continued the unsinkable conversation of the previous meeting, Cindy described how, to the Forest Service, there is a difference between the Bear Dance ceremony and the Bear Dance site. She suggested that the Bear Dance Foundation needed to understand that other Maidus have rightful interests in the site. Visions of long-term development of the site would need to include Maidus other than those on the Bear Dance Foundation. With broader participation/consensus, there would be the possibility of long-term permits for the ceremony and for the site, which would mean the possibility of building a roundhouse there. In order to get to this stage, though, there would have to be consensus-building with the Rancheria Maidus, and "we'd need to get past parking and firewood," to really outline the kind of relationship that would exist with the Forest Service. Cindy suggested that another foundation could be formed for site development, and she offered the Forest Service building and the Forest Service's professional facilitator for a meeting open to all Maidus interested in a "cultural development project at Roxie Peconom." Cindy said that this kind of arrangement would not mean complete freedom from the Forest Service, because the Forest Service would still be interested in engineering and the environmental specs for any building plans. What the facilitator added was telling: "Perhaps this is a situation of coming together to get what you want, or not getting what you want."[22]

The fiery, eighty-one-year-old Viola, who was fairly quiet throughout the decidedly (and thus, to me, ominously) cool-headed meeting, was obviously considering from all angles this idea that working with the rancheria might be the only way forward. At the meeting's end she piped up, "I like the idea of a portable roundhouse. How about that?" Her novel—and strange—suggestion would maintain the Maidu political status quo, but also incorporate the important ceremonial structure. And the Honey Lake Maidus could remove it when it was not in use so that no other Maidus, Paiutes, or non-Indians (whether they be tourists, "Paiute Renegades," boy scouts, or cattle) could mess with it when they were not around.

The Forest Service clearly feels that the Indian community should come together, because it's the law that they work with all of them. Yet Bob Andrews' and Cindy Diaz' feelings about this, and perhaps their anger in having to get involved at all, come down to a patronizing judgment that the Honey Lake Maidus probably aren't a tribe. They insist that they're just a family, and because they're just a family, they need to rely too heavily on the Forest Service for help running their event. Bob told me, "The real contradiction on Ron's side is that Ron doesn't think that he should be ruled by the Forest Service, but then he demands county prison crews to clean up the site and cut and split wood!"

He has a certain point; prison crews have been used to clean up before and after the Bear Dance ever since the first Bear Dance was held on the Lassen National Forest in 1989. The Bear Dance Foundation used to arrange this without the Forest Service. Jack Osborn at the California Correctional Center (CCC) in Susanville used to find Ron Indian inmates to do the work. It should be emphasized, however, that contracting out inmates from the CCC is a common practice among organizations in Susanville, a holdout from the era of the town's congenial relationship with the prison industrial complex. Thus, rather than revealing the tribe's inauthenticity, it seems to point out how much of an accepted local institution the Bear Dance Foundation really is. Somehow, over the years, using prison labor (especially that of Indian prisoners) became part of the tradition of hosting the Bear Dance at Roxie Peconom Campground.[23] When Jack Osborn retired, the Bear Dance Foundation began contracting a crew through the Forest Service.

When Bob Andrews questions this practice, he emphasizes that the Forest Service is doing the Bear Dance Foundation a favor by contracting the prison crew for them. Because it's just a favor, he wants Forest Service personnel to have a say over what the crews do out there, not Ron. Fundamentally, Bob thinks that since the Forest Service does not sponsor the event, the Honey Lake Maidus should do the work. "Get the young men to do it! I really want to help Ron—he shoulders too much of the burden. But what/where is this Honey Lake Maidu 'community'?"

Lynne Guerrero, an attorney with California Indian Legal Services, was eventually retained by the Bear Dance Foundation (at Ron's insistence) to negotiate with the Forest Service on its behalf. Before the third and final meeting I will discuss, Guerrero prepped the foundation, telling it that in order to "work with the Forest Service" (itself an assumption about the Bear Dance Foundation's intentions, which caused grumbling, but less than usual) the foundation should be expanded to include more than just Leona Morales's descendants. The Honey Lake Maidus thus began to prepare a new counterstrategy. "The Forest Service is never going to work with just one family," Guerrero repeated. This was the very language her colleague Will Jackson, as we will see in the next chapter, used to express the state's position on Federal Recognition: "The BAR is never going to work with just one family." I preview this because the parallels are important to recognize: both the Forest Service and BAR demand reorderings of Honey Lake Maiduness in order for it to be acceptable. According to Guerrero, "We'll have to show that the foundation is composed of many Honey Lake Maidu families" in order for the Forest Service to take it seriously as a Mountain Maidu organization. "The Forest Service's perception is that they're only dealing with a few Maidu individuals when they're dealing with the Bear Dance Foundation. And they think that's inappropriate. Andrews is under pressure from other Maidu people, and he knows that the Forest Service doesn't have to work with individuals." In other words, because the Forest Service did not think that family hosting was appropriate, that tradition, a very old one that predated any kind of coalition hosting, would have to be changed! The Bear Dance Foundation, this time, perhaps because of Guerrero's pressure, could see that compromise was in order. It voted to add members to its ranks. It was not hard to find that Brad Peconom, Gene Ryan (a Bob Junior descendant) and Amelia Garcia (an Old Tom descendant) were interested. Their efforts at the next Bear Dance took a great deal of pressure off of Ron, Viola, and Linda Hutt, the Bear Dance Foundation's treasurer. As a result, too, the foundation began to reflect the Honey Lake Maidu tribe rather than just one tribal lineage.

Guerrero's presence at the next day's meeting (May 4, 2001) between the Bear Dance Foundation and the Forest Service seemed unnerving to District Administrator Mike Zunino and District Ranger Bob Andrews, the Forest Service representatives who were present. Bob, as we've seen, is terrified of being sued, and I thought perhaps that this was why he was so terse, even in his patronizing decision to not allow any cars on the north side of the creek this year because of past problems, and in his comment to the Bear Dance Foundation that "your track record works to your detriment." Later, he revealed that he had expressed his "disappointment" over his relationship with the Bear Dance Foundation to Maidus from the rancheria. And he pulled out a letter that had been hand-delivered to him that morning by Allen Lowry, a letter that made clear why he was acting so cornered. It read:

May 4, 2001

Dear Mr. Andrews:

This letter is to inform you that the Maidu people of the Susanville Indian Rancheria ("SIR"), wish to express their continued desire to participate in any and all decisions concerning the use of "the Bear Dance site" on Willard Creek. As you know, the majority of the Maidu families in Lassen County are represented within the SIR Tribal membership. Many of these families have a long and ancient history of participation in our annual ceremony. Over the last few years, a growing concern among the Maidu People, traditional Bear dancers, and Ceremonial Leaders has developed because of the way the U.S. Forest Service has allowed a few individuals to control the Bear Dance Site.

Traditionally, the Maidu People select their own leaders and especially when a ceremonial is concerned. The simple fact that the U.S.F.S. continues to allow the same person to control through Use Permit or otherwise a ceremonial site of the Maidu puts the U.S.F.S in a position of selecting our leaders. The SIR feels that for the last few years the U.S.F.S. has allowed an individual and few members of his family to desecrate the Bear Dance on Willard Creek. The so called organization you have been dealing with has little or no connection with the Maidu People in Lassen County, the SIR or anywhere else. It is our belief that this organization was dissolved years ago, and the name was picked up and used by people and persons to promote their own interests. We demand that U.S.F.S. no longer allows this situation at the Bear Dance Site to continue.

We propose that our government to government relationship be honored and that this Tribe be recognized for who we are and that we be consulted regarding any decisions being made with our ceremony on U.S.F.S. lands.

Sincerely,

[signed] SIR Chairman, Ike Lowry[24]
[signed] Allen Lowry, Maidu Cultural Rep.

Each party to this Maidu conflict has its own understanding of Mountain Maidu history in the area, and particularly of the history of the Lassen Yah-Monee Maidu Bear Dance Foundation. But as Wanda Brown was careful to enunciate, buoyed by her anger at Andrews' use of this letter to make his point about how he has tired of working with the Bear Dance Foundation, "This is Maidu business, not Forest Service business at all."

It was convenient for the Lowrys to put the Forest Service in the middle of their conflict with Ron. I believe this was solely a strategy, however, for I cannot reconcile the sovereignty the SIR struggles for with the town of Susanville with the idea that it is the Forest Service that allows Ron to host the Bear Dance and doesn't allow them to. Thus, what I believe we really see here is more about how local Indian people get something from the state by manipulating its bureaucracy. In this case, the SIR letter crushed the possibility of Andrews negotiating a compromise with the Honey Lake Maidus. The meeting ended soon after this letter was shared, and in its aftermath, there was only a widening impasse between the Honey Lake Maidus and the Forest Service—and Ron and Bob in particular. The SIR Maidus, meanwhile, must already have been planning their own Bear Dance, which, in 2002, was held in Mountain Meadows. While this might seem a logical and perhaps traditional solution to the problem, the fact remains that it took place, with divisive effect, on the same weekend as the Honey Lake Maidu Bear Dance. It forced local Maidu people to make personal choices that were construed as political.

MAIDU BUSINESS

There is a longer history of cooperation among the Mountain Maidu tribes than today's relations would indicate. Telling the story of some of these alliances and feuds in the Honey Lake Maidu petition for Acknowledgment was important in order to show the Branch of Acknowledgment and Research that its own administration had led to the difficulties faced in the Honey Lake Maidu community today. But because of the state's history of trying to erase tribal differences, revealing tribal cooperation was risky and unappealing to the Honey Lake Maidus: they already knew that the "Susanville Indians" period left them in the position of having no legal sovereignty to speak of. Under pressure from the Forest Service to open hosting of the Bear Dance to all Maidu, they girded themselves against state-driven change by turning to Federal Recognition as what they believed might be their last hope for satisfactory sovereign resistance. And the tribe turned, with my support and that of others, to certain tellings of a noncooperative tradition as a bulwark for both its petition and its position contra the Forest Service.

But as they tried to turn their back to the state's trespasses into their history, the Honey Lake Maidus revealed how their defensive strategy was also an "offensive" one. The ugly—offensive—side of their relationship with other Indian people (particularly other Mountain Maidu people) is emphasized in daily conversation and at meetings, despite clear connections between them today and in the past: Ron and Viola's first cousin's daughter (née Carole Madero) is married to Ike Lowry, the chair of the SIR who had signed the letter to Bob Andrews quoted above; Gene Ryan shares family with Allen Lowry; Ron's children both have a child whose other parent is an SIR member; and two of Viola's daughters live on the rancheria. What is more, both groups share similar struggles against the federal government, the state, and the local non-Indian community. Finally, SIR Maidus attend the Morales-sponsored Bear Dance in a heartfelt way every year. Yet the fact remains that the offensive aspect of petitioning (in both senses of the word) means conflict with other Indian peoples.

CONCLUSION: COYOTE IS IN POLITICS

At the sweat I attended in 2001, Radley Davis said, "Coyote is in politics," and prayed for healing in and between Indian communities. A member of the Susanville Indian Rancheria I spoke with at the ceremony implied the same; he said that he had been warned by neighbors not to come to this Bear Dance, that his food would be poisoned, whether literally or symbolically I am not sure. Yet he came nonetheless. The final point I would like to emphasize in this chapter is that the Bear Dance is a Big Time, a coming together of different village/tribal communities, which even in the old days was a dangerous time despite being a time of spiritual celebration. In 1928, Bill Joe, a Konkow Maidu informant for the anthropologist Hans Uldall, described Big Times in the following manner:

When they went to a Big Time in the old days . . . they sent two or three to the roundhouse [of the host village] with orders to look and listen, and when [they] came back they told the chief everything.

"Everything is good," they said. At daybreak [the rest of the people] went up to the roundhouse. Then the speaker greeted them from the top of the roundhouse, "Go ahead, you fellows, all is well, there is nothing wrong, it is good!" he said. "Go in, hurry up, go in!" he said. Then one went back to fetch the women. The men sat on their haunches inside. Then the women went in. Only then did the man sit down and put down his bow next to him all well strung, which he would grab at once if anything went wrong. (Uldall and Shipley 1977, 77–78)

Perhaps, then, Coyote has always been a guest, in one form or another, at the Bear Dance. He is certainly a vibrant figure in modern Mountain Maidu consciousness. Although sometimes called by the name Devil, in the myths he is a figure who moved, dialectically, alongside the World Maker.[25] Gary Snyder has poetically (and eclectically) captured some of this essence in his introduction to William Shipley's *The Maidu Indian Myths and Stories of Hanc'ibyjim* (1991), a new translation of Tom Young's (or Hanc'ibyjim's) stories recorded by Roland B. Dixon in 1902 and 1903. Snyder writes, "As Earthmaker fantasizes a world in which unmarried girls remain virgins and married couples remain celibate, Coyote calls for tickling, lovemaking, and whispering to each other" (1991, viii). Indeed, there is, as Shipley put it elsewhere, a Rabelaisian quality to the Mountain Maidu oral tradition. Hanc'ibyjim's stories include one about how Coyote managed to marry his own daughter, and countless tales about how he convinced different women to have sex with him although they didn't intend to. My favorite is about how he convinced a group of women he was one of them by presenting his erect penis as his baby. Bill Simmons has put it this way: "Coyote is clever, selfish, self-destructive and comical, while Earthmaker is more group than self oriented and therefore heroic, but also incapable of defending himself at times" (n.d., 25). I would add that Coyote is competitive, angry, and dangerous in complement to the World Maker's traits. Neither side is complete without the other. Without Coyote, the Bear Dance's renewal would not feel so sweet, nor be so necessary.

The man I spoke with who came to the Susanville Bear Dance despite the warnings from his family and friends said he was there because it was the celebration he had attended as a young man—it was *his* too. His words offer a way to understand the spirit and tradition of the Bear Dance as it articulates with the Forest Service, the Federal Acknowledgment process, and with Indian people of many tribes. The Bear Dance has long been part of the history of the state's attempts to administer Indian identity and existence. But this very old role the state has played is surpassed by an even longer history of division (whether by tribe or tribelet seems unimportant) among Maidu groups as well as by a very long history of the dance of the bear, rattlesnake, and community in concentric circles. The Bear Dance is a ritual for renewal, coming together, and healing that works despite and beyond the politics of its staging, hosting, or planning.

CHAPTER FIVE

PETITIONING AND FREEDOM

For the Honey Lake Maidus, non-Recognition has come to mean a lack of freedom—a lack of freedom, for instance, to celebrate the Bear Dance without intensive Forest Service intervention. Because of this, they are eager to work within the frame of the Federal Recognition process. Yet the price of their submission of a petition is a postural submission to the state, and the loss of other freedoms. To understand their engagement of this contradiction as petitioners we must understand how freedom is a means of governance even as it is also, by another definition, simply the opposite of oppression. I turn to sociologist Nikolas Rose (1999), who crosses genealogical descriptions of power—those that explore power's history— with sociological descriptions. Rose writes in *Powers of Freedom* a "glossary," as he puts it, of Foucaultian techniques of the self.

To be governed through our freedom: the very idea seems paradoxical. . . . The politics of our present, to the extent that it is defined and delimited by the values of liberalism, is structured by the opposition between freedom and government. But the critical force of these investigations does not arise from the familiar paradox that to make humans free it has been necessary to subject them to all manner of compulsion. . . . Freedom is an artifact of government, but it is not thereby an illusion. (1999, 62)

Rose wants, as I do, to distinguish "between freedom as it is deployed in contestation and freedom as it is instantiated in government" (ibid., 65). Though tacit, the beams he leans heavily upon are Althusser's idealogical apparatuses, which elaborate and reinforce the Gramscian conception of hegemony: in his explication of the creation of "free societies" with "free markets," using Britain as his main example, Rose writes,

The previously unfree subjects of these societies cannot merely be "freed"—they have to be *made* free in a process that entails the transformation of educational practices to inculcate certain attitudes and values of enterprise, changes in television programmes ranging from soap operas to game shows to implant the desire for wealth creation and personal enterprise, as well as the activities of marriage guidance consultants and a host of other psychological therapists to sort out the difficulties that arise when personal life becomes a matter of freedom of choice. (ibid., 65)

Both the directness of the Gramscian language of hegemonic domination as well as the subtleties of Rose's Foucaultian description of freedom are appropriate to the Honey Lake Maidu case.

First and foremost, however, the words and actions of my Honey Lake Maidu informants told me that in the name of freedom (and inclusion, justice, and equality) they found righteous struggle. This orientation aligned them with Gramsci's "war of position," a concept that invokes the metaphor of sustained trench warfare, and adds important stakes such as the political, racial, and economic orders of society. Indeed, Honey Lake Maidu tribal members believe that their Acknowledgment petition stands between the contrary positions of the Federal Acknowledgement procedures and their people's original sovereignty. They envision that the petition has the power to move both "armies," though it is clear to them that the Branch of Acknowledgment and Research is programmed to favor the state's positioning. But though I cannot answer whether the Honey Lake Maidu petition will move the state, which is to say the assistant secretary–Indian affairs and BAR (it will take many years to receive that answer), it is possible to see how the petition, or, more properly, petitioning, as a practice, process, and powered discourse, has moved the Honey Lake Maidus. Indeed, as Gramsci himself noted, only permanent victory can change a subaltern's standing in a war of position, and even then, "not immediately" (1980, 52).

MONEY: EMBARKING UPON THE HONEY LAKE MAIDU PETITIONING PROJECT

One of the more benign ironies of the Federal Recognition process is that the Administration for Native Americans (ANA), an office of the Department of Health and Human Services, offers competitive grants for tribes that decide to petition for Federal Recognition. In 2001, these funds were reduced to awards of approximately sixty-five thousand dollars (including extensive in-kind contributions) for one year's time. ANA grants thus afford tribes the experts—anthropologists and attorneys—that BAR itself strongly encourages tribes to hire in order to get the job done. They also cover the cost of paying one or perhaps two tribal members (or nonmembers) for the full-time effort petitioning demands, as well as the cost of photocopies, postage, printing, and long-distance telephone calls.[1]

The Bear Dance Foundation eventually won one of these sixty-five thousand dollar ANA grants, but not without a good deal of worry and frustration. After missing the May deadline in 1999, Jim Reid, the grant writer from the California Indian Assistance Program, submitted the Bear Dance Foundation application for the October 1999 deadline. By December, the funds had ostensibly been awarded. However, in February, when the paperwork caught up, the Honey Lake Maidus were asked to submit a new budget to reflect the fact that instead of funding for a two-year project, it had awarded them funding for only one. Wanda Brown and I rushed to make changes but then found that there was only more waiting in store. It would not be until May that the preliminaries were settled. Five months of waiting on the ANA monies meant five months of uncertainty and confusion (had they or had they not won the grant?), hardship (for those who had agreed to fill positions created by the grant and were waiting for the office to open so they could be paid), and close contact with cold bureaucrats who seemed to forget who the Honey Lake Maidus were every time the phone rang.

On May 1, 2000, for example, I called the Honey Lake Maidus' ANA contact for an update on the status of the application. When she told me, "We just got a new ruling. We cannot award any monies until September or October, the new funding cycle," it occurred to me that the tribe had truly entered the belly of the governmental beast. I told Ron this latest news, not hiding my feelings of defeat and hopelessness. He said he'd call the Honey Lake Maidu contact and tell her, in so many words, that she was a petty bureaucrat who had no right to toy with him or his people. Without knowing the outcome of Ron's conversation, I left Susanville for three days.

When I returned, the money was ready to be "drawn down" into the Lassen Yah-Monee Maidu Bear Dance Foundation's account. We all felt like we'd won an important battle. Significantly, the Bear Dance Foundation understood that it was their agonistic philosophy —might equals right—that got the grant rolling. Now the Honey Lake Maidus were ready to play offense with BAR.

BASKETBALL METAPHORS

Ron and I attended his grandson Michael's football games throughout the fall, and during the winter we relished his basketball games. Eighth-grade boys' basketball provided a break from the one-sided company of the TV for Ron and a break, for me, from the alternating cycles of freezing and burning that I found characterized living in a wood-heated cabin. The games were usually packed with other people happy to be out, the gym was always warm, and the games were exciting.

Basketball games were also one of the few places in Susanville where Indians and non-Indians mixed. A grandson of the famous Maidu runner Seymour Smith (who raced from Medford, Oregon, to San Francisco in 1937 to celebrate the opening of the Golden Gate Bridge) was on Michael's team, and so was a grandson of Tommy Merino, the Maidu-fluent elder from Greenville. Some of Ron's distant relatives were usually in the stands too; Ron greeted them with gruff "How-yadoin'"s and nods of the head. In low tones on the bleachers, he would tell me about "Indian basketball" in his younger days, forty or so years ago, how tough the players were on each other. Ron has told me many stories about the violence of his youth, "when Indians were *wild*." The basketball stories involve tales of players dragged off the court bloodied, their arms broken or teeth smashed.

I turn to basketball as my own elaborating symbol for the Honey Lake Maidu understanding of their relationship to the state as petitioners. There are four aspects to this choice. First, the image of a basketball game exemplifies the clear-cut manner in which the Honey Lake Maidus conceive of the state and the possibility of beating it. In a basketball game, might equals right in the same, clear-cut way. There are many ways to describe this, but I will note here that basketball is taken seriously, is played wholeheartedly, and its bodily tolls are accepted as just part of the game.

Second, the basketball metaphor matches the Honey Lake Maidu understandings of the state as an opponent team. Though there are many branches of the Bureau of Indian Affairs, and though one of them, the Branch of Acknowledgment and Research, describes itself as composed of "teams" of scholars (a genealogist, an anthropologist, and a historian on one team, and three such teams composing BAR), the Honey Lake Maidus approach Washington as a unified opponent. They are not distracted by bureaucratic differentiations. What I call "the state" to refer to the system of administrative, legal, and bureaucratic apparatuses, is glossed in a similar, monolithic way by the Honey Lake Maidus as "the government," "Washington," and sometimes by its agents, "the feds." The *systematicity* of "the government"/"the state" is quite obvious to the Honey Lake Maidus. Despite its many factions —the BIA, the Forest Service, the court system—it works as a single, grand team. Thus, though the tribe, and particularly its oldest members, express a long-term historical understanding of partisan positioning in Washington, which is to say that having Democrats in power is generally valued, change is conceived as occurring in tiny increments across a very broad, bureaucratically contradictory field. But Federal Recognition is the key on all the courts. The Honey Lake Maidus approach BAR with the understanding that Federal Recognition will mean finally getting what they need from the state and, ultimately, being free to turn their backs on it.

The basketball metaphor also resonates with particular histories of literal basketball playing in Honey Lake Valley, which I will briefly relate. Susanville's all-Indian leagues were part of a history of enforced racial apartness, but they were also, as Ron's prideful stories indicate, spaces in which Indian people happily turned their backs on non-Indian society in sovereign posture.

During the 1970s, the American Indian Organization of Lassen County (AIOLC) ran tutoring and enrichment programs for Indian kids. Ron and Viola's brother Richard (or "Shine"), who died in 1997, helped run the AIOLC's basketball program. As his obituary described, he moved to Cleveland, Ohio, "encouraged" by the government's Indian Relocation program, but he later

returned to Susanville [where] he promoted an all Indian sports program including basketball, softball; the teams consisted of young students of both genders. . . . His programs focused on elementary, junior high, and high school. Richard started the first all-Indian little league team consisting of youths from various tribes.

Playing basketball (and softball/baseball, though I maintain that basketball works as the key symbol more readily than either softball or baseball does) with other local Indian kids was conceived as a way to build confidence, pride, and community in an otherwise non-Indian–dominated society. Today, the AIOLC has dropped the sporting aspect of its programs, but only because the Susanville Indian Rancheria runs its own basketball teams in a league with other Federally Recognized teams.[2]

Though the members of the rancheria have maintained such sovereign separateness (based though it was, originally, in white-on-Indian racism), for the Honey Lake Maidus, basketball and other sports became activities that seemed to offer the possibilities of gaining symbolic capital and/or successful integration into non-Indian power structures. Indeed, my Susanville Honey Lake Maidu consultants proudly told me stories of not only respect for Richard Morales throughout the Indian community, but of "Shine Morales Day," which was held annually in Susanville to honor him for a string of years in the 1950s and represented for them how well-liked their (to some, great-) uncle/brother/cousin was, "even by the non-Indians."[3] In this vein, the history of Honey Lake Maidu non-Recognition is reflected in Michael's participation on the middle school basketball team: the boys from the rancheria who I tutored at Lassen High are still part of all-Indian leagues, but the Honey Lake Maidus are only part of the integrated, public school league; they have fewer resources for insulating their culture from the dominant one.

Finally, I choose basketball as a metaphor because it highlights the ways in which the Honey Lake Maidu strategy in petitioning the government is problematic. Basketball games are agonistic in a satisfying way that the petitioning process, a war of position, is *not*. The contradiction is that in a basketball game, even if there are no referees, once your arm is broken, you are done playing. Winners get declared after a certain period of play—a basket's a basket, usually. Yet in a war of position, the battles are multiple and the outcomes inconclusive, and in this case the referees are the state's, and they play by a different set of rules. Indeed, we will find that BAR consistently denies the agonism that Indian people see (and experience) in the Acknowledgment procedures: one cannot help but read experiential irony into BAR's *Guidelines*, which state that "part of the purpose of the administrative procedures is to remove the influence of political pressure from the acknowledgment process" (1997, 5). BAR insists that the Federal Application process is impartial, apolitical; it prefers to think in terms of administrative determinations, not "matches." And so we will find that the shortcomings of the basketball metaphor were the shortcomings or blind spots of the Honey Lake Maidu approach to the state.

ORGANIZING THE PETITIONING PROJECT: TALLYING SCORES

> It is just a game
> we are told by those
> who cannot play it
> unless it is play.
> For us, it is war,
>
> often desperate
> and without reason.
> We throw our body
> against another
> body. We learn to
>
> hate each other, hate
> the ball, hate the hoop,
> hate the fallen snow,
> hate our clumsy hands,
> hate our thirsty mouths

when we drink from
the fountain. We hate
our fathers. We hate
our mothers. We hate
the face in our mirror.

We play basketball
because we want to
separate love from
hate, and because we
know how to keep score.

> —From "Why We Play Basketball," in *The
> Summer of Black Widows*, © 1996 by Sherman
> Alexie, by permission of Hanging Loose Press
> (see appendix C for the poem in its entirety).

I remember one basketball game in January with Ron after I
had heard some favorable (but misleading, as it turned out)
news from the ANA regarding their grant. Our spirits were
very high. Our talk turned to who would run the ANA project
as its director. What about Viola's daughter Wanda? Wanda
had been let go from her job at Lassen Modoc Indian Housing
when the rancheria decided to run its own housing office. A
few weeks later, the Bear Dance Foundation had the meeting
at which a reduced budget was worked up and resubmitted to
the ANA. Talk eventually turned to the position of project
director. Wanda said she did not feel confident enough to
hold the position, and wanted to suggest that her old boss (a
non-Indian) at Lassen Modoc Housing be chosen for the job.
Ron was absolutely opposed to this individual. She was not
Honey Lake Maidu, he said. Worse, she was living with a member
of the rancheria, and thus had a connection to the rancheria.
Ron in no way wanted the rancheria to find out about the
Honey Lake Maidu petitioning project; he said he didn't want
"any weak links."

Already, the prospect of the project to come was causing
tension between Wanda and her uncle. Neither side wanted

to listen to the other, neither could see the fear and concern behind the other's position. Yet in the end, Wanda accepted the job.

There were structural tensions within the Bear Dance Foundation that the petitioning project would aggravate. In chapter four, I showed that, as chair of the Bear Dance Foundation, Ron tended to try to dominate the other members of the foundation who, in turn, tended to band together against him. At the same time, there was immense respect between these "sides." Ron was appreciated for his willingness to take the leadership role and for his hard work organizing and running the Bear Dance. But while both Ron and Viola should be thought of as expert "keepers of tribal knowledge," Ron was critical of his sister's attempts to express any memories or histories that were different from his own. Ron, in the final tally, came to dominate the Federal Recognition project, partially because Viola was a little less willing to share her materials with me and partially because of her poor health and age. Petitioning demanded significant work on the part of elders, and this in-kind contribution from tribal members was calculated into the ANA's award. Viola did not have as much free time for this kind of contribution as Ron did. And even though Ron sometimes tired of my repetitive questions, his own intellectual projects were tightly wound up in the documentary evidence that the Federal Application process demanded—a happy confluence, as it turned out.

But another way to think of it is that Ron and I worked very closely together over the course of the petitioning project, and he needed me to separate myself from Viola, even in a small way, in order for him to share certain things with me. This was also true of how he reacted to my interviews with other tribal elders who live outside the Honey Lake Valley, elders such as Carole Mickens, John Peconom, and Inez Valenzuela. And thus the "Honey Lake Maidu" petition that was drawn up was a petition carefully shaped by Ron Morales's understanding of his people's history. In part, this was because the petitioning project was being run by the Bear Dance Foundation; the official Honey Lake Maidu Tribe was something still inchoate at this point.[4]

And so even as there was excitement at this early meeting, there were problems everyone could see, lurking ahead. Happily, but somewhat ominously, Ron had talked about "adopting" all of his relatives into the tribe after Recognition (not just Honey Lake Maidu relatives), and had mentioned that "they would be members, but wouldn't have a vote."[5] Wanda had worried aloud about how the Honey Lake Maidu constitution and bylaws would have to be clear on "blood quantum." She was concerned that "if you left it at less than one quarter blood, you'll end up with a Mexican tribe"; there was a risk of Maidu blood losing its place. She had motioned up the hill, toward the rancheria. Viola recognized the direction in which both the evening's talk and her daughter were pointing: she said, "Let's don't start fighting just because we have a little money to spend now." Unstated was, "like the rancheria does."

CALIFORNIA INDIAN LEGAL SERVICES MEETS THE LASSEN YAH-MONEE MAIDU BEAR DANCE FOUNDATION

One way that the ANA money was spent, and that the Honey Lake Maidus went public as petitioners, was through California Indian Legal Services' (CILS) involvement with the tribe. After May's coup—the arrival of the funds into the Bear Dance Foundation's account—attorneys Will Jackson and Lynne Guerrero drove to Susanville. They met with the Bear Dance Foundation (Ron, Viola, Wanda Brown, and Linda Hutt) and myself in order to organize the petitioning work to come over the next thirteen months. Jackson and Guerrero explained the government's strategy and some appropriate responses from the Honey Lake Maidus, and the Bear Dance Foundation struggled to translate the lawyers' perspectives into their own terms.

Jackson told the foundation members that, although they'd already waited long enough for Recognition from the government, "unfortunately, you'll probably have to continue to wait—for the long haul. Probably seven years or more, while the petition's reviewed." Ron said "Wow," and let his hands drop to the table from their place under his chin. (Later, he would tell me, "It almost blew me off my chair when he said that.") Viola asked why it would take so long, and Jackson explained that it was because of the volume of petitions the BAR team receives. He explained, "It's just not a priority for the Department of the Interior. They have no incentive for Recognizing more tribes." And "Petitions make more work and more trouble for them."

I would soon be used to Jackson's skeptical realism about BAR, and his willingness to drive five hundred miles (literally, from Oakland to Susanville and back) for the Honey Lake Maidu Tribe. Jackson seemed to think of his job as that of opposing BAR on every legal tack possible, and simultaneously that of not letting his clients feel too hopeful about the outcome of the process. However, as the petition drafter, I was in the position of making, and believing, the Honey Lake Maidu case to be the most convincing case BAR had ever seen. My hopes were mixed with those of my friends and employers, and I felt the ironies of this project strongly when Jackson spoke that night. In going for "tribe," the Honey Lake Maidus were opening up to the possibility of losing that status as much as gaining it. Losing Federal Recognition was forever. Not possessing it was, at least, suffused with hope.[6]

Finally, Jackson's assertion that "this is a direct quote from BAR: 'We will never Recognize just one family'" made concrete a worry that I had been putting aside since we had first started tackling Federal Recognition. It was a worry about figuring out who else besides Roxie Peconom's descendants made up the Honey Lake Maidu Tribe and how bringing these people together, as a tribe according to the government's model, would work.

THE OFFICIAL TRIBAL ROSTERS: PRELIMINARY LISTS

When I had asked Ron and Viola who composed "the Honey Lake Maidu Tribe" soon after I first met them, in the fall of 1997, it seemed to me that they had evaded the question. This was probably because it just was not an important concern for them at this point in time; they knew who they were and that they were a tribe. More recently, at my repeated attempts to bring the Honey Lake Maidus to the Federal Application process's table, Ron had pulled out three manila envelopes from the wooden magazine rack of important documents he kept by his favorite plush reclining chair. They included family lists sent to him by elders from the Jack lineage, and those sent to him by his grandmother's and great-uncle George Davis's descendants. Some families had made computerized lists, others were submissions with members' names and birth dates written in curlicue handwriting. Ron had solicited this information in the mid-1990s when Bill Simmons told him it was what he would need to do to get started with Federal Recognition.

Now, these lists had to be read with strategy in mind. BAR demanded archival proof of the genealogical connections of the proposed tribe, and I would need to go to the National Archives and Records Administration in San Bruno, California, and collect federal evidence about the ancestors of the people on Ron's lists. Then Ron, Viola, and I would have to evaluate the membership and the genealogical documents in light of how to make the most successful petition possible. This seemed the imperative course of events at the time, although now I can see this as a Federal Acknowledgment–driven strategy that I was helping to impose in the face of BAR bureaucracy. The work of "ambivalent experts" to install "capacities for self-determination and self-mastery" (Rose 1999, 89) in their clients—literally bringing them the "freedom" of government control—was part of the history I both enacted and uncovered in the archives.

SOLIDIFYING HONEY LAKE MAIDUNESS
AS A GENEOLOGICAL "FACT"

I talked with Ellen Bera, an archivist with expertise in Record Group 75, "Records of the Bureau of Indian Affairs," on the phone before my first visit to the San Bruno Archives. She told me, "I'm hit or miss here because of the pulling and the filing." In other words, although she was a professional door-keeper of state records, she might not be able to access specific information because of filing errors and lapses. This sent me into a five-second nightmare about how, because of a bureau-cratic expert's mishap, I might never know that certain documents critical to the Honey Lake Maidu case existed. Yet this scenario troubled me less and less as I began to understand that even the most "critical" documents in the archive were not without their flaws. I came to understand that a consequence of bureau-cracy is that no single piece of paper holds the complete answer to anything. For me, it is this simple horror that best summarizes what lies behind the state's door for petitioners.

Yet when I arrived in San Bruno, instead of being consumed by such negative thoughts, I came down with a bad case of archival gold fever. I was hungered by the possibility of what I might uncover—Bera may have realized that she needed to give me a taste of the dusty reality, because she promptly told me that most California Indian people come to San Bruno because of Federal Recognition research or because of some kind of "intra-tribal split due to fighting" and that most do not "go away happy." She said, "For most it's really difficult. They don't know how to find [what they need] in these records." I wish I had suggested that perhaps what they imagine should be there in fact never existed. In any event, Bera assured me that I was on a well-beaten path. She said that she could "pull by"—this native terminology makes me think of commercial fishing[7]—"Konkow," "Lassen," "Susanville Indian Rancheria," and "Greenville Rancheria." She'd let me use the finding guides to locate anything else I was interested in. I had her pull everything, and then got to photocopying.

The way we worked was that I would drive down to San Bruno, make a haul (usually over two days), and then, back in Susanville, Ron and I would pore over the catch. We found the allotment files particularly fascinating. Often, they appeared to contain every scrap of official correspondence ever made about or with a particular Indian person. Ron picked names from an alphabetical list of Indians who had received allotments (a list copied from the San Bruno finding aid), and I looked for those individuals and copied any and everything interesting in their file. One night as we leafed through Indian allotment files Ron told me, "I really dig this. But a guy could really get around in these allotments, if you know what I mean"; someone might forge or change or remove documents from the archive rather easily. I had not considered it, but he was right. Despite the security precautions, it was hypothetically possible.

On my first trip, it had occurred to me, however, that anyone could walk into the archive and collect information about Indian persons in an entirely above-board fashion. I do not think anyone could find out information about my family, for instance, in quite the same way.[8] As one of the finding aids organized by the archivists put it, "The Bureau's programs have had an impact on virtually every phase of tribal development and individual Indian life including education, health, and ownership, financial affairs, employment, and legal rights." In light of the petitioning effort, it was clear that this accessibility had both wonderful and terrible aspects. The allotment files, for instance, were extremely helpful to Honey Lake Maidu projects, both individual and corporate, but they also reflected histories more painful. Reading about Ron and Viola's parents and aunts and uncles and their financial stresses and family traumas in the files seemed to me to be endorsing the government's meddling administration of their lives, and became more and more distasteful to me, despite the fact that I had been hired to collect and think about these stories.

The uncritical way the archival finding aid presented the government's actions was equally distasteful: "Many persons of Indian descent are not mentioned in any of the Bureau's records because they severed all connection with any tribe," it read. There is a flaw to such logic: calling them (and filing them as) Indian persons stripped them of their tribe from square one, and thus just because they had slipped through the state's net did not mean that they were not tribal members.

But beyond the marks of historical subjection and statistical savoir that I found in the archives, Ron's fears about potential manipulation of the documents reflected an understanding of Indian agency and an understanding of the political uses of the archives, which had implications, first of all, for our own project. Though we were researching genealogy that might connect possible Honey Lake Maidu members back to ancestors from the Honey Lake Valley, one individual Ron wanted me to research was someone who had never been mentioned to me as possibly Honey Lake Maidu, and had, in fact, been described to me as a Greenville Maidu. Ron said that it was imperative that he find out who her relatives were so that he could make sure that Honey Lake Maidus were not related to certain members of the rancheria in an ironic or inconvenient way. Thus the archival research, the fisherman role I took on for the tribe during this phase of the project, may have been as much about coming up with a definition of Honey Lake Maidu based on who wasn't Honey Lake Maidu as it was about finding out who was.

THE ARCHIVE AND A UNIFIED, MULTILINEAGE TRIBE

Ron based most of the decisions about which family names to research on his mother Leona Morales's tapes and notes as well as on the membership lists I've mentioned. Ron eventually played me one of the tapes Leona had made for her children. She began by saying, "The Honey Lake Indians, the Maidu Indians, no other tribes were here," and she proceeded with a spontaneous list of families in the valley and where they lived. Yet whether she was listing families of the "Honey Lake Maidu Tribe" as we were trying to define it remains ambiguous. She told the tape recorder, "I know that the Maidus lived in Quincy to Honey Lake Valley. They were married into one another; they were different families." Was she describing the Mountain Maidu tribelets with their family-based structures? I maintain that she was. Through Leona's tapes, the voice of an older, departed generation remained in the present, but although her words provided the grounds for understanding most of the archival materials (particularly regarding the Old Tom and Wetajam/Momolo lineages), there were some important contradictions that the Honey Lake Maidus did not override. For one instance, in her description of the Honey Lake Indians, Leona made no mention of the Jacksons, although we found evidence that the Jackson family has longstanding roots in Honey Lake Valley. Yet she included Cap DeHaven and his wife, Emma's, family on her list of old-time families in the valley. She said that DeHaven's father and mother lived in Honey Lake Valley. Ron and I were excited about researching DeHaven's line: Cap DeHaven was relatively well known in Susanville, well represented in historical news clippings and the field matron's notes, and a strong case might be made for his role as a sociocultural leader in the Honey Lake Maidu community. The only problem that we eventually found, according to his and his wife's allotment files and the 1928 California Indian Roll applications, was that they were not Honey Lake Maidus. In both cases, we stuck close to the archive. Adding a third family line, the Jacksons, to the Jacks and Peconoms was strategically wise, as was founding these three lineages in archival information, even though it meant leaving out the DeHavens and several other families said to be Honey Lake Maidus who had left no traces—or only contradictory traces—in the government's files.

An example of how Leona's words outweighed the archive on the tribe's scales can be found in the Bear Dance Foundation's interpretations of 1928 California Indian Roll applications. The Honey Lake Maidu applications to California's Indian (land) Claims Commission case, kept on microfilm in San Bruno, contain extremely important information about applicants' parents' and grandparents' names, as well as the California county in which these individuals had been born. Some of this was quite contradictory information. For instance, Lamb Samson's 1928 application "documents" that his father was Lamb Charley and that his paternal grandfather was Secouya, a Butte County Maidu. Lamb Samson was Roxie Peconom's half brother through their father, Lamb Charley, and thus on the 1928 Roll, his paternal grandfather should have been hers as well—Wetajam, who was born and raised in Lassen County.

In this case, Ron and Viola argued that the federal representatives made a mistake when they wrote Secouya and Butte instead of Wetajam and Lassen. On this matter the archive contradicts everything Ron and Viola know. Nonetheless, standing behind oral tradition when it is contradicted in the archive seemed to me to be a risky maneuver, simply because the Federal Acknowledgment process does not value oral history as historical evidence for a tribe's case. Furthermore, I was beginning to feel that backing oral tradition put the tribe in the position of picking and choosing from the assembled state evidences to the point of destabilizing the grounds for making any decision about what evidence to uphold. While for Ron and Viola it was a simple fact that Lamb Samson's father was Roxie Peconom's, regardless of the documents, for me, because I was trying to bridge between the Federal Acknowledgment procedures and the tribe, it seemed a bigger problem. In the end, though we counted Lamb Samson's 1928 application among the applications that can be traced to the Honey Lake Maidu tribal community, we did not send along his file for inspection by BAR. I worried about this decision: Would the Honey Lake Maidus get called on it? If they sent in Samson's 1928 application later, would it work against Honey Lake Maidu Recognition, even though the tribe has other evidences that contradict it? In short, my fears of BAR's judgments' arbitrary omnipotence were the strongest precisely at such points of documentary departure. This is perhaps a typical example of the kind of conservative consciousness written into a petition, a conservative consciousness that reflects the way that tribal realities (in the past or present) are almost impossible to document unambiguously.

MATCHING THE ARCHIVAL TRIBE TO TODAY'S TRIBE

Even aside from the problems with noncorrespondence between oral history and the governmental archives, there were problems of present-day noncorrespondence. While we found that the Jacksons could be traced to Honey Lake Valley, Ron did not want to contact any of their contemporary lineage because he said they would not want to be a part of the Honey Lake Maidu Tribe. Wanda said she would contact the Jackson lineage, but she never got around to it. Finally, I contacted Al Jackson and he said, No, he and his wanted nothing to do with "Honey Lake Maidu." Nonetheless, the Honey Lake Maidus decided to include the Jacksons in their discussion of the pre-Contact and early twentieth century periods in the petition, because adding more lineages made the Honey Lake Maidu case stronger. My position on the issue vacillated right up until December 2000, when the Honey Lake Maidu Constitution Committee and California Indian Legal Services recommended that the Jacksons be included. In the end, the petition explained that because of the non-Recognition of the Honey Lake Maidus in the historical period, the Jackson lineage had affiliated with their Pit River relatives. This illustrates clearly the strangeness of working backward from the government's records: the Jacksons were being "made" Honey Lake Maidu (in the past), whether they wanted to or not. The tribe was allowing the archive to steamroll modern nonaffiliations in the same way that it had ejected the well-liked and well-remembered Cap DeHaven from the history of the Honey Lake Maidus.

There were also other problems that contemporary relationships would pose for the petition. Bob Junior, Roxie Peconom's brother, had left Honey Lake Valley very early in the twentieth century, to work, as I've mentioned, cutting post for ranchers near Red Bluff. His descendants had clear genealogical connections to Honey Lake Valley, but would their distance from the "center" in the 1900s work against the tribe's claims to social, political, and cultural cohesion?

Furthermore, by this point, the Old Tom lineage (also referred to as "the Jacks") needed to be included in the petition, for, as Will Jackson had put it, "the BAR will never Recognize just one family." But couldn't the Old Tom lineage "bring down" the Honey Lake Maidu case in the way the Junior lineage could? Inez Valenzuela (great-granddaughter of Old Tom) was a well-informed Honey Lake Maidu elder, but she had supposedly not passed on much of Honey Lake Maidu tradition to her children and grandchildren, and had integrated herself into her father's, and later, her husband's Mexican American community. Still, there had been a marriage between Isabel "Curly" Peconom and Lawrence Jack, and this section of the Old Tom lineage had stayed close (both genealogically and geographically) to the Honey Lake Valley, as well as to tribal traditions.[9] As Jackson would put it, the past was a certain "two points" in the game, but how would we make the present day a slam dunk?

BLOOD AND NATION

This hurtful, even violent, way of judging what a tribal lineage's "contribution" to the petition would be reflected clearly the pressures of the Acknowledgment procedures on the Bear

Dance Foundation that I felt, and then mirrored in the advice I gave. These pressures and this violence indicate how the Acknowledgment process itself is based in hegemonic under-standings of American Indianness—popular national construc-tions of race, culture, and how much difference is too much for the state, or in this case, too little for it to accept. Such understandings of difference have great bearing on the shape BAR desires successful Federal Acknowledgment petitions and their petitioners to hold.

The Federal Acknowledgment process has no blood quantum requirements, but this is not to say it does not have biogenetic requirements for petitioners. First, a potential member's lineal ancestors must be documented as Indian persons. This infor-mation is most easily culled from the Dawes Act allotment files and the 1928 California Indian Roll applications, and behind both lie the logics and statements of blood quantum: Dawes Act allotments were only awarded to those Indian persons with one half or more "Indian blood." And when question number twelve of the 1928 California Indian Roll applica-tions asked applicants to name their California Indian ancestors living on June 1, 1852, a line was included for their percentage of Indian blood.

Next, establishing documentary connections back to these bona fide lineage ancestors for contemporary tribal members is crucial to creating a successful petition. This means that contemporary members must each submit either a BIA card or a federal roll number. Barring the existence or availability of either of these identifications, a birth or baptismal certificate must be presented so that the member in question is formally connected back to an "officially documented" member—that is, a member such as a parent or grandparent with either a BIA card or a roll number.[10] Significantly, both identify Indian-ness in terms of blood quantum.

This kind of blood thinking lends itself, quite obviously, to restrictive definitions of Indianness. And as I've described, the Federal Acknowledgment procedures are built upon the 1934 Indian Reorganization Act, which established the precedent that Indians "now under federal jurisdiction" possess one half or more tribal blood. As Representative Howard, one of the IRA's cosponsors put it, the quantum provision was included because "the line must be drawn somewhere or the government would take on impossible financial burdens in extending wardship over persons with minor fractions of Indian blood" (quoted in Anderson 1978, 10). Such a focus on Indian blood alongside this kind of economic calculation of Indianness resulted in the creation, with the passage of the IRA, of "Applied Anthropology Units" for assessing Indianness through anthropometrical measure. Perhaps the most notorious Applied Anthropology Unit was that of Carl Selzer, who concluded by reference to phenotype, cranial measurements, and blood type, that only twenty-two out of two hundred Lumbee Indians were eligible for an IRA government, regardless, even, of their family relationships (in one case, he divided biological brothers [see Blu 2001].)

It does not seem mere coincidence that the Lumbees were barred from Federal Recognition in the second half of the twentieth century. Today, for the situations of both ancestors and living members of tribes petitioning for Acknowledgment who must be "documented," the FAP has quantum reckoning at the foundation of its genealogical analysis, hidden deep within the paperwork. I have shown how the Acknowledgment criteria focus on aspects of "culture," defined open-endedly, with social or political activity, language use, communal proximity, in-marriage, ritual practice, and legal affiliation among the potential proofs. These cultural requirements, combined with the requisite genealogical/blood evidence, make Indianness into a kind of mathematics. It's as if culture and blood exist as their own continuum, which, when plotted on a plane, overlap in a region of authentic Indianness. (See figure 1). In theory, then, the Federal Acknowledgment process has established a

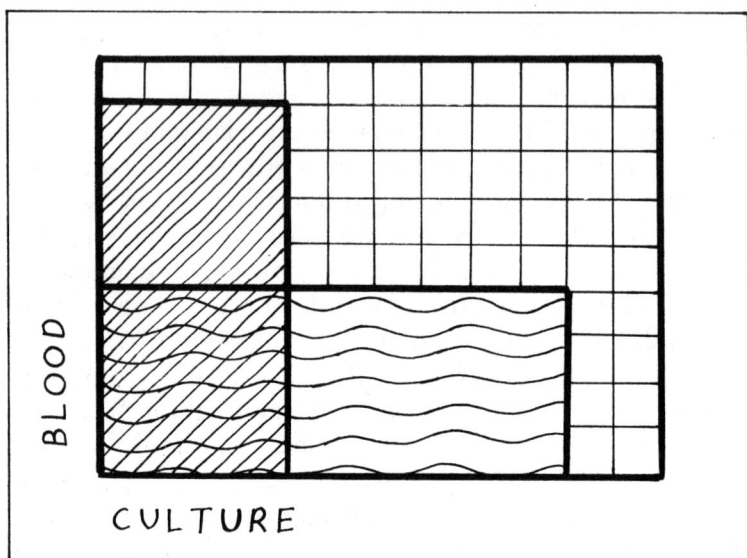

AUTHENTIC INDIANNESS

An imaginary of BAR decision making. Illustrated by John Isaacson, © 2005.

quantum reckoning of culture traits such that the right amount, in combination with the correct blood/genealogical mapping is deemed Acknowledgeable. In practice, however—as the history of BAR decision making shows—what that right amount is varies from case to case in an unpredictable way. Considering the case of Carl Selzer, one might be thankful that BAR considers both aspects, blood and culture. Yet the way this plays out unjustly for non-Recognized peoples today is in the multiplication of subjective variables of culture that figure 1 brings to light. Figure 1 represents an imaginary of BAR's decision making in the same way that BAR's adjudications invoke the national imaginary of Indianness. Though neither imaginary works as a realistic reflection of experience, both are terribly elucidating.

Wanda's fear about "Mexicanizing" the tribe mentioned earlier can be interpreted to reflect a pragmatic absorption of the ideas of racialized exclusion and race-culture "accounting" that are fundamental to the Federal Acknowledgment procedures. In federal contexts, conservatism in terms of both blood and culture is pragmatism, in service to cultural survival, cultural sovereignty, and freedom.

Yet in tribal context, though blood in the sense of descent remained the one main unifier of Honey Lake Maidu membership, it was blood's poetic, emotional force, rather than its biological materiality, that truly built their Nation. In other words, Wanda's fears about Mexicanizing the tribe were not only reflections of federal pressures. They were, she explained, anxieties about losing connections to the past, connections to literal ancestors as well as to cultural orientations. Although, for a tribe as small as the Honey Lake Maidus, no member is expecting a rebounding of biological Honey Lake Maiduness, tribe members nonetheless believe that affective connections to tribe, conceived in terms of genetic descent, have regenerative power.

Kiowa-Cherokee author N. Scott Momaday has famously described cultural memory as something that resides in his body and blood: "I think that each of us bears in his genes or in his blood or wherever a recollection of the past. Even the very distant past. I just think that's the way it is. . . . In the case of the Kiowa, it's a remembering of the migration. A remembering of coming out of the log. A remembering of crossing the Bering land bridge" (quoted in Strong and Van Winkle 1996, 561). Although this might be understood as a Lamarckian idea that verges toward a reckoning of one's culture as residing with one's blood quantum,[11] Momaday, like Wanda, in fact steps beyond Western social-scientific models and speaks of descent's affective orientations: a connectedness to the past that becomes part of his own personal psychology as he goes about his life. The past becomes, through emotional transub-stantiation, something that can be experienced in the present. For the Honey Lake Maidus, this affective understanding of cultured blood is part of the lived truth of their culture and descent that defies quantification. And it is the lived truth that so often slips past the system of reckoning employed by BAR in the Federal Acknowledgment process because its emphasis is not on degrees or distances from, but on blood's generational span.[12]

In this manner, the Honey Lake Maidus chose "connection to" rather than "distance from," and in the end sent member-ship applications to all the descendants of Wetajam and Momolo and all the descendants of Old Tom. Similarly, the Honey Lake Maidu tribal constitution, in the end, made no reference to blood quantum. Both these decisions reflect how Honey Lake Maidu policy fundamentally challenges U.S. racial hierarchies and the policies of approximately a quarter of the Recognized tribes, whose constitutions reflect the Indian Reor-ganization Act's biogenetic membership requirements (Strong and Van Winkle 1996, 55). Furthermore, in making these decisions about membership, we can see how the Honey Lake Maidus challenge the Federal Acknowledgment process's ability to identify something that they maintain is only their own to identify. Their tribal prerogative spills over the edges rigidly drawn by the government.

WASHINGTON, D.C.: OPEN DOORS, BUT INVISIBLE WALLS BARRING THEM

In November 2000, I traveled to the National Archives in Washington, D.C. I was searching for allotment evidence, which, if it existed for the Honey Lake Maidus, would be crucial to their case. Yet in both my work and my recesses from work I found a sense of coldness at the nation's capital for non-Recognized

Indian people and their researchers. I found that the price of all the nickel-and-dime freedom of the museums and monuments is walking along the endless Mall and feeling like you are getting nowhere, that you are, in fact, a warm-blooded anomaly in a world of impressive, oversized marble temples and benchless lawns.[13] November in Washington made the starkness more real. I felt it in the hollows of my bones.

Inside the National Archives, the hallways were bedecked with displays about survivors of the Holocaust, Japanese American internment camps, Federal Indian schools, and African American slavery, all under the optimistic banner, "Research Will Set You Free." The displays told brief stories, such as how the documents that helped establish monetary restitution for Japanese American internees were researched here. It made me feel a deep sadness because I had just met the archivist and discovered that despite the freedom of the archive—the open door—there was still very little access for Native peoples.

Despite several volleys of hopeful letters in the months preceding my trip, when I met the archivist face to face, he told me there would be nothing for me to research: "We're only 'Federally Recognized' here." It was horrifying to me that he might not know or care to know how important archival research is to the non-Recognized in this country. He did not seem to understand that the government could have r/Recognized an Indian tribe at some point in the past, even though they might not be r/Recognized today. Shades other than black and white apparently fell outside the finding guides.

And so I came upon some of the bureaucracy's marble walls. The central office's correspondence files, for instance, contained stacks of onionskin cards, three inches by five, indexed by correspondent. I asked for nine names (including those of Albert Jackson and Old Man Joaquin to try to document their work creating the Susanville Indian Rancheria), and the only records available were under one of these names, that of George Davis, Roxie Peconom's brother. Ron and I had been unable to turn up much information about George, and we considered it important to our research for the tribe. The Davis section of the National Archives letter files included easily 250 entries including at least fifty different men of that particular name. None were my man, George Davis, Honey Lake Maidu. I suppose the government would conclude that he never existed as a tribal person. The Archives' apparently open, but nonetheless invisible, doors emphasize the foundational argument of this book: that the Federal Acknowledgment process is both broken, from the tribes' perspective, and completely functional, from the state's. State bureaucracy functions to keep the non-Recognized tribes out, yet it interminably includes them.

On a warmer day at the National Archives, away from the archivist I began to call "the Doorkeeper," I found some of the materials for which I had traveled across the country: the neither black nor white evidence of the receipt by Honey Lake Maidu ancestors of allotments from the Public Domain under Section Four of the 1887 General Allotment Act. The 1928 Department of Interior regulations explain, "An applicant for an allotment under the fourth section is required to show that he is a recognized member of an Indian tribe or is entitled to be so recognized." George Roth, a member of the Branch of Acknowledgment and Research, whose Roth Report goes to admirable scholarly lengths to prove his document-centered position on Recognition, emphasizes that this means that it was not sufficient to possess Indian blood/heritage in order to be eligible for a Section Four allotment; it was necessary, as well, to be a member or have the right to membership in a functioning tribe (Roth 1996, 40–41).

In the petition we argued that, in granting individuals Section Four allotments, both the federal agents who operated in the field and the federal government had affirmed the de facto existence of the tribe in which the allotted individual held membership. We said that on the basis of the thirty-five Section Four allotments in the Honey Lake Valley and surrounding area (amounting to 5,964.82 acres) made to these members of the historic Honey Lake Maidu community, though they were not identified as such, it is clear that the federal government Recognized them as members of a functioning tribal entity. We asserted that the federal government officially interacted with this functioning tribal entity on a government-to-government basis from 1892 to 1950, when the last Section Four allotment was finalized.

The other project of my trip to Washington, as I've mentioned, was an appointment at the Department of the Interior to meet with John Dibbern, George Roth, and Lee Fleming, who are BAR historian, anthropologist, and genealogist/chief respectively. John Dibbern met me at the security checkpoint inside the Department of the Interior building and told me, as we walked down a maze of hallways, that since it was in BAR's interest to have the tribe write the best petition possible, its members wanted to take time to answer any questions I had.

He also said that I'd have to bear with him; the route to our meeting place was deliberately confusing because there had been an attack on BAR when its office was the first floor. Providing a sense of the volatility of issues surrounding Recognition as perhaps nothing else will, Peter Beinart has described how

the branch stopped meeting visitors in its offices a few years ago, after an anonymous caller announced that unless a certain tribe was recognized, there would be ten thousand bodies in body bags. At about the same time, a canister of mace was thrown through an open window into a nearby women's bathroom. After that, the branch moved from the first floor to the third floor. Its exact location is now a secret. (1999, 34)

Assembled (I cannot say how safely) in a conference room far from the first floor, Fleming opened our discussion with a comment about getting the notice of the Honey Lake Maidu formalization of the petitioning process into the Federal Register—"It's coming," he said, and all the men present chuckled in an embarrassed way about how even registering a tribe's Intent to Petition letter took such an unforgivably long time. The Honey Lake Maidu letter had been mailed in May and it was now November. "You and fourteen other groups are waiting to have your letters of intent registered. And there are 230 applications [petitions] in right now," he said. Later, they specified that the Honey Lake Maidus are actually 223rd on the list of petitions to sift through—slightly higher in the queue, which was moving at about three decisions a year.[14] This made me feel guilty about meeting with these gentlemen at all; I wanted to rush them off to a quiet place so they could get some work done!

Dibbern and Roth had a lot of specific advice about which government documents to track down. They told me, "Get hold of the federal censuses of 1850, 1870, 1900, 1910 and 1920." Also: the Honey Lake Maidus would need to find the California Indian judgment rolls—1928 (which I already had from San Bruno), but also the 1944, 1955, and 1968 rolls.[15] They further advised that the tribe prove that the Honey Lake Maidus lived in a historic settlement in each decade of the twentieth century via local tax records and that the Honey Lake Maidus demonstrate that as a tribe they are quite distinct from other area petitioners.

As far as the Section Four Public Domain allotments were concerned, I would need to find out whether tribe members were allotted near one another or in a scattered manner. The allotments would need to be placed on a map. As I scribbled notes and questions across the pages of my notebook, I was reminded of Nikolas Rose's discussion of inscription devices like maps, as "material technologies of thought that make possible the extension of authority over that which they seem to depict" (1999, 37). In this spirit, throughout our meeting, Dibbern and Roth encouraged me, as the Honey Lake Maidu researcher, to discern the "logic of the state"—they thought it wise to reveal the rationality of the allotting agent's methods, which would hopefully reveal his understanding of the tribal nature of the Honey Lake Maidus. They told me to research the allotting agent's correspondence, which might provide such information, as it had for other "California Indian entities." They had the call numbers of the materials I'd need to work through memorized. Dibbern knew that researching this would take a long time, and he joked about how I'd have to travel back and forth from the National Archives to the College Park, Maryland, archive to get much of the information.

The logic of the state would have to be proved, yet also its illogic, I thought to myself. Roth and Dibbern assumed a perfectly documented world, yet when I asked, Susanville was not able to dredge up its tax records for me (they mentioned something about a leaky attic), and when I searched the BIA correspondence files, I found that Allotting Agent Bernard Arentzen did not always make notations about the peoples he awarded Section Four allotments. No personal details or interactions between himself and the Honey Lake Maidus are mentioned; no "logic" is revealed. What comes of this is a sense of the racial politics of "truth"—a sense of how the weight (and bulk) of a petitioner's documentary evidence depends on the whims of the documenters.

Before I left, I asked Dibbern and Roth about the political atmosphere surrounding Federal Recognition. Roth told me, "The prevailing winds aren't about to change. But there *are* winds out there, this *is* Washington." He acceded that some politicians against gaming want a really tough process. And Dibbern said that (then) Assistant Secretary of the Interior Kevin Gover would not hand Federal Recognition over to Congress, but would create a separate organization, if anything.

Their mention of Washington's "winds" was a clear reference to the recount of the 2000 presidential election, and the Gorton-Campwell recount had been specifically invoked in our conversation earlier that morning.[16] The politically liminal aftermath of the 2000 election was just part of "living according to Law" is what I heard them telling me. It was as if to say, "Sometimes our interpretations differ and we have to hold ourselves to our national procedures, as we do for Federal Recognition." Roth explicitly mentioned a need to keep to the law, the procedures, the criteria. I realized that part of me understood these men from BAR. The attorneys at California Indian Legal Services might tell me that as petitioner-writer, I wouldn't want to tell BAR the whole truth, but at this moment that seemed just lawyers' tactics. At BAR, the idea that they grounded themselves in was that the truth will set you free! Well-trained in the hegemonic ideals of freedom as a means of governance, I, too, wanted to believe that the truth could set this tribe free.

Indeed, the push and pull I was feeling encapsulates the tease of the Roth report: Roth lays out how a hypothetical California tribe might go about proving previous Federal Recognition through research in government archives, but to have the documents line up so neatly would be like lightning striking the same spot twice. And so it is that only the *right* kind of truth can set you free. I had the feeling that Dibbern and Roth really wanted the Honey Lake Maidus to come out with a strong case for Federal Recognition. But they did not seem to take the step of thinking about the injustice of the procedures. What if the truth excluded or robbed you? What if the government's one-sided evidence did not reflect what the Honey Lake Maidus knew to be truth?

I think that in the BAR staff's ideal world and in mine, there would be a whole team on this project instead of just me, Wanda, Ron, Viola, and some of the others. Because the fact was that Dibbern had exhausted me when he had explained how to research the government's interactions with the Honey Lake Maidus in just the period between 1881 and 1907. I felt like what lay ahead was an ascent of the Washington Monument via the stairs, with a Xerox box full of documents in my arms.

CALIFORNIA INDIAN LEGAL SERVICES
MEETS THE HONEY LAKE MAIDU TRIBE

We walked off the court,
left the ball waiting

. . . .

Somehow, we
grew families while

that ball waited, in-
ert, suspended, till
we remembered, with
a complex rush of
pain and joy, what we'd

left behind, how we
loved the ball as it
finally dropped in-
to the net, after
years of such patience.

(Alexie 1996, 22)

On September 17, 2000, the Honey Lake Maidu Tribe assembled for the first time with that explicit title as its business.
According to the lawyers, the agenda was to inform all those who
had returned official membership applications of the seriousness
of the Federal Acknowledgment process, and the difficulties
of proceeding. According to the Honey Lake Maidus, it was a
tribal reunion after, in some cases, a generation or two, a symbol
of unity grounded in people's willingness to meet together once
again. Federal Recognition was proving to be a tribal project that
could move people to literally reverse the route they or their
parents, grandparents, or great-grandparents may have taken when
they left Honey Lake Valley for opportunity elsewhere. The
approximately fifty members gathered at the meeting from all
generations had a mental impact on the cumulative vision of
tribe. The power of this expression of tribal presence was immense.

Will Jackson and I made presentations from our particular perspectives—mine, that every single member needs to think about what he or she may have in his or her attic, memory, or experience that might help the tribe win Recognition; Jackson's, that the tribe needs to plan for the worst. He warned,

Remember that 'the Honey Lake Maidu' in the past, that's a slam dunk. But the petition is not a history lesson to the United States. It needs to show that this is a continued, contemporary tribal entity. And it's going to take a long time, so we shouldn't delay. Remember: the BAR sends [Obvious] Deficiency Letters but rarely gives advice.

Carole Mickens, Ron and Viola's elderly cousin who'd driven up by herself from Oakland, clearly identified with Jackson's hint of sarcasm and, adding to his presentation, called out, "Fix your own problems! Ha!"[17] Also spontaneously, Gina Garcia, who had traveled from Los Angeles, presented the idea of creating committees to work on both the tribal constitution and family histories to include and use in the petition. Tribal members volunteered to head these committees and signed on participants.

In his presentation, Jackson had expressed that many Indian people think that once they've sent in a Letter of Intent to Petition, their work is done. I was already struggling with a feeling I perceived among tribal members that they could sit back now that petitioning had begun. I believe now that this was because the tribe was not thinking like CILS; although it realized the Recognition game (itself a simplification of the multiple battles of a war of position) would be played on the state's court, members chose to focus on the confidence of their own game and were not as interested in the bureaucratic details. The slam dunks of the early period—the burials in Lassen County, the published article describing the tribe's creation story and Honey Lake Valley's sacred places—boosted their confidence and their general morale, which they knew they'd need to make it through the process. Having CILS and myself to keep one set of eyes on the law and the other on the Branch of Acknowledgment and Research was critical to their own posture of turning their backs to the state.[18]

The September 2000 meeting was dominated by my presentation and Jackson's. Sadly, the decision had been made to put off lunch after a late start, and by the time we were done talking and forming Gina Garcia's committees, many members had time only for a quick bite to eat before they had to head for home; tribal time in a social sense was sacrificed to the political at this meeting. But I did get a chance to talk to one of Old Tom's great-great-great-granddaughters, who lived in Oregon. She said, "It's something else to see this group all together." She was never told about her people's history because of bad blood—family feuding. "And I hope it's behind everyone." Later, I would find out that this bad blood was mostly because of George Peconom's abusive relationship with Celia Jack. His physical abuse is said to have led to her death.

Inez Chavez Valenzuela was born in 1920. She describes how her immediate family's feelings of connection to tribe soured as result of Celia's death. Celia's children, Ernest, Lanora, Inez, Emma (all Old Tom's descendants), and Hazel Peconom (Walter's daughter—Celia's first marriage had been to George Peconom's brother, Walter) were orphaned when she "passed"; "All of the Jack children [were taken away] to Indian school in Greenville and Hazel was sent to an Indian school in Haskell, Kansas." Lanora and Inez Jack (Inez Chavez Valenzuela's mother) eventually went on to high school at Sherman in Riverside, California, hundreds of miles south of Honey Lake Valley.

"So there were things my aunts, uncles, no matter how I asked, would not tell," Inez said. She had lost her mother at a young age, and by twelve she'd gone to live and work in the fields with her father's Mexican American community. And so there were other reasons for silence too. As she wrote me in a letter,

My great grandmother Julia Saunders [Old Tom's daughter and Bob Tail's sister] passed away 6 months after my mother passed away on April 12, 1928. While in her dying bed, she left a very harsh will, with her attorney. She left her land, Home and all her money to Uncle Ernest Jack, Aunt Lanora Jack and Emma Jack as well as her estate. To my Aunt Hazel Peconom, her grand-daughter she left $1.00. To my mother Inez that would have been divided between our family, she left us $1.00. To my sister Christina, brothers Manual, Joe and myself, she left $1.00 a piece. She disliked my father because he was Hispanic.

Inez, nonetheless, maintained a strong connection to her memories and experiences in Honey Lake Valley. In the 1950s she discovered that she and her siblings had inherited her Aunt Emma's share of her great-grandmother's land in Janesville. Another aunt, Lanora, however, was logging the land, despite the fact she was not the sole owner. Her letter continues:

When I went and told my attorney, Pancero, to probate Aunt Emma's estate I had [him divide it between the descendants of] Aunt Hazel Peconom, Uncle Ernest Jack, Aunt Bessie, Lawrence Jack, Harding Jack. My mother's share was divided between [me,] my sister and brothers. We all received a portion of the timber money. We put the 160 acres up for sale in 1982 and in February of that year it sold. This was the last of my great grandmother Julia Saunders' land. It all came to an end. Aunt Lanora lost a son George Wilson while logging [that land.] George was riding on the top of one of the contractor's caterpillars when it rolled down the hill and crushed him. It was a sad end, but sometimes we pay for our mistakes we make in life. I've always tried to do the right thing in caring and share whatever I have. To understand each other is the Legacy I leave for my family.

As her final comments indicate, for Inez, Federal Recognition means reattaching to tradition, and smoothing over the angry relationships of the past that were founded in violence and racial hatred and elaborated by fear and a sense that there was not enough to go around. To her thinking, having an official tribal structure, a byproduct of the Federal Acknowledgment process, means that her grandchildren (among them, Gina Garcia) and their children will have a structure through which to resolidify their bonds to the Honey Lake Valley. Their land is gone, but in the final analysis, maybe the land, itself only a remnant, represented the divisions the tribe had gone through and the divisions that had arisen between families.

As this example indicates, the FAP's requirement of giving, revealing, and laying bare opened the tribe to its hard past. If it was not reminding people of economic powerlessness or violence directed toward the tribe, it was reminding them of intratribe violence—or the utter loneliness of never having been taught tribal history. Petitioning is a process that reorders and transforms community. Consideration of Federal Recognition means consideration of power and how it has shaped understandings of identity. There is great difficulty to this memory work, for as the Honey Lake Maidus filled out their genealogies, for example, both the holes and the lines of connection could represent the painful memories no one wanted to address. Moreover, in so doing, each tribal member was making a symbolic pact with the Federal Acknowledgment process, the System, which had done them wrong before.

Over the course of the summer of 2000, I watched as the membership applications poured into the Honey Lake Maidu office. I would read them and enter the information into a genealogy program. Wanda and I had set an August 31, 2000, deadline for membership applications, but in the end we continued to take them through March of the next year because we did not want paperwork to stand between a potential member and his or her membership. But, nonetheless, we had picked a deadline, and the paperwork was daunting and stressful to the people seeking to meet it. These words themselves—*deadline* and *meeting* a deadline—indicate the way that applying for membership was a sacrificial death for a hopeful rebirth. Because of this, they evoke the spirit of Coyote.

Fear of what might happen if the membership applications were completed incorrectly characterized some people's
procrastination. For others, despite their dedication to Honey
Lake Maidu Recognition, it was not clearly in their best interest
to sign on as members, particularly if they were associated with
another rancheria; they were already Recognized, why risk it
to join a non-Recognized tribe?

Still others were stalled on genealogy—apart from the
problem of who's who, there was the work of summoning the
patience and the graciousness, despite their gall, to fill out the
chart. Filling out the genealogical chart was part of a fundamental violence that came with the creation of the Honey
Lake Maidu Tribe. First, there was the exclusion of other, non-
Honey Lake Maidu relatives.[19] Next, it was the archival violence
that, for instance, seemed to trample Leona Morales's words and
the histories passed on. Not to mention the hurtful reminders of
state racism found in the government's files. Genocidal violence
was of course invoked through the act of trying to remember
the past, and this meant recognizing loss at the very moments
of coming together. But now, the tribe itself, in capitulating to
the FAP, was asking members to justify themselves, asking for
enrollment numbers and "pedigree charts."[20] What I found
was that a tribe must subscribe to the logic of violence itself to
move forward with the FAP.

At the very least, it was clear that petitioning involved a
recapitulation of bureaucracy. Tribal members complained
about tribal applications being lost (in one case, a member's
genealogical and application materials had to be submitted to
the Susanville office three times), of only ever talking to the
answering machine when calls were placed to the office, or of
names being left off the list of tribal members. General suspicions
of Wanda's manner of running the office and my own work there
seemed to abound, while praise or gratitude was rare. Complaining about problems with the Honey Lake Maidu office
became a way of letting off steam about petitioning and working

closely with other tribal members. A relatively benign example might be provided by one tribal member from the Jack lineage who called me at home one morning and said, "Wanda's not doing her job. Not all of my family has received their newsletter." She suspected that all the Peconoms had, though.

Furthermore, CILS's involvement was shaping a certain kind of legalistically bureaucratic tribe. On December 18, 2000, for example, the Constitution Committee met to discuss constitutional issues with Will Jackson. He had prepared a constitution, and over the course of the meeting he went through it with the committee and others present, explaining its implications. Certain changes were made—the number of Tribal Council members, the addition of a cochairperson, the number of times the council had to meet per year—and it was voted in as the Honey Lake Maidu Draft Constitution. The document agreed upon set in motion a series of General Council meetings—first for the council's approval of the constitution itself—each of which necessitated the presence of a lawyer. It even laid out a program for its own adoption: an Interim Election Board had to be established, and a notice of the election and a copy of its agenda had to arrive at tribal members' residences no later than ten days before the election. Quorums and "Robert's Rules" were discussed—this was, Will Jackson insisted, so that BAR would know that the Honey Lake Maidu petition was in shape, above board, and, well, *legal*.

However, Jackson had prefaced his guided tour of the tribe's options for creating their constitution with an expression of his feeling that all of this was ludicrous, "just an exercise." The Honey Lake Maidu Tribe had been operating as the non-profit Bear Dance Foundation for years, and tribal authority was probably much more informally enacted and respected the way it was than anything that he could put into the legal vernacular. An "ambivalent expert" in Rose's full sense, equipped with "a radical politics of rights and empowerment" (1999, 89), he essentially felt the tribe could take or leave the constitution once it was enacted.

Instead, much like involving themselves in petitioning and thus becoming petitioners, once the constitution was voted upon, tribal members quite naturally had expectations that tribal government would be run according to its specifications. They felt they needed something to direct them through the murky waters of federal tribalness.

SHIFTING GROUND

The Oakland meeting with California Indian Legal Services also highlighted for me the demographic changes that came with organizing as an official tribe, itself concomitant with the momentum of the government grant and the tribe's progression through the petitioning process. One shift that seemed to take place before my eyes was a geographic one: once the tribal applications were in, it was clear that the greater portion of the membership no longer lived in the Honey Lake Valley. The final tally had only fourteen out of 212 members living in the Lassen County vicinity. This was reflected in the attendance at the Oakland meeting. No one from Susanville had traveled to attend the meeting. Brad Peconom, a Wetajam/Momolo descendant who lives in the San Francisco Bay Area was present, however, and he argued successfully for the constitutional principle of cochairpersons. Although he and a few others were primarily concerned about "lineage balance" in the Tribal Council positions, the cochair case was won through the logic of geography: most present were worried about the dominance of Susanville, which is remote and often inaccessible to the rest of California during the winter because of icy mountain passes. They were hoping that tribal meetings could be held in central or even Southern California once in a while.

It was agreed that the next meeting—for tribal elections and the vote about the constitution—would be held in Sacramento, in February. Ron and Wanda later agreed to this venue, but at the last minute Ron called me and told me that there was no way he was driving to Sacramento: Susanville was the Honey Lake Maidu homeland, and it was the center from which all decisions should be made, despite the fact that snow would most likely cancel any meeting we scheduled there. When Wanda announced that the meeting would be changed from Sacramento to Susanville, I was suddenly in the position of fielding irate phone calls, and in the end a huge February blizzard did, indeed, cancel the meeting. At the makeup meeting in early March, a quorum was not reached.

But finally, on a warm day at the end of March, the third attempt met with success, and tribal elections were held, in Susanville, to everyone's great joy and almost complete consensus. Ron Morales and Diana Sears were made cochairs; Gina Garcia, secretary; Art Chavez, treasurer; Wanda Brown, Margaret Ulleseit, and Brad Peconom, members-at-large. This was a well-balanced council, in my opinion. Sears represented the Bob Junior descendants, an important branch of the Wetajam/Momolo lineage; Garcia, Chavez, and Ulleseit the Old Tom lineage; and Peconom, a Bay Area branch of the old Susanville crew, represented by Wanda Brown and Ron Morales. An important scrimmage felt like it had been won: here were the Honey Lake Maidus, organized as officially as any Federally Recognized tribe.

After the tribal elections, members spent time visiting sites in the Honey Lake Valley and Mountain Meadows. Inez Valenzuela and her descendants spent time, as usual, at the Jack cemetery, *Wdojykom*, which is located on private land that changes hands quite frequently, thus thwarting Honey Lake Maidu attempts at creating lasting sympathetic relationships with its owners. They went to make sure nothing had happened to their burials, and, devastatingly, found evidence of all-terrain vehicles in the area.

A Tribal Council position called tribal historian had been conceived at the Oakland meeting for coordinating actions against precisely this kind of desecration. Creating this position reflected the young tribe's desire to learn its history and/or renew it through education and grant writing for revivals of language, dance, and traditional doctoring.

But though these actions reflect motions toward traditional orders of cultural integration, they also mark the shifts in power that occurred slowly over the period between the September 2000 meeting with CILS at Roxie Peconom Campground and June 2001, when the petition was sent to Washington: a new Honey Lake Maidu was being created, with many new members, particularly from the Jack lineage.

The work of advocating for sacred sites and burials is work in keeping with core Honey Lake Maidu values of "fighting for the tribe." But radically breaking with the status quo of Honey Lake knowledge keeping, the position of tribal historian was founded on the premise of equal access to tribal knowledge for all. With the coming together of minds that accompanied the assemblage of members to the Honey Lake Maidu tribe for petitioning, members of the Jack lineage and from other families outside the Susanville core had ideas for sharing and spreading cultural knowledge. One member told me that if Ron was going to insist on keeping all his grandmother's baskets in his own home, he should open it to visitors. He should also copy all his photos and give them to members and share his papers and files. This orientation also reflected an openness to BAR that differed from that of the core Honey Lake Maidu community in Susanville.

Ron used his knowledge as cultural capital (or, alternatively, as a personal artillery) in an environment threatened on all sides, by the state/Forest Service, by the Paiutes, by other Maidus, and even by his own tribe members. But, though we might see the "outside" lineage's reorderings of the tribe and its concepts of knowledge/secrecy as a break from Leona's, Ron's, and Viola's

ways of going about their lives as Indian people, it is critical to see
that this was not the birth of something new. It represented, I
believe, a return to an older order of existence, before Honey
Lake Maidu culture was so threatened that it needed to erase
itself in all apparent aspects, before someone like Leona Morales
felt she had to keep petroglyph sites from even her children.

Eventually, the Bear Dance Foundation would become a
vestige of a past period. Ron, Viola, and Wanda interpreted this
change, this shifting ground, as the rebirth of their people,
despite the twinges of personal pain it brought them. In Wanda's
case, the more organized the tribe became, the farther it traveled
from the space of her stories, memories, and hopes. She conceived of her efforts for the Bear Dance Foundation and as the
ANA grant's project director as efforts made for her mother,
for her grandmother, and for all those who came before them.
She also had other generational reasons for wanting to see the
Honey Lake Maidus gain Federal Recognition: she wants her
children's children to have a sense of tribe to call home, as she did
as a girl because of her close contact with her grandmother.

In the 1980s, when the Susanville Indian Rancheria needed to
expand its enrollment in order to receive government funding,
Wanda was one of two Honey Lake Maidus who were accepted
onto the Susanville Indian Rancheria rolls. Yet she describes
this as no real tribe for her children, who she believes always
felt excluded in certain ways: because of their light skin (she
claims it would have been easier if their Indian blood had
been mixed with Mexican blood, "like the rest of them up
there," rather than Anglo blood), and because of their particular
historical, tribal, and familial connections in a Joaquin-/Paiute-
dominated political environment.[21] She understands tribe and
history as integral, and knows what it would mean to her mother,
Viola, to finally have that history a/Acknowledged in a validating way. Yet, feeling the stress put on her by her Uncle Ron,
and watching him denigrate her mother's and her own contri-

butions to the Bear Dance, and, finally, to the tribe, she gradually withdrew from both the Bear Dance Foundation and the Tribal Council. After the March 31 tribal elections (when she was elected member-at-large), she informally stopped participating with the tribe. The fact was, she'd never even sent in a membership application—though she handled everyone else's—she had not wanted to jeopardize her house on the rancheria. As her mother also expressed, Wanda was happy to see the tribe "take off," but she felt that others could pick up where she had left things.

Ron, too, was tired of always fighting the Forest Service at the Bear Dance and hoped that the "new blood," as he put it, would mean a lessening of his own role as fighter, worker, organizer. He was happy that the "young people" wanted to get so involved. It meant the tribe was in good hands and that he could begin to relax and step away, despite the power he seemed to possess as a symbol for everyone.

The Bear Dance Foundation, which had already been unraveling, was officially absorbed by the Honey Lake Maidu Tribe with only a few meetings' discussion. It seemed, to those I spoke with, part of the natural progression of events, part of the momentum of tribal freedom.

Yet the real question remains: as Greg Sarris[22] asks in his fictional account of petitioning, *Watermelon Nights*, What kind of nation does the Federal Acknowledgment process lead to? What kind of sovereignty will this be?

These questions bring the sociology of power I have outlined back to genealogical understandings in both Foucault's and my grandmother's senses of the word *genealogy*: the genealogy of the discourses that have sought to define Indianness via what it is not are quite grounded in investigations of Honey Lake Maidu tribal members' literal genealogies in the National Archives. There is a ceaseless circulation of cause and effect, powered act and empowered response, within this continuing history of federal-Indian relations. But Nikolas Rose, whose own analysis links the Gramscian and Foucaultian, ultimately looks to breaking this open, asking "if there are ways of organizing our concern for others that [do] not seek to set them free— relations of obligation, of commitment, perhaps evoking an older sense of care" (1999, 97). The answer I have come to is that this older sense of care for the Honey Lake Maidus is old-time tribal care for community that, in many ways, as we've seen, is opposed to the libratory care of Federal Recognition. The great contradiction, however, is that Federal Recognition appears to be their best hope for its return.

FROM "THE POLITICS OF RECOGNITION,"
BY CHARLES TAYLOR

There is a form of the politics of equal respect, as enshrined in a liberalism of rights, that is inhospitable to difference, because (a) it insists on uniform application of the rules defining these rights, without exception, and (b) it is suspicious of collective goals. Of course, this doesn't mean that this model seeks to abolish cultural differences. This would be an absurd accusation. But I call it inhospitable because it can't accommodate what the members of distinct societies really aspire to, which is survival. This is (a) a collective goal, which (b) almost inevitably will call for some variations in the kinds of law we deem permissible from one cultural context to another. (1994, 60)

CHAPTER SIX

FEDERAL RECOGNITION AND THE POSSIBILITIES FOR HEALING

THIS FORM OF LIBERALISM TAYLOR WRITES ABOUT IS GUILTY AS charged by the proponents of a politics of difference. This form of liberalism, as inscribed in the Federal Acknowledgment procedures of the Branch of Acknowledgment and Research, Bureau of Indian Affairs, Department of the Interior, has produced the non-Recognition of the Honey Lake Maidus and other tribes and is complicit in a continuing form of ethnocide. The demands of cultural integrity in 25 CFR Part 83.7 are so ahistorical that they essentially work against cultural integrity. Yet the closed-but-a-crack door to the law holds these tribes by its very exclusion of them—the cultural sovereignty believed to exist beyond the door of the law is so palpable that it reifies tribal imperatives and makes legal reorganization worth the effort, worth the risks to individuals or groups and their goals and practices.

In the Honey Lake Maidu case, the collective goals to which Taylor refers are not so wholly collective: their specific collective goals can work, at times, against those of other collectivities. And so the politics of difference is itself a stone-strewn route.

I believe that the divisive effect of Federal Acknowledgment gatekeeping can be linked to the two incompatible sociopolitical frameworks under which the Branch of Acknowledgment and Research operates.

The first frame is an older, paternalistic model of the governance of problem cases, such that the "Indian problem" is conceived in terms of primitivity of custom and its connection to too many blood quanta. The Federal Acknowledgment criteria closely conform to this vision of quanta of blood and culture: in their stricture, the criteria enact the early-twentieth-century vision of the happy extinction of difference. The key difference is that today the Indian problem considered by the bureau is that the non-Recognized tribes are not different *enough*. In this context, tribes must compete with one another over the right to certain histories, certain blood, and certain cultural activities.

The second frame under which BAR works is the neoliberal envisioning of the government of the Indian problem, which is focused upon accountability: the BIA is pressured to run itself as a business, minimizing inputs and maximizing outputs. According to this model, Indianness is evaluated according to the testimony of experts, budgetary considerations, and political expediency. Here, would-be tribes are encouraged to reflect discrete identities, and, in their petitions, cut-and-dried histories with easy-to-read self-representations.

The two frames are inextricably connected, of course.[1] And there is hope for a tribe like the Honey Lake Maidus in under-standing the BIA as a business and themselves as consumers of the state who might clamor for recognition of their needs. Yet they find that in order to do so, they must rely on older, paternal imaginaries of Indianness: they have to depict themselves appro-priately to be r/Recognizable. Together, the way Honey Lake Maidus blend these sociopolitical framings creates an approach to petitioning that would transform the state into a grand piñata, to batter at, then enjoy.[2] Yet the pertinent question is whether the modern liberal state has the philosophical space or practical inclination to support the cultural survival for which the Honey Lake Maidus are truly asking. The reality of the metaphor is that the Honey Lake Maidus are looking for meat—one might predict that the state's piñata sugar will not sustain them.

Indeed, the state, from the core Honey Lake Maidu per-spective, is a place in Washington, D.C., from which faceless bureaucrats throw Indians a few bones and then watch them snarl over them. The image is one of Ron Morales's favorites: "There's no meat on them bones, even, but they throw them and the Indians fight over them," he says. The meat that the state seeks to retain control over is the meat of resources, resources such as money and land, as well as those more intangible, like recognition, jurisdiction, the ability to cast blame, the moral high ground—and the meting of justice. For their part, the Honey Lake Maidus seek a bone to gnaw, but preferably a fleshy one.

To understand this situation, that in which the goal of survival leads to anything *but* monolithic collectivities, I have worked in this book to restore the original and continuing state violence toward Native peoples to the role of catalyst in the equation of California Indians and what is sometimes reputed to be their notorious factionalism. Doing so helps make sense of factionalism as a political process for dealing with change that has a very long history.

HOPE AND FACTIONALISM

The continuous regeneration of people's hopes, even after generations and generations of abuse, calls to mind the regenerative prowess of Coyote. The effervescence of hope is tied, too, to Coyote's gift for causing strife and factionalism because of the context of struggle that is part of what it is to be an American Indian: the construction of tribe in different historical periods has created situations of stress in which factional hopes have arisen (and still arise) as healthy, but sometimes destructive, responses.[3] Community survival is often both constructive or destructive, and almost always political for Indian people: community survival involves negotiating power structures and choosing between either compromise or division for the sake of a better future (see Sider 1993, 207).

An example of this kind of community division over decision making in the context of strategizing for survival can be furnished by the story, in summary—the actual discussions, of course, do not remain—of the Honey Lake Maidu people's division over how to fit into the non-Indian world in the early twentieth century. Their struggles and choices are similar to those of other California tribes, in a general sense.

Three Honey Lake Maidu lineages survived the pre- and early historical period epidemics, violence, and social transformations: the Jacksons, the Peconoms, and the Jacks. As I have described, members of each chose different paths in the early 1900s. Some of the Jacksons moved to the Susanville Indian Rancheria when it was purchased in 1924, others moved to Dixie Valley in Pit River country. Most of the Peconom lineage, particularly the descendants of Roxie Peconom, moved to Susanville and purchased private homes near the rancheria. The decision (encouraged, perhaps, by Field Matron Young) to live in Susanville rather than on the rancheria or elsewhere has been described by my consultants as a compromise based on the hope that adapting to some of the white social structure would be the route to their people's best possible future. Recalling, too, that in the 1980s Peconom descendants Wanda Brown and her sister Linda Hutt chose to move their families to the Susanville Indian Rancheria, we can also think of this decision as based on an economic understanding that adapting to the government's system might be the best option for a family that did not own a house or any land.

The Jack lineage families, meanwhile, remained living on or near their allotment lands in the Elysian Valley and Janesville areas. Later, most of this lineage found that adapting to the dominant economic structure successfully would mean moving away from Honey Lake Valley (though they retained Julia Saunders's allotment into the 1980s.) Such reasoning, too, had led to a separation within the Peconom lineage, when Roxie's brother Bob Junior moved away to Manton in the early years of the twentieth century. Today, one might say that these choices have left the Honey Lake Maidu non-Recognized, and isolated, to some degree, from one another. Yet these choices might also be said to have been immensely successful—the survival of the tribe was witnessed by the coming together of the lineages and generations in March 2001, when the Honey Lake Maidu tribal constitution and Tribal Council were voted into existence. And so there was power in the multiplicity of the Honey Lake Maidu strategy even as this multiplicity has, over time, made understanding what is in the tribe's interest and acting upon it more complicated.

But, ultimately, there are still the issues of sugar versus meat and of inter- and intratribal factionalism as a reflection of the violent judgments of larger society, both of which beg the question of what will come of Federal Recognition for the Honey Lake Maidus. In the meantime (not even the BIA knows how long that might be—maybe ten or more years) I have focused upon the kind of reorientations waiting before the law demands, like the plot of one of Kafka's short stories in which a confused protagonist engages (and is abused by) the capricious bureaucracy. I believe that by closing in on the Honey Lake Maidu Tribe's engagement *with* their non-Recognition—their recognition of both their power and powerlessness in the face of developers and the Forest Service—as well as their engagement *of* their non-Recognition—that is, their choice to embark upon the Federal Acknowledgment process—this work has described some of the crucial realignments that occur in the ever-extending liminal period of petitioning that will move, with the tribe, into the post-Acknowledgment period.

These realignments constitute a war of position between tribe and state that is integral to a history of control and both internal and external struggle to cope with domination. One of the most important changes for the Honey Lake Maidus that I have described was the constitutional ordering of the tribe, previously represented formally only by the Bear Dance Foundation.

THE HONEY LAKE MAIDU TRIBE DIGESTS
THE BEAR DANCE FOUNDATION

Hope will turn out to be created not simply in the context of struggles against the dominant society but also in the context of a people's internal struggles—the same factional struggles that have often also had such destructive consequences.
—Gerald Sider 1993: xviii

The Honey Lake Maidu Tribe was organized throughout 2001, and by the middle of that year, members' thoughts had turned to what would happen after the ANA money ran out and the project was finished. The Bear Dance Foundation was encouraged to turn the computer and fax/copier/printer purchased under the tenure of the ANA grant over to the tribe. Yet the foundation was not convinced that this was in its best interests. This tension came down, once again, to geography: Ron and Viola argued that they would need the computer to write letters, because protecting cultural resources in Honey Lake Valley required constant vigilance. The federal prison was now under construction in Herlong—letters needed to be written urging the use of backhoes to dig deep test holes at the site because of the extensive earthmoving by the army in the recent history of the area. Having the tribal secretary, who lived in L.A., write these letters on the tribe's computer would require too many expensive long-distance phone calls.

Yet the Tribal Council saw this position as an act of defiance. The Tribal Council, balanced between Jack and Peconom descendants, was largely "technocratic" in Bruce Miller's (1988) sense—well educated and administratively talented, but for the most part lacking in forms of authority based in old-time cultural knowledge. The exception was Ron, and this was his power. In fact, the reader may recall that Ron was actually only a cochair of the tribe. The other chairperson was Diana Sears, a descendant of Roxie Peconom's brother Bob Junior. As her campaign statement had noted, she knew something of tribal government because of her experience as an Indian Health Service nurse. Professional, thoughtful, and responsible about attending Tribal Council meetings, Sears nonetheless played second fiddle to Ron, who was considered an authority in a way she was not. This was true not only in terms of cultural authority but also gender and age.

These differences within the Tribal Council formed an axis for division. Furthermore, Ron and Viola constantly held the nascent, officializing tribe to the standard of what they had been told by their grandmother. And to these two, and certainly to their lineal relatives, Roxie Peconom was *the core* of the tribe.

The Tribal Council saw this dichotomous way of thinking, in terms of core members and peripheral members, as a divisiveness that would work against larger tribal interests. Inez Valenzuela, for instance, had lived since the 1930s outside the Honey Lake Valley, but had an unfaltering understanding of her Honey Lake Maiduness. Her great-grandmother, Julia Saunders, had been a major matriarch of the tribe, and Inez's own personal experience of cultural connection despite geographical dislocation was reflected in her hope for the future of the tribe. This future included the possibility of buying land near the Bay Area and building a casino. More generally, from the perspective of the so-called periphery, the core needed an infusion of new ideas; it had been whittled away for far too long. From this vantage point, Ron's informal, family leadership needed revitalization. It had taken months too long, for instance, for Wanda to hand over the tribal membership application forms for Margaret Ulleseit's taste, and now the computer and printer, long pursued, were going to be held back by the Bear Dance Foundation. Margaret Ulleseit and Art Chavez's[4] feeling was that, in order to survive as a community and in order to get Recognized, things had to be done according to the liberal procedures of justice . . . and simple business sense. This meant that there would have to be organizational hierarchies and orders of procedure. Organizational hierarchies would mean a subsuming of the Bear Dance Foundation within the Honey Lake Maidu Tribe.

Yet throughout the Bear Dance Foundation and Tribal Council meetings, Ron and Viola were obstinate about not submitting to the authority of the council. California Indian Legal Services attorney Lynne Guerrero strongly encouraged the Bear Dance Foundation to defer to "tribal law and custom," by which she meant the new Honey Lake Maidu tribal constitution, but this legal language made no sense to the Bear Dance Foundation. To them, the Bear Dance constituted tribal law and custom if anything did.

The key to the resolution of these threatening issues was Ron's position as a member of both the Tribal Council and the Bear Dance Foundation, as well as his organic ability to read, then reform and express, the interests of the general membership. Despite an agreement not to discuss the tensions between the foundation and the Tribal Council with the general membership, at the tribewide General Council meeting in Reno, Ron suddenly introduced a topic not on the agenda. He boldly proposed that the tribe take over the work of the Bear Dance Foundation. This was one step further, even, than having the Bear Dance Foundation placed under the tribe's umbrella as had been discussed: it meant uniting the two organizations inextricably.

The proposal was met with much enthusiasm. Ron had essentially proposed dissolving the core and periphery distinctions that had been mapped to the control over and participation in the staging of the Bear Dance for so long.[5] This was a true move toward ceremonially integrating all tribe members.

What's more, Ron had obviously read the opinion of the foundation well: Linda, Viola, and the other members were happy to have the burden and stress of staging the event every year taken off their (small) committee's shoulders. (At the time, I thought that perhaps this had been why they had been so loathe to give up the ANA resources: they had so little help, why would they give up their only assets?) By uniting the Bear Dance Foundation and the Honey Lake Maidu Tribe, Ron had administratively, as chair, demonstrated to the Tribal Council that the Bear Dance Foundation was behind the tribe 100 percent. He helped establish a single position behind a single tribal interest: cultural preservation—the safeguarding and staging of the Bear Dance—of which Acknowledgment would be a crucial part.

But in this way, too, I recognized that he had established that tribal interests are the interests of the Honey Lake Valley, and that the computer needed to remain there. Later, Viola was the most stubborn proponent of this view, and probably to this day the computer takes up space in the back bedroom of her daughter Wanda's house, a kind of hostage against Viola's marginalization within the tribe and by her brother.

The union of the Bear Dance Foundation and the Honey Lake Maidu Tribe was understood as the ultimate wedding of the informal, familial system of ceremonial leadership with a more flexible, "open," or legalistic system. For me, this understanding makes sense of a comment Wanda had made the night before, at the Bear Dance Foundation meeting: she had told all present that *she felt she'd never been part of a functioning tribe.* Wanda was looking to the future of Honey Lake Maidu leadership, and her point was about how Ron's exercise of the kind of "familial ceremonial authority" I described for the petition was not satisfying to her—nor, as I increasingly understood, to Viola, Marvin Benner, or Brad's father, John Peconom. Wanda and these others were struggling with the shape of their tribe, a practice with a long history. In the current context, ordering the community along the lines of a constitution and bylaws and California Indian Legal Service's legal orders of procedure allowed political dissent a fighting chance in a way it was not currently permitted (without disastrous consequences) because of the family structure of the Bear Dance Foundation.

Though I will emphasize that the union of the Bear Dance Foundation and the Honey Lake Maidu Tribe in no way erased the old-time tradition of internal/external struggle, in many ways tribal members had come to embrace that form of the "politics of equal respect" that Charles Taylor found guilty and Nikolas Rose described as a contradictory freedom. What I found was that this politics of equal respect had come to match tribe members' individual and collective goals, on the tribe's own terms. For example, I was happy to see that something of the eclectic, charismatic nature of informal tribal leadership remained, particularly through Ron's easy leadership in the face of a weighty issue at the General Council meeting. With the procedural skeleton in place, the Honey Lake Maidus are adding flesh to the bones in the shape of their version of tribalness. The Honey Lake Maidus were reenvisioning a substantive political unity, based on the liberal, legal, procedural tools of freedom, such as their constitution and bylaws, and emblemized by their decision to blend the Bear Dance Foundation and the tribe's structures. This was an internalization of the liberal values and techniques of self-actualization, a kind of liberal self-Acknowledgment . . . and, one might argue, a slight retreat from the belligerent approach and the metaphors of war.

A SUMMARY OF THE HONEY LAKE MAIDU CRITIQUE

Yet the struggle remains, however diminished, for the government's and the Honey Lake Maidus' definitions of tribe conflict, even as they articulate with one another. First, in the Honey Lake Maidu version of tribe, traditional territorial boundaries have a concreteness that extends beyond BAR's intent. At the same time, as is true throughout much of indigenous California, the geographic location of members' residences is of less importance, thus defying BAR's envisioning of a geographically located community steeped in "traditional" Indianness. Second, the Honey Lake Maidu petitioning effort authenticates instrumental economic desires for Federal Acknowledgment. There simply *are* material stakes to Indian identity, and Federal Recognition has, logically enough, become a kind of economic resource. Nonetheless, this is ignored by BAR, and taken up by critics of Indian gaming, in ways that marginalize the real issue, which is the need for survival as a community. This is linked to my third point of critique, a critique about the way that the Honey Lake Maidu Tribe confronts the politics of Federal Recognition as it takes it on, though BAR denies that there is anything political about the process at all. I have shown that it is absolutely political to not include space in the Federal Acknowledgment process for the state's role in culture change, for Indian silences, or for the full ramifications of Indian struggles with reconciling the past and the future. Fourth, I have shown how the Honey Lake Maidus' and the government's understandings of blood and descent differ. For the Honey Lake Maidus, blood connects and rebuilds rather than dilutes and distances. And it saturates the tribe's petition for Acknowledgment.

Finally, it is important to understand that the Honey Lake Maidu story is a California story: the way the tribe has approached petitioning reflects pressures and histories that weigh heavily on indigenous cultures across the state. In other words, this is not just the story of one tribe's experience of injustice.

OTHER CALIFORNIA TRIBES

The similar experiences of California tribes stem from the similarities of their historical experiences. Working together as the Advisory Council on California Indian Policy, the state's tribes made this point to Congress in 1997, proposing a bill to change the Acknowledgment criteria. In particular, what the ACCIP called "the California approach" took on the criteria that ask for identification as an Indian group on a substantially continuous basis (Criterion A), evidence of community

(Criterion B), and exercise of political influence or authority (Criterion C). It proposed that the Acknowledgment process's assumptions be reorganized in order to allocate more fairly the burden of proof, which the current system has the petitioner alone bear. To this end, it proposed that if three alternative requirements could be met, the petitioner should be presumed to be qualified according to the first three criteria, A, B, and C. These three alternative requirements were: (1) that no less than 75 percent of the current members are descendants of the California Indian group upon which it bases its claim for Acknowledgment, (2) that the membership of the petitioner is composed primarily of persons not members of any other Indian tribes, and (3) that the petitioner is the successor in interest to a treaty or treaties (ratified or not ratified), or has been the subject of other (specifically named) federal actions.

The Advisory Council also suggested that gaps of up to forty years during the period between 1852 and 1934 be permitted according to the Acknowledgment process. It stated that "it would be unconscionable to force California Indian groups that suffered through this period to provide evidence that, for the most part, does not exist because of the actions or neglect of the federal and state governments" (ACCIP 1997a, 22). The California approach would also have the term *community* defined more broadly than at present to account for genocide and state-sanctioned slavery and indentured servitude, as well as economic violence, which often caused the widespread dispersal of the tribal members. "The focus of the term should be on networks of social interactions between group members, regardless of territorial proximity, though the geographic proximity of members to one another and to any group settlement or settlements would still be a factor in determining whether a community exists" (ibid., 23). Finally, rather than requiring that a "predominant portion" of the membership comprise a community, the Advisory Council advised that a "substantial portion" should be the standard.

Of course, the historical experiences of California tribes also differ, and it is certainly true that they have confronted the Recognition process in different ways, in part because the ACCIP bill was not adopted. Time has shown a sustained tension between the tendency to work together as a unit (reflected in the work of the Advisory Council) and a tendency to balkanize— along the lines of the many clear linguistic and cultural tribal lines the state's tribes possess. In what follows, I will focus on the separate experiences of five California tribes, beginning with the success of the Federated Indians of Graton Rancheria.

Representative Miller's California Tribal Status Act of 1997 (an ACCIP successor bill) was not approved, but a direct result of work begun with the ACCIP was that the Federated Indians of Graton Rancheria (Southern Pomo and Coast Miwok peoples), with Greg Sarris as their chair, were Acknowledged via Congress in 2000 as part of the Omnibus Indian Advancement Act (PL 106-568). Appealing directly to specific legislators to carry their voices to Congress, the Federated Indians of Graton Rancheria were able to parlay connection and a moving description of their particular experiences as a tribe into congressional Recognition, thus avoiding the BIA's Federal Acknowledgment process. In sum, the Graton triumph truly has an epic quality: turned from their lands, transformed by necessity into domestic servants and seasonal farm laborers, given a tiny rancheria, members of this tribe of powerful healers and awesome basket makers were finally Acknowledged as a people through sheer strength of will and political savvy. It is a California story with an ending the Honey Lake Maidus and so many others can look to with hope.

The story of the Ione Miwoks, on the other hand, is the quintessential Kafkan narrative. In contrast to the Honey Lake Maidus, and similar to the Federated Indians of Graton Rancheria, this tribe was formally Recognized by the federal government at a specific date in the past, and was therefore permitted to bypass some of the requirements of the regular Federal Acknowledgment process. Most notably, according to hard-won reforms made in 1994, a petitioner with this status—called "Previous Acknowledgment"—needs only to complete the process from the date of the last instance of its Federal Acknowledgment.

Yet the Ione Miwoks had already been waiting on their Acknowledgment for fifteen years when CILS attorney Allogan Slagle's investigations revealed incontrovertibly that the BIA had made a series of mistakes that had obscured their Previous Federal Acknowledgment. The government had listed them, instead, as regular petitioners, and further, it was denying any knowledge of their current petition.

Although the Ione Miwoks stalwartly maintained that they had received a letter from Commissioner Louis Bruce in 1972 advising them that the BIA possessed evidence of their Previous Recognition as a tribe, the BIA claimed that Commissioner Bruce had no authority to say such a thing and that no written evidence of such a letter exists today or in fact ever existed. In response to these denials, in 1990 Slagle located a February 24, 1975, memo that Assistant Solicitor Scott Keep wrote to the associate solicitor of Indian Affairs expressing his confusion about the actions of the bureau; however, in 1990, Keep denied writing the memo. Keep's alleged 1975 memo, as reported by Slagle, reads,

The Ione Band of Indians is a small California group residing on a 40 acre tract of land in the central part of the state generally east of Sacramento. The department has been trying to acquire land for this group for almost 60 years. The Bureau's excellent "Note to the Reviewers" recounts the tragic chain of circumstances which had thus far frustrated the acquisition in trust of the land on which the band lives. It reads like a Kafka short story [Slagle's note: "This last sentence was struck through."]. The Bureau's memorandum that is in for review is framed in terms of extending Federal recognition to the Ione Band. [M]y review of the available materials convinces me that the Ione Band has previously been recognized by the federal government. . . . From the materials that I have it is not clear why the Area Director did not complete the action directed by the Commissioner [Slagle's emphasis] (1990, 48).

Keep's memo exemplifies an arbitrariness, a back-and-forthness or capriciousness on the part of the BIA. In essence, the Ione Miwok Tribe's legal identity (historic and future) quavered in flux for almost twenty years because of bureaucratic fumbling. And for Slagle, the reference to Kafka testified to a not-so-petty bureaucrat's epiphanous moment of understanding his own role, and the larger system's role, as obstacles, instead of enablers, of Native people's rights. Indeed, in the end, the Bruce letter of 1972 was said to have been neither a contract nor an agreement, and was thus meaningless for the Iones.

It was not until 1994 that the Ione Band was finally Acknowledged. Their Acknowledgment—which occurred by perhaps embarrassed direct action of the assistant secretary of the Interior *outside* of the BIA's Federal Acknowledgment procedures—only betrays more of the absurd capriciousness of the process.

The Muwekma Ohlones, a tribe that covers a large expanse of the heavily impacted San Francisco Bay Area (which, for instance, was "served" by no less than three Spanish missions, where policies of Native enslavement devastated the community), are experiencing a similarly Kafkaesque situation today. The Muwekmas were awarded status as "unambigously previously Recognized" in 1996, yet tribe members found that this preferential status still meant that they would have to wait the twenty or more years before reaching the front of the queue and receiving BAR evaluation. And so the tribe took BAR to court, arguing that making it wait so long was unjust. It was the first instance of this kind of direct judiciary attempt on the Federal Acknowledgment process. The Interior Board of Indian Appeals, which offers the only recourse the tribes have in the process,[6] ruled that BAR should immediately consider the Muwekma petition. Despite the tribe's strong support by then-Lt. Gov. Cruz Bustamonte and Congresswoman Zoe Lofgren, and despite its unambiguous Previous Acknowledgment, the tribe was denied Federal Acknowledgment in September of 2002. The Muwekma Ohlone Tribe is currently appealing this decision.

As I have mentioned, there has been only one California tribe Acknowledged by the federal process, the Timbisha Shoshones of Death Valley, in 1983, though one could hardly call it a story of justice served. Living in poverty in the shadow of a luxury inn in a national park, the core Timbisha community made it through the process on the strength of its living language and cultural practices. Certainly, the tribe's longstanding relationship with the National Parks Service (NPS) was useful to its tribal documentation. Yet achieving federal status—Acknowledgment—did not change the tribe's material situation or serve to protect its culture. Rather, a long struggle with the NPS ensued. It was not until 1999 that the NPS was willing to begin negotiating with the tribe, government to government, for the return of a piece of the tribe's aboriginal lands. In 2000, three hundred acres were awarded the tribe, three hundred extremely hard-won acres that remain wrapped tightly in red tape.

This story of bittersweet success is further marred by a closer look at the tribe's 1983 Acknowledgment, one that has been impossible to replicate for other California tribes. Writes Mark E. Miller, "Although the Timbisha Shoshones had a strong case and almost certainly would have succeeded at a later date, they clearly had the fortune of going through the FAP in its early years when the levels of proof and burdens were not so onerous. As BAR evaluations are historically situated, Allogan Slagle, an expert on Tribal recognition in California, guesses that the Shoshones' twenty-two page petition would not survive the FAP today" (2004, 154).

It quickly becomes clear that the most success route California tribes have found is the congressional route to Federal

Acknowledgment, as is true across the nation. Congress is more sympathetic to the tribes and their histories, perhaps because it cleaves closer to the idea of bringing justice to the nation's tribes that was the original intent behind the Federal Acknowledgment procedures. Perhaps, too, Congress recognizes the role its refusal to ratify the treaties it made with the California tribes in the 1850s has played in creating their current situation: the state's approximately 320,000 Indians are the poorest and most underserved of the Indian *and* non-Indian populations in the nation. Yet taking the congressional route to Acknowledgment requires Previously Acknowledged status (because Congress is unwilling to step on the BIA's toes), a good deal of perseverance, and most important, a very powerful political ally. Before the Acknowledgment of the Federated Coast Miwoks, for instance, a small ruckus was made over the fact that the son of Senator Barbara Boxer, who was backing the tribe, was working with them on their casino plans. These kinds of connections are simply hard to come by for most un-Acknowledged tribes. And one can imagine that from a congressperson's perspective, casino politics complicates the meaning that allying with Indian people holds.

The sober truth is that even among California tribes with Previous Acknowledgment, there are still many who remain un-Acknowledged. One such tribe is the Strawberry Valley Maidu Tribe, a Konkow people who were left out of California Indian Legal Services' class-action suit because of a misunderstanding (*Tillie Hardwick et al. v. the United States*, 1989). The Strawberry Valley Maidus are most well known for owning the smallest reservation in the United States—the one-acre Strawberry Valley Rancheria. Ron's cousin Mona Davis is a member. Being surrounded by two Konkow tribes with casinos—Mooretown and Enterprise rancherias—has provided the Strawberry Valley Maidus certain opportunities, such as health care. But because members are unsatisfied with joining their more distant relatives as "adopted" members without voting privileges, and because they are proud of their particular tribal history, the Strawberry Valley Maidus won an ANA grant to begin their petitioning work for Restoration through Congress. Though they are having a hard time getting their bill introduced (in part because they refuse to work through California Indian Legal Services because of *Tillie Hardwick*), they are preparing a petition according to BAR's requirements, in the hope that there will be a breakthrough and that they will be able to move ahead through Congress.

In this context, the Honey Lake Maidu situation appears unique. Landless and mostly forgotten by the government, their case is not one of unambiguous Previous Acknowledgment. Yet their story is thus doubly important. It is the tribes that are "unattractive" to Congress that define the limits and, ultimately, the true flaws that lie within the Federal Acknowledgment process.

RECOGNITION AND THE MASSACRE AT EAGLE LAKE

I have not yet taken up the question of how external relations—relationships with other tribes and with non-Indians—are transformed in the face of Federal Recognition, but this, too, offers a powerful critique of the process as it works in California, connecting back to this chapter's focus on factionalism. I will now describe how, as petitioners with opposing claims on the valley, the Susanville Indian Rancheria's Wadakut Paiutes of Honey Lake Valley and the Honey Lake Maidus face off against one another, ironically working toward mutual erasure as they seek the town's and the state's r/Recognition. Afterward, I will turn to the possibilities for alliance in the Honey Lake Valley.

In September 2000, Harold Dixon came "down into town"— that is, off the rez—to give what the Lassen Land and Trails Trust called a "Whistle Stop Lecture" at the old Susanville train depot. "The Paiute of Honey Lake Valley" was a lecture on his people's primacy in the Honey Lake Valley, for an audience of about fifty-five Indians and non-Indians. The materials were based on the tribe's documentation for its Acknowledgment petition. The evening started out in the parking lot with a prayer in Paiute, and continued with dancing. All the old white ladies loved Mata, one of the dancers and "the littlest Indian," as I heard one of them call him. Emphasizing conflict by his very name, *Mata* is also a spectacular former village site in Milford that the Honey Lake Maidus claim for their own.

Seventy-one-year-old Harold "Utie" Dixon's presentation, the central attraction of the evening, was about Old Man Joaquin, his grandfather, the family patriarch, who is as important to his family as Roxie is to the Peconoms. Old Man Joaquin was born in 1834 and lived (like Roxie) to be 108. Joaquin married Mattie, and together they raised ten children. Today they have over two hundred descendants. At the mention of their daughter, Kitty Joaquin, and *her* daughter, Gladys Mankins, who sponsored the Bear Dance at Janesville for so many years, the audience broke into murmurs and whispers as people remembered their connections to the event and the family. When Dixon spoke further of the Bear Dance, I began to see the full extent of his deliberate erasure of the Maidus from Honey Lake Valley: "[Janesville] was where it started," Dixon said. "Then it kind of faded out—don't know what happened to it." No one mentioned the obvious contemporary nature of the annual Maidu celebration. It was clear to me that the Wadakut Paiutes were trying to write a new history, revised and excised.

Why this would seem necessary became clear later, when Theresa Dixon, Harold's daughter, stood up and told the story of western expansion, in round phrases: "They had a westward policy. But then they got to California. So they made a termination policy. It was a genocide policy." She explained that "there was a massacre at Eagle Lake. June 1866. And in June 2000, 134 years later, we had ceremonies and prayers there."

She told the story of the U.S. soldiers' attack on the village site in what is now the Forest Service's Eagle Lake Ranger District, a place that her family wants "taken off the Forest Service map," that is, left unnamed, "so that those who died there can find peace. . . . Children, animals, dogs, horses were slaughtered there," she said simply, quietly. Mothers were killed before they could retrieve their babies, hung in their baskets on tree branches. One was heard crying after it was all over. Theresa's great-grandfather, Joaquin, had barely escaped.

The biggest impression her words left was of the trauma suffered by these people, suffering that they cannot help but have held on to.

But in choosing to write the Maidus out of her presentation, Dixon neglected to mention the terrible role the Maidus played in the massacre. This incredible choice of simmering hatred over recognizable accusation is much like the Honey Lake Maidu refusal, at the cost of local recognition, to be depicted in uptown Susanville's "intertribal" murals. To be together before the town in any medium would be too much for either side's delicate construction of its history.

Nonetheless, all evidence points to a Honey Lake Maidu role in the massacre. Kitty Joaquin's version of the story of the Papoose Massacre, collected and paraphrased by Fritz Riddell in the late 1940s, follows.

A short time after white people came to Honey Lake valley a band of Wadátkut[7] people, including Joaquin (Kitty's father), was on a hunting trip to Eagle Lake (Kitty stated on another occasion that they had gone to the lake to escape the soldiers). A group of soldiers, augmented by a number of Maidu men, were also in the vicinity. Hog-die Jim . . ., Joaquin's uncle, was afraid that the soldiers and the Maidu would attack the Wadátkut camp, so advised Joaquin and the others to move their camp. Joaquin, however, felt that there was no real danger, so was not willing to move camp. Hog-die Jim then took the dried meat, a rabbit skin blanket, and all the horses and left. . . .

The soldiers and the Maidu attacked Joaquin's camp and killed everyone except a baby in a cradle board, two women who jumped into the lake and swam to safety, a half-grown girl, and Joaquin. Joaquin, too, jumped into the lake to escape, but while in the water he was shot through the body by a soldier, John Mulroney. Killed at this time was Joaquin's brother. Joaquin escaped and was cared for by the others who had gotten away. For the remainder of his long life Joaquin felt bitterness toward the whites and the Maidu. (1978a, 28)

Ron and his family corroborate this story, but they deny the massacre. Viola explained that Joaquin was one of Winnemucca's soldiers who would waylay and kill whites in the valley. "Then the Maidu and the whites chased them up to Eagle Lake." "Oh," I said, putting it together, "the [Eagle Lake] Massacre."[8] "No," Viola said, "there was no massacre." By this she did not mean that no one died at the edge of Eagle Lake, but that no one was *killed*. She said the soldiers were just chasing the Paiutes and the Maidus were helping them, but the Paiutes were not murdered. They (simply) jumped in the water and drowned, and "some were captured and the soldiers fired back—if they were shot first." I believe that one reason why Viola couldn't consider it a massacre is because of the rest of her socialized understanding of the history of Honey Lake Valley, which had the Paiutes in the role of foreign interlopers who came, made trouble, and then tried to pose as indigenous to the area. According to this thinking, allowing them anything more might jeopardize Honey Lake Maidu Acknowledgment.

Stepping back from this precipice, we could say that, for the Honey Lake Maidus, the everyday struggle of non-r/Recognition with the county and with the federal government includes a struggle with other local Indian peoples. At the same time, there are serious tensions, if not animosities, between the Indian and non-Indian segments of Susanville (and particularly between the SIR government and the City of Susanville). If the roots of Maidu-Paiute conflict tie back to the massacre at Eagle Lake, then this extratribal conflict might also be tied back to non-Indian readings of the massacre: Asa Fairfield's *Pioneer History.*

In Susanville, Fairfield's is the standard history of what took place in June of 1866 at Eagle Lake that is taught in the schools and recited around town at events like Isaac Roop Day. In Fairfield's *Pioneer History,* the white pioneers were merely would-be victims who, increasingly, were able to outsmart the Indians. Old Tom is depicted as helping the Paiutes by selling them guns and ammunition, which he stole from frontier wives while their husbands and sons were away. Fairfield writes that the soldiers went up to Eagle Lake to the Paiute camp as a preventative measure. Once there, not only were the Paiutes massacred, but Old Tom himself was hunted down and murdered. In this telling, the white emigrants were simply protecting their womenfolk and property.

The reader might see how Viola's version of the story is sensitive to this pioneer motive: she, too, implies that the whites and Maidu guides were just "keeping the peace." Also significantly, her telling does not include mention of the murder of Old Tom, Honey Lake Maidu. I suggest that this is because there are surprising ways in which the economic and political positionings of the Indians and the pioneers (and particularly the Mountain Maidus in Honey Lake Valley) are constructed in parallel even today. In fact, I believe that the situations of the local Indian people and the town are similar: both groups are looking for their own variety of federal recognition. The non-Indians don't need Federal Acknowledgment but they want, for instance, to be acknowledged by the government with a new prison: federal prisons mean federal jobs.[9]

Len Rousch's relationship with Ron and Viola provides an example of the alignments of interests in the Honey Lake Valley that involve alliances between Indians and non-Indians—a mapping of community imperatives despite structural positions that conflict. Rousch comes from a long line of ranchers in Susanville and is a member of the Lassen County Cattlemen and Cattlewomen's Association. His forefathers were the ranchers who took Honey Lake Maidu land when they moved into the valley with their cattle and their pioneer dreams. But despite his relatively recent acquisition of the land, he feels a deep connection to it, and an urgency to protect it. Rousch has become good friends with, and a good ally to, Ron. Ron has shown Len where his family's gravesites are so that Len can watch those areas closely to keep pot hunters away.[10] The Honey Lake Maidus and Rousch are united in their opposition to the proposed federal prison—Rousch, for the economic changes it will bring to his ranching community, Ron for the disturbance of possible graves in the area. When grouped together in early 2000 as members of Citizens Against More Prisons (CAMP), the Honey Lake Maidus were looked to as critical opponents of the prison plans. What CAMP hoped was that Ron and his people's claims to possible burials in the area would at least buy them some time to investigate what they believed was the Bureau of Prisons' inadequate consideration of water sources in the area.

Rousch, meanwhile, also supports the Honey Lake Maidu petitioning efforts. This is a motion toward a Honey Lake Valley where Indian interests and debates are not ignored (or "administered"), but acknowledged and included in local debates. Thus it is also a motion toward a Honey Lake Valley where Paiutes and Maidus might not need to fight over local recognition, because each tribe could find economic and social security.

ANTHROPOLOGISTS AND INDIANS

On this note of alliance and relationship, and in the mode of concluding, this book has not only been a narrative of the Honey Lake Maidu petitioning efforts, but a document of my voyage, as an anthropologist working for the Honey Lake Maidus, to the door of the state, neither an altogether pleasant nor altogether hopeless journey.

The scholarly discipline of anthropology has long expressed ambivalent attitudes toward applied work such as mine. Ever since the academic eclipse of the practical scholar of the James Mooney vein in the early 1900s, there has been a tendency to marginalize this type of research. I believe that this marginalization represents a fear that is similarly mirrored in the government's insistence on the apolitical nature of the Federal Acknowledgment process. In both cases, stepping back from political contexts in the name of objectivity has meant retreat into self-reference rather than engagement. My understanding is that the anthropologist's role in Federal Acknowledgment advocacy today is best thought of in terms of the ambivalent expert Nikolas Rose described. The anthropologist is ambivalent because of an understanding of the larger contexts of law and the relationships that any advocacy will surely affect. It is an ambivalence that reflects an orientation to justice rather than truth. As Allogan Slagle wrote in 1987 when he was working for the Recognition of California's Tolowa Nation,

The petition may succeed as scholarship but may fall short of its goal as advocacy. On the other hand, if it is found to be better advocacy than scholarship and helps achieve the goal of federal acknowledgment for the Tolowa Nation, perhaps it will have brought us all a step closer to recognizing the sovereign rights of an aboriginal community which has the purpose of surviving *as a community* [Slagle's italics] whatever may befall it. (1987, 117–18)

It is fair to say that I have been guided in my work by an admittedly idealistic vision of "the good anthropologist," which, for me, has meant an advocate and ally committed to justice, something like Slagle was.

Yet, aside from the vexing discursive problem of what is justice and for whom is it just, this quest for the noble anthropologist (opposed, of course, to that of the savage anthropologist) cannot help but to some degree go hand-in-hand with a classic "victim anthropology," which Laura Nader critiqued in her

1972 call to "study up." In the case of the study of Native North America, victim anthropology echoes historical processes of domination on a recurrently new tack. Biolsi and Zimmerman explain this well in the introduction to their edited volume, *Indians and Anthropologists*:

The continued economic and political oppression of Indian communities still makes Indians (more or less) available for anthropological research. Anthropologists as individuals—or most of them—have not been directly involved in the colonial disempowerment of Indian people, but their choice of Indians as subjects of study has been directly enabled by it. To some extent, this relationship is undergoing change as Indian communities have come to question and even control research. (1997, 12)

It is in this last point that I believe the anthropology of Native North America will find its reformation. One might think of this in terms of the metaphor from the Honey Lake Maidu story of Coyote at Wepum Mountain, the metaphor of fleshing out the bones. In the ethnography of Federal Recognition, and in their work for Federal Acknowledgment, the bones of the skeleton are the linguistic, ecological, geographical, religious, and material pieces early California anthropologists and other scholars documented, often quite sensitively. The flesh is the humanity—the Native voices and intellect—needed to narrate and animate the complicated whole of contemporary California Indian cultures. The anthropologist should not play a part in this work at all if he or she is not willing to let Indian people themselves do the shaping and editing. And the anthropologist should be prepared: such editing will most likely involve whittling away the anthropologist's power, and even the anthropologist's role.

This points, too, toward a vision of reform of the Federal Acknowledgment process. Speaking before the House of Representatives at a 1995 hearing on the Acknowledgment process, in fact, Jack Campisi has argued that "if you can set a system up that gives the petitioner some equality in the debate, if you can set a system up that makes it more collegial, or if I can set a system up that gets both the bureaucrat and the anthropologist out of the debate, which may be the best solution, you may be able to move [on] these [problems with the Acknowledgment process]" (U.S. House 1994, 214). Moving beyond anthropological evidence and, as Ron pointed out, the use of anthropologists in such an inbred way in the determinations of the Federal Acknowledgment process might finally lead to justice for the tribes. But, radically, this might mean throwing away cultural adjudications altogether. It would certainly mean a national commitment to cultural survival, and quite probably a plan for tribal adjudication of tribal status cases. If the tribes could then move beyond factionalism, a higher vision of indigenous justice might emerge.

SENDING THE ANTHROS AWAY

The final piece of the story of the petitioning and transformation of the Honey Lake Maidu Tribe is what I think of as a sign of its success in both these endeavors: by the close of the ANA-funded petitioning project, the Honey Lake Maidu Tribe was ready to digest the Acknowledgment petition. What this meant was that the document I wrote so closely with the Bear Dance Foundation (and so close to Ron's vision) was rescinded from BAR shortly after it was submitted.

Honey Lake Maidu tribe members could not completely own their petition until I was no longer employed by them. Indeed, an advantage of the employment of ambivalent experts is that, when it is necessary, their roles can be interpreted as interference, with minor impact upon the relationships among tribe members.

After the Bear Dance in June of 2001, my work for the tribe was complete. I sent the petition and supporting documents to Washington, D.C., in a packing box. It probably amounted to fifteen pounds of material. After two months, I sent an e-mail of inquiry to BAR, to make sure that it was considering the Honey Lake Maidu materials. The BAR replied that further organization of the genealogical documentation was necessary (in and of itself, this was extremely aggravating because BAR regulations and explanatory materials provide absolutely no guidance on how it should be organized in the first place). I then suggested to the tribe that we discuss with the BAR gene-alogist what kind of organization BAR needed to see, and that the tribe keep its place in the government's queue. Yet after BAR's comment that more work was required, some members of the tribe felt angry that the job had not been completed to BAR's complete satisfaction. These tribe members, including Gina Garcia and Margaret Ulleseit, ended up approaching another anthropologist, Dotty Theodoratus (known for her thorough tribal genealogies), for advice. After talking with Theodoratus, the tribe decided to pull the petition from the queue. In particular, it began to rework the narrative and membership materials in order to include more Mountain Maidu families, like the Salems of Big Meadows. If the ANA grant had been awarded for the two years the Bear Dance Foundation had originally intended, this work would have been supported. As it was, the tribe was passing the hat and talking about holding yard sales to raise money for revising the petition during tribe members' free time.

By the time the 2005 Bear Dance rolled around, the petition had still not yet been resubmitted. Even so, I am confident that it will happen because I can see the kind of strength and commitment tribe members show to the tribe. I almost cannot help but think of this seeming failure as part of the tribe's great success: they made a submission to BAR (a literal sub-mission of a petition), but it was a "full submission" in neither the literal nor the figurative sense. And because of the way the tribe is beginning to reinterpret and radicalize what turned out to really be just my draft of the petition, it hopefully never will be.

Looking back, I cannot say that I was untroubled by tribal members' unhappiness, but I believe that truly skillful ambivalent experts have the capacity to shrug some of this off because of their very ambivalence—that understanding of the role they play for (and between) both the tribes and the state. Nonetheless, it is also my experience that anthropologists are not immune to the symbolic violence that ricochets from the door to the law, and throughout the waiting room before it. Both the history of the state's political and economic abuse and traditional modes of anthropological domination contribute to this violence. Practitioners at the intersection of these spheres must learn to live and work with these facts.

CONCLUSION: BLOOD CYCLES

For the Honey Lake Maidus, tribe is an ethos—a history, an orientation—that a bureaucrat in D.C. is not going to be able to quantify according to the criteria as they stand. But in their and my own attempts to translate it for Washington via their petition, this ethos has been solidified and spread among tribal members and has thus become stronger. Key to this ethos is the factionalism discussed earlier in this chapter: that direct, basketball-like approach to the state, other Indian peoples, and internal issues of Honey Lake Maidu membership. This posture reflects a willingness to struggle, a hope for the future that lies in continual agitation for r/Recognition and the redistribution of resources.

Coyote's antics are reflected in such agitation and tied to an understanding of regeneration fundamental to the practice of a politically circumscribed and thus evolving tradition. The motif of regeneration calls forth both bloodshed and blood hatred by non-Indians, as well as the connection of the bloodline that is most important to the Honey Lake Maidus as they seek to rebuild and refortify their collective organizations.

Ron Morales invoked the cycle of generation and degeneration as he told me the story of his life, and it is clear that he believes his individual experience mirrors tribal regeneration and healing. Ron's grandmother Roxie believed that he was repeatedly saved by the Creator for an important reason, which he and I understand is his people's Federal Recognition. "Anyone else would've died, the things I've done," he explained after some stories of his early years. "I had the devil in me." Of all the "rough Indians" he used to spend time with in his youth, he is one of the few left; he has survived repeated car wrecks, fights, games of Russian roulette, and, even, one dark night, the experience of picking up a hitchhiker in Hat Creek who turned out to be the Devil himself—"with red eyes, dark skin, a leather hat and clothes"—who told him and his friend, "Oh, I *like* you guys," and had to literally be kicked and pushed from the car.

Ron says that though his grandmother was not a sucking doctor—a ritual specialist who can suck pain and illness from patients' bodies, ceremonially—she could see things and heal some sickness, and she saw that though he seemed to ignore her stories, he'd nonetheless be able to remember them later in life. Thus, though he says that there do not seem to be many doctors of the old-time power left, because of his personal experience, Ron knows that doctoring, too, will come back when the time is right. All of it will.

AFTERWORD

THE WASHINGTON FRONT

IN THE FALL OF 2000, CONGRESS'S GENERAL ACCOUNTING OFFICE (GAO), spearheaded by representatives from antigaming states, proposed an "audit" of the Federal Acknowledgment process. Its report, issued the following year, proposed harsher requirements for Acknowledgment and more space for third-party critique of petitioners, and seemed to indicate a serious congressional backlash against un-Acknowledged tribes. Whether or not this is so, the GAO report was the only congressional action to have an effect on BAR procedures over the course of approximately twenty years of congressional nagging. The effect was that, on October 2, 2002, BAR announced a grand overhaul, part of a larger, Bureau of Indian Affairs reorganization that left it with a new name: OFA, the Office of Federal Acknowledgment. OFA would be under the command of the "Principal Deputy Assistant Secretary-Indian Affairs," a new position within the Office of the Assistant Secretary–Indian Affairs.

BAR's reorganization tripled its staff to thirty-three employees, expressly so that it could address (1) the Freedom of Information Act requests from interested third parties (such as local towns) that purportedly take up 40 to 60 percent of the current staff hours each week, and (2) the litigation that BAR—er, OFA—finds itself embroiled in (and preparing documentation for) over and over again. The report concluded that "approximately half of the cases since 1987 have gone to the Interior

Board of Indian Appeals (IBIA) for review and/or litigation in district court" (BIA Strategic Plan 2002, 6). Yet rather than systematic analysis of the concerns these tribes have voiced, concerns that turned them to the judicial branch after both the BIA and Congress had failed them—BAR hired more staff to help with the demands of its involvement in such cases. Rather than attempting fundamental reform, it turned inward to an expanding bureaucracy.

At the end of 2002, BAR reported that there were fifteen Technical Assistance reviews to provide tribes, fourteen Preliminary Findings to write, and twenty-one to thirty-one Final Determinations to make, amounting to "55 professional staff-years" (ibid., 8), though it promised that with six teams of three, the backlog could be addressed in four years. BAR's priorities were clear: its backlog action plan addressed third-party concerns at the cost of the concerns of the first party—the tribal petitioners. It prioritized processing speed over assistance and sensitivity to the needs of petitioners while seeking congressional approval for a sunset provision that would slowly shut the door to the law. Alarmingly, its intention was to "limit each petitioner to one technical assistance review" (ibid.) What this means is that, today, petitioners to BAR have one and only one opportunity for feedback before their petition's (and their people's) Final Determination.

Under its "Procedural" recommendations, BAR explained that it would

eliminate letters of intent to petition and remove groups with only letters of intent from the document maintained by the BIA showing the status of petitioners for acknowledgment; or, require that letters of intent include a governing document, membership list and names of individuals in the governing body and offices they hold. (ibid., 18)

It is a reordering that essentially makes the queue at BAR *appear* shorter, thus signifying a national failure to recognize or address the needs of the tribes as yet just beginning the bureaucratic ascent to the Acknowledgement machine.

BAR's reorganization, thus, made no substantive revisions of the way the Federal Acknowledgment process works for tribes.

THE LOCAL FRONT

Currently, Ron is on the board of the directors of the Mountain Meadows Conservancy, which has as its mission "to conserve, protect and enhance the natural beauty and health of the Mountain Meadows watershed; to protect its significant Mountain Maidu burial and cultural sites, and to provide recreation and public access for generations to come." Its latest victory is getting Pacific Gas and Electric to quit leasing its land in Mountain Meadows to ranchers from Red Bluff who run their cattle there. "They are going to treat all their lands as if they are cultural or burial sites," Steve Robinson, the director and founder of the Conservancy, and a longtime supporter of the Bear Dance, told me hopefully. Robinson is working with Ron on the possibility of trading a portion of the Mountain Meadows wetlands with the Forest Service for a space in the Lassen National Forest where the Bear Dance could be held. This land would be the Honey Lake Maidu Tribe's, and the Honey Lake Maidu Tribe's alone.

Though the tribe's revised petition for Recognition has still not yet been resubmitted, lowercase r recognition just might be slowly beginning to occur.

25 CFR PART 83.7

The Mandatory Criteria for Federal Acknowledgment

(a) A statement of facts establishing that the petitioner has been identified from historical times until the present on a substantially continuous basis as "American Indian" or "aboriginal." . . . Evidence to be replied upon in determining the group's substantially continuous Indian identity shall include one or more of the following:

    (1) Repeated identification by federal authorities;

    (2) Longstanding relationships with State governments based on identification of the group as an Indian;

    (3) Repeated dealing with a county, parish, or other local government in a relationship based on the group's Indian identity;

    (4) Identification as an Indian entity by records in courthouses, churches, or schools;

    (5) Identification as an Indian entity by anthropologists, historians, or other scholars;

    (6) Repeated identification and dealing as an Indian entity with recognized Indian tribes or national Indian organizations.

(b) Evidence that a substantial portion of the petitioning group inhabits a specific area or lives in a community viewed as American Indian and distinct from other populations in the area, and that its members are descendants of an Indian tribe which historically inhabited a specific area.

    (1) This criterion may be demonstrated by some combination of the following evidence and/or other evidence that the petitioner meets the definition of *community* set forth in 83.1:

(i)   Significant rates of marriage within the group, and/or, as may be culturally required, patterned out-marriages with other Indian populations;

(ii)   Significant social relationships connecting individual members;

(iii) Significant rates of informal social interaction which exists broadly among the members of a group;

(iv)   A significant degree of shared or cooperative labor or other economic activity among the membership;

(v)   Evidence of strong patterns of discrimination or other social distinctions by non-members;

(vi)   Shared sacred or secular ritual activity encompassing most of the group;

(vii) Cultural patterns shared among a significant portion of the group that are different from those of the non-Indian populations with whom it interacts. These patterns must function as more than a symbolic identification of the group as Indian. They may include, but are not limited to, language, kinship organization, or religious beliefs and practices;

(viii) The persistence of a named, collective Indian identity continuously over a period of more than 50 years, notwithstanding changes in name;

(ix)   A demonstration of historical political influence under the criterion in 83.7 (c) shall be evidence for demonstrating historical community.

(2) A petitioner shall be considered to have provided sufficient evidence of community at a given point in time if evidence is provided to demonstrate any one of the following:

(i)   More than 50 percent of the members reside in a geographical area exclusively or almost exclusively composed of members of the group, and the balance of the group maintains consistent interactions with some members of the community:

(ii)   At least 50 percent of the marriages in the group are between members of the group;

(iii) At least 50 percent of the group members maintain distinct cultural patterns such as, but not limited to, language, kinship organization, or religious beliefs or practices;

(iv)   There are distinct community social institutions encompassing most of the members, such as kinship organizations, formal or informal economic cooperation, or religious organizations; or

(v)   The group has met the criterion in 83.7 (c) using evidence described in 83.7 (c) (2).

(c) The petitioner has maintained tribal political influence or other authority over its members as an autonomous entity from historical times until the present.

(1) This criterion may be demonstrated by some combination of the evidence listed below and/or by other evidence that the petitioner meets the definition of political influence or authority in 83.1.

(i)   The group is able to mobilize significant numbers of members and significant resources from its members for group purposes;

(ii)   Most of the membership considers issues acted upon or actions taken by group leaders or governing bodies to be of importance;

(iii) There is widespread knowledge, communication and involvement in political processes by most of the group's members;

(iv)   The group meets the criterion in 83.7(b) at more than a minimal level;

(v)   There are internal conflicts which show controversy over valued group goals, properties, policies, processes and/or decisions.

(1) A petitioning group shall be considered to have provided sufficient evidence to demonstrate the exercise of

political influence or authority at a given point in time
by demonstrating that group leaders and/or other mech-
anisms exist or existed which:

(i)   Allocate group resources such as land, residence
       rights and the like on a consistent basis;
(ii)   Settle disputes between members or subgroups by
       mediation or other means on a regular basis;
(iii) Exert strong influence on the behavior of individ-
       ual members, such as the establishment or mainte-
       nance of norms and the enforcement of sanctions
       to direct or control behavior;
(iv)   Organize or influence economic subsistence activi-
       ties among the members, including shared or
       cooperative labor.

(3) A group that has met the requirements in paragraph
    83.7(b)(2) at a given point in time shall be considered
    to have provided sufficient evidence to meet this crite-
    rion at that point in time.

(d) A copy of the group's present governing document including
its membership criteria. In the absence of a written document
the petitioner must provide a statement describing in full its
membership criteria and current governing procedures.

(e) The petitioner's membership consists of individuals who
descend from a historical Indian tribe or from historical Indian
tribes which combined and functioned as a single autonomous
political entity.

(1) Evidence acceptable to the Secretary which can be
    used for this purpose includes but is not limited to:

(i)   Rolls prepared by the Secretary on a descendancy
       basis for purposes of distributing claims money,
       providing allotments, or other purposes;
(ii)   State, Federal, or other official records or evidence
       identifying present members or ancestors of present
       members as being descendants of a historical tribe

or tribes that combined and functioned as a single autonomous political entity.

(iii) Church, school, and other similar enrollment records identifying present members or ancestors of present members as being descendants of a historical tribe or tribes that combined and functioned as a single autonomous political entity.

(iv) Affidavits of recognition by tribal elders, leaders, or the tribal governing body identifying present members or ancestors of present members as being descendants of a historical tribe or tribes that combined and functioned as a single autonomous political entity.

(v) Other records or evidence identifying present members or ancestors of present members as being descendants of a historical tribe or tribes that combined and functioned as a single autonomous political entity.

(2) The petitioner must provide an official membership list, separately certified by the group's governing body, of all known current members of the group. This list must include each member's full name (including maiden name), date of birth, and current residential address. The petitioner must also provide a copy of each available former list of members based on the group's own defined criteria, as well as a statement describing the circumstances surrounding the preparation of the current list and, insofar, as possible, the circumstances surrounding the preparation of former lists.

(f) The membership of the petitioning group is composed principally of persons who are not members of any acknowledged North American Indian tribe. However, under certain conditions a petitioning group may be acknowledged even if its membership is composed principally of persons whose names have appeared on rolls of, or who have been otherwise associated with, an acknowledged Indian tribe. The conditions are that the group must establish that it functioned throughout history until the present as a separate and autonomous Indian tribal entity, that its members do not maintain a bilateral political relationship with the acknowledged tribe, and that its members have provided written confirmation of their membership in the petitioning group.

(g) Neither the petitioner nor its members are the subject of congressional legislation that has expressly terminated or forbidden the Federal relationship. (25 CFR Ch. 1 [April 1, 1999 edition]: 237–43).

COYOTE AT WEPUM MOUNTAIN, TOLD BY RON MORALES

I'M GOING TO TELL THE STORY ABOUT MOUNTAIN MEADOWS, where my grandfather was born. This story was told to him by his grandfather, and it's the story about Wepum Yamani—it's a mountain over there, Coyote Mountain. It sets right in the middle of Mountain Meadows.

The story goes like this, that there was an old Coyote. He's a big guy, he lived right on top of that mountain. And he's a no good son of a gun. He lay up there and he would look down. He'd watch the women dig wild potatoes and dig wild onion and dig wild tobacco and he'd run down fast, he'd run down the hill down there, and he'd try to get them ladies when they were stooped over trying to dig their roots, and he would sometimes put his paws over their eyes and he'd say, "Aw, this is your honey," he said. He even talked in Indian— he could talk good Maidu, this Coyote. He could talk good Maidu, and he could also walk upright like a man. He was very clever. And the Indian, well, he was just a big bad fellow and they'd like to get right of him.

He said that sometimes the pickin's would be really poor in Mountain Meadows—the potatoes would be small, the onions would be small. But that goddamn Coyote, they would sneak up on his mountain and look over at him in the evening time and he'd have his fire going and they could see from the light that in his Indian baskets—he had baskets around there he had stolen from the women that had made baskets in that Mountain Meadows area—and his baskets were plum full of big potatoes and big onions and all of the stuff that was in that valley. But his was all big and looked the best you could ever imagine. So the old Indian guys, they got together—the Indian doctors and all of them—they got to together, "How are we going to get rid of this guy, he's the main Coyote, he's the *wiswalulu*." That meant the Devil, like the Devil; he's a no good son of a bitch.

So they were deciding what they could do about this guy and everything was quiet in that Mountain Meadows, but then that son of gun would holler, cry in the night, make his old sound. That would start them all up, all the shittin' Coyotes, they would holler around. But they wouldn't holler until that son of gun would holler on the mountain. He would holler, then, shit, pretty soon a chain reaction: it went all over, them son of a bitches Coyotes all woke up. And so they were having a hell of a time, trying to figure what the hell to do, how to catch him. They tried to catch him before, shit, they tried to sneak up on him, they tried to set a trap for him, they couldn't do shit, they couldn't catch him.

Finally this old woman, she said, "I know how you can catch him," she said. "You go over to Big Meadows," which was Lake Almanor. "There's an old man over there," she said, "that makes nets for to fish with," she said. "You guys get some nets," she was telling them. And she said, "You get around his mountain," she said, "You men," she said, "you go up," she said, "and you'll catch him. He can't get away from those nets, they're strong," she said. So them men they listen good, them Indian doctors, they listen good, so they did, they went over to Big Meadows.

Time went by, too, months, years, and they were still living next to this Coyote, and he was still a no good son of gun.

So finally they had enough net, they come back, and so they said, "We'll fix that son of a gun, we'll catch him. We'll get him," they said, "because he's bad," they said. "All the time molesting the women, jumping around down there, grabbing the ladies and he's just got all the food up on his mountain, and he's got all the plenty of stuff on his mountain. We got to rid him of that."

So they planned to catch him. They all took that old net and they went right around that mountain, all these men, and early in the morning before the sun come up, they said. They went up in there and they just walk quiet and then here that old Coyote come down and—boy! He got tangled in that net and they round him up in the net and the men jumped on him and he was just a hollering! He said, "Gee, why you want to do this to me?" he said. He said, "I'm your friend," he said. "Man," he said, "guys," he said, "all I wanted, I would share my mountain with if you share your women with me. I've always wanted to share," he said. "You guys go on and share," he said. "It's you guys, not me! I'm trying to be a good guy," he said. "Shoot, I'm a nice one. Shit, I'll share my food with you. Look at all my potatoes, look at all my onions, look at all my tobacco there," he said. "I'll share all my tobacco with you guys," he said. "If you'd just share your ladies with me, that's all you have to do," he said.

They never listened to him. They were digging a big hole right up on top, digging. Finally, they rolled him out of that net and right into that hole and they put that net over him and put some heavy limbs over it and they said, "We'll fix you. And you stay there," they said. They were—gee, well, they were just getting into his potatoes, they were getting into all his stuff up there, the Indians. They put it in their old pack and they packed it down from there.

They watched him. They watched that Coyote. That old Coyote, he was just really talking, trying to talk them into letting him loose. He was telling them all the good things he done in the world for everybody. Them Indians, they never listened. They watched him. At night they would build a fire, and they never took their eye off him. That's what the Indian doctors said: "Whatever you do, don't take your eye off this fellow, because he could get away." So they wouldn't even sleep, they would have to take turns to watch him.

This went on for days and days. Ole Coyote he would talk every shittin' day, trying to talk his way out of it. The ladies they would go out picking and they weren't bothered, Coyote wasn't hollerin' at night. And, shit, like I said, he was really talkin' like hell. And they wouldn't give him no water, they wouldn't give him nothing. The shittin' old sun would shine down on him and he was getting weak, he was getting skinny, and his hair fell out, was falling out. And pretty soon his old eyeballs were getting kind of sunk in there, and they said he was lookin' really rough, that's what the old people said, he was lookin' pretty rough.

So what happened is that they watched him and watched him and pretty soon his old eyeballs fell out. And his old hair fell out, then his old skin was falling off his bones, and pretty soon his old bones were just getting all scorched from the sun, sun beating down. Pretty soon it was starting to stink real bad so here come the old Red Tail Hawk, he fly by and here come the old Magpie, he fly down, and here come the old Black Bird, he come. And the Blue Jay, he was the worst one, hollering around. They come to see what stink so bad in that hole. So they look in there, and they say, "Eww, he stinks," they said, "He stink bad." So that's why my uncle said the scavengers of the air, they won't touch a Coyote, because they're no good. He said, they'll eat any kind of varmint, they'll eat a rabbit, they'll eat whatever, but they won't touch a Coyote because they're bad, no good suckers. They just were bad guys.

Finally, the old Indian fellows, they felt real good that they captured this old Coyote and they got him there. They were still watching him, though, and here this one morning they seen these old two cousins, the old wolf and the fox, they were down there having a hell of a good time, catching mice, diggin' potatoes down there, there at the bottom of the hill. And finally this old Indian doctor, he hollered at them, he hollered in Indian what the wolf's name was, "Hey," he said, "come on up here and get your cousin," he said. "Get your cousin." The wolf and the old fox, they run on up the hill, and they looked in the hole there and here was old Coyote, he was laying in there. He was just bones, is all, and some hair laying there. Even his old eyeballs were dried up by that time. Just his bones were all bleached, real white, laying there. And so he said, "Take your cousin, we don't want him here. This is our hill now," the old Indian doctor said. Old wolf, he said to fox, "Jump down in there and throw our cousin's bones out. So the old fox, he jumped in that hole there and he throw his old cousin Coyote's bones out, Old Wepum's bones out. The old wolf he had his old pack sack there, it was made of a deer hide and he put the bones in there, threw them in there. Finally, he told his cousin, "Let's go. Let's go," he said. He talked in Indian to his cousin fox. "Let's go," he said, "We'll take our cousin and we'll take care of him."

They went down the hill singing their song. They went down and down, and the Indians, them old Indian guys, they had these young guys that watch out and followed them. They followed this old wolf and this old fox, and they were sneaking— the fox and them didn't know that they were following them. But when they were singing their song, they were saying, in Indian, they were saying, "Boy, them Indians think they're so smart, but our old cousin ain't dead, he's just as alive today as when they put him in that hole. Well, them old Indians think that they're so smart, but they're not smart."

So they watched them anyway, and pretty soon, they said, pretty soon the old wolf and fox they just dumped the old bones of their cousin out and they put the old arm bones there and the finger bones there and they laid it in the shade—it was real hot—and they laid it in the shade. And these two young Indian guys—they were trackers, they said, "Well, I guess they're just going to lay him out and bury him, I guess." They left, they didn't want to see no more of it.

So they come back, and they reported back to the Indian doctor who was up on the hill. They covered the hole up. It was their hill now, it was their hill. They were going to have plenty of food and plenty of good stuff. It would all be there for them. So what they did was they said, we're going to have a big time. Tell everyone at Big Meadows to come to our Big Time. So, the word was that they were going to have a Big Time. They rid the world of the Coyote; they'd just got rid of the bad ole wiswalulu. So they were happy, shit, the women went out and they dug. They prepared for a whole month. They were going to have that Big Time.

Boy, they just laid everything out a big old log. They had all the food they said there. Even the birds came to have a good time. Shit, them old red tail hawks and Blue Jay and them fellows—even them sand hill cranes, they all come. All animals were happy because they rid the world of Coyote. So when they start to sit down, it was just getting evening time, about to set down to eat and celebrate getting rid of this old Coyote. They were all happy, the women were happy, the men, the kids. They were all playing and having a good time. So they were getting ready to eat dinner. And pretty soon it was evening time. There was this old Indian doctor giving a speech, about how happy he was that the world was rid of the Coyote, about how he was so proud of his relatives for catching him and everything.

And just before they were about to eat, [my Uncle George told me,] "Shit, old Coyote holler like a son of bitch up on the hill up there." He said, "Shit, he was alive as hell." They looked up there, they could see him—they could see his old shadow up there, big old Coyote, hollering like anything.

So that that's pretty much what it is about, that Coyote Mountain. It was a powerful mountain: it was a mountain where there was power and the Coyote, he claimed his power. The Indians had it for a little while, but Coyote, he reclaimed it. Like I said, you can't rid him of it, the only time there'll be no more Coyotes is when the Creator comes back—that's in the end of this world.

"Just call me Coyote."

APPENDIX C

SHERMAN ALEXIE'S "WHY WE PLAY BASKETBALL"

1.
In December, snow
covered the court. We
wrapped our hands in old
socks, soaked the white snow
with kerosene, lit

the match, and melted it
all down to pavement.
We were Indians
who wanted to play
basketball. Nothing

could stop us from that,
not the hunger in
our thin bellies, not
the fear of missed shots,
not the threat of white

snow. We were small boys
who would grow into
small men. We played ball
until dark, then played
until we could see

neither hoop nor ball.
We played until our
mother and fathers
came searching for us
and carried us home.

2.
We play because we
remember the first
time we shot the ball
and knew, beyond doubt,
as it floated toward

the hoop, that it was
going to be good.
We walked off the court,
left the ball waiting
as we fell in love

with Indian girls
who grew past us, who
grew into Indian
women. Somehow, we
grew families while

that ball waited, in-
ert, suspended, till
we remembered, with
a complex rush of
pain and joy, what we'd

left behind, how we
loved the ball as it
finally dropped in-
to the net, after
years of such patience.

3.
We wanted to know
who was best, who could
change the game into
something new. We knew
about Seymour. Blind

and deaf, he played by
sense of smell. Leather
balls drove him crazy.
He identified
his teammates by tribe:

Spokanes smelled like bread;
Flatheads smelled like pine;
Colville smelled like snow;
Lester smelled like wine.
Seymour shot the ball

when the wind told him
it was time to shoot.
In basketball, we
find enough reasons
to believe in God,

or something smaller
than God. We believe
in Seymour, who holds
the ball in his hands
like you hold your God.

4.
It is just a game
we are told by those
who cannot play it
unless it is play.
For us, it is war,

often desperate
and without reason.
We throw our body
against another
body. We learn to

hate each other, hate
the ball, hate the hoop,
hate the fallen snow,
hate our clumsy hands,
hate our thirsty mouths

when we drink from
the fountain. We hate
our fathers. We hate
our mothers. We hate
the face in our mirror.

We play basketball
because we want to
separate love from
hate, and because we
know how to keep score.

5.
We play basketball
because we still love
the place where we lived.
It was a small house
with one door. We lived

there for twenty years
with crazy cousins
and one basketball.
We fought over it
constantly. I climbed

into a tall tree
with the ball, refused
to come down unless
they made me captain.
My brother dragged me

from the tree and punched
me so hard I saw
red horses. We play
because we believe
in our skins and hands.

These hands hold the ball.
These hands hold the tribe.
These hands build fires.
We are a small tribe.
We build small fires.

NOTES

INTRODUCTION

1. More recently, Ron urged that he didn't wish to give his nemeses so much credit. Coyote is much more clever and deserves much more respect than they do, he says. Nonetheless, describing someone as Coyote-like is an important figure of his and other tribal members' speech that bears different meanings. First, Coyote is the mythological character who was present at the creation of the world, acting as foil to the World Maker. This was sometimes explained to me through Christian analogy: Coyote is the Devil to the World Maker's Christ. Capital C *Coyote* in this sense is a maker-of-schemes with supernatural backing, a selfish, comical transgressor of social norms. *Coyote* in its lowercase *c* sense can refer to the animal itself—perceived as a pest (and, in Ron's words "a real *ugly* guy"), a coyote is a troublemaker in the this-worldly realm, that can, at times, invoke the larger spirit of Coyote.

2. The Heritage Commission was established in 1976 to mediate between Native interests and developers and/or archaeologists. It maintains a confidential file of lands sacred to California peoples.

3. Perhaps, like me, many readers' parents had Theodora Kroeber's *Ishi: Last of His Tribe* (1964) on their bookshelves.

4. See Bruce G. Miller (2004) for excellent comparative descriptions of the situations of non-Recognized peoples across the globe. The way the Federal Acknowledgment process in the United States compares with other national systems is particularly fascinating (see also Tolley 2004).

5. Please note that in 2003 there was a mostly titular reorganization of BAR. It is now known as the Office of Federal Acknowledgment, or OFA.

CHAPTER ONE

1. Other anthropologists and historians of California Indians have begun with genocide as well. Please consider Jaime de Angulo's approach to *Indians in Overalls*, which infuriated Alfred Kroeber (see Gui de Angulo's "Afterword" in Angulo 1990), or consider his wife, Theodora Kroeber's, *Ishi in*

Two Worlds (1961). Nancy Scheper-Hughes's discussions of the California genocide (2001), (2003) are quite apropos, as are Heizer (1993), Heizer and Elasser (1978), Hurtado (1988), Rawls (1984), and Sarris (1998), among others.

2. This BIA statistic was cited in the Advisory Council on California Indian Policy, "Recognition Report: Equal Justice for California" (1997, 6).

3. Cook does not mention that between 1803 and 1841 the Russians also colonized part of California. Labor extraction, rather than integration into Russian culture and society, was emphasized. Kashaya Pomo tribal members were employed in various jobs in support of the international trade in sea otter and seal pelts, though the major workforce of the industry was an imported group of Aleutian Indians.

4. See Powers (1975) for a moving story of the kidnapping, enslavement, and escape of two Koncow Maidu children, Woalockie and Yoatowee.

5. My phrase "bore the brunt," in fact, understates the terror of these early European encounters. Burrill (1988) has attempted to explain the painful destruction of lifeways by using fiction to heighten the reader's empathy. Jewell (1987) tells the "Tales and Legends of Concow Maidu of California" with a focus upon contemporary Konkow informants' memories of these and other historical events. Both authors convey some of what it may have been like for Indian peoples in those days.

6. Today, Lake Almanor/Big Meadows attracts summer vacationers and fishermen, as it did in the 1880s and 1890s, when the young engineering student Julius Howells toured the area. Howells was later employed by Pacific Gas and Electric to design the damming of the Feather River and the flooding of both the Big and Mountain meadows, beginning in 1910. This second meadow, Mountain Meadows, now shelters two PG&E waterworks, Walker Lake and Ole Salem Dam, the last of which is named after John Peconom's brother.

7. Please note that this is different than a figure for "all persons of partial Maidu ancestry," though such a figure has not been calculated.

8. Whether Lassen and Meyerowitz or Isaac Roop first settled the Honey Lake Valley is debated by local history buffs. Asa Fairfield, author of *Fairfield's Pioneer History of Lassen County, California* (1916), has written that Roop built a cabin a year before Lassen did, and that he stayed through the winter of 1854–1855.

9. See Fairfield 1998, 111.

10. Skirmishes and acts of mutual terrorism characterized the early years of European settlement of the Honey Lake Valley, at times effectively isolating the valley's whites from their population center at Reno. Finally, on January 5, 1858, a peace treaty was signed with the Paiutes of Winnemucca's band. Yet by 1860, conditions along the Nevada border had deteriorated

such that the U.S. Calvary was called in, precipitating the Ormsby Massacre, in which Major Ormsby and forty-five white soldiers were killed by starving Paiutes two miles south of Pyramid Lake. The Ormsby Massacre spread the fear of "renegade Paiutes" far and wide (see Fairfield 1998, 211–17; Sarah Winnemucca Hopkins 1994.)

11. I believe that this situation is similar to that described by Raymond Fogelson, who has written of "nonevents," or "events that actually occur, and can be documented, but are so traumatic they are denied. In my field-work with and ethnohistorical research on the Cherokees," he writes, "I have found surprisingly few Cherokee accounts of the painful events that accompanied the actual Removal exodus. . . . It would seem that the Removal experience was so degrading, so incredible, so brutally real that it became unreal to the Cherokee mind" (1989b, 143).

12. It is well documented that in 1859, Pit River people were removed from their lands and marched to Round Valley, near the coast. The Bancroft Library, at the University of California, Berkeley, has letters from army offi-cers regarding their work to subdue the Pit Rivers between 1850 and 1861 (MSS 91-35c). The Reports of Capt. Nathaniel Lion (May 22, 1850) are particularly interesting in this regard.

13. See the (Susanville, Calif.) Lassen Advocate, "Henry Vanetti Killed by Walter Peconom," June 28, 1900, and "Walter Peconom Killed," July 29, 1910.

14. Slagle (Keetowah Cherokee) passed on in the spring of 2003. He gave much of his time to fighting for the acknowledgment of California's tribes.

15. Since filing the petition, the membership rolls have increased to 212, due to "late" submissions of membership information.

CHAPTER TWO

1. The man from the country waits for the rest of his life. When he dies, the doorkeeper shuts his door.

2. This thought first occurred to me as I read the work of Allogan Slagle, the attorney and activist mentioned in the previous chapter. For Slagle's thoughts on the relation between non-Recognition in California and Kafkan scenarios involving the Ione Miwoks, see his 1990 column in News From Native California.

3. Furthermore, two more of these sixty-four tribes have been Acknowledged, but not through the BAR process. The Ione Miwoks had their status clarified by direct action of the assistant secretary–Indian Affairs; the Federated Coast Miwoks of Graton Rancheria were restored to Acknowl-edged status by an act of Congress.

4. Instigated in large part because of Helen Hunt Jackson's depiction of the romance and hardships of Indian life in Ramona (1934 [1884]), the

Smiley Commission had authorized the same for Southern California. Its report had resulted in the Act for the Relief of Mission Indians (1895), which set aside fourteen small parcels for homeless Indian persons. Across the state, another thirty-six *rancherias* had been added by 1930, for a total of 117 by 1950.

5. A second series of acquisitions of rancheria lands occurred between 1914 and 1933, as a response to the 1914 Homeless Indians Act and the Indian Reorganization Act.

6. Unless otherwise noted, the materials referenced in this segment of this chapter come from the National Archives and Records Administration's Register 75 BIA: Records of the Greenville School, Administrative Records, Quarterly Field Matron Reports.

7. The cover page of the quarterly report form for field matrons in the Indian Service reads:

The position of field matron has been created in order that Indian women may be influenced and instructed in their home life and duties as farmers and mechanics are supposed to direct Indian men in their avocations.

The duties of a field matron, therefore, are to visit Indian women in their homes and give them counsel, encouragement, and help in the following lines:

1. Care of a house, keeping it clean and in order, ventilated, properly warmed (not overheated), and suitably furnished.

2. Cleanliness and hygienic conditions generally, including disposition of all refuse.

3. Preparation and serving of food and regularity in meals.

4. Sewing, including cutting, making, and mending garments.

5. Laundry work.

6. Adorning the home, both inside and out, with pictures, curtains, home-made rugs, flowers, grassplots, and trees, construction and repair of walks, fences, and drains. In this connection there will be opportunity for the matrons to give to the male members of the family kindly admonition as to the "chores" and heavier kinds of work about the house which in civilized communities is generally done by men.

7. Keeping and care of domestic animals, such as cows, poultry, and swine; care and use of milk, making butter, cheese, and curds; and keeping bees.

8. Care of sick.

9. Care of little children, and introducing them the games and sports of white children.

10. Proper observance of the Sabbath; organization of societies for promoting literary, religious, moral, and social improvement, such as "Lend a Hand" clubs, circles of "King's Daughters," or "Sons," Y.M.C.A., Christian Endeavor, and temperance societies, etcetera.

8. The "Susanville area" was first administered by Greenville, until 1909, when it was switched to the jurisdiction of Roseburg, only to be returned to Greenville's purview in 1918. After 1923, Susanville was administered by the Sacramento Agency. Susanville is roughly fifty miles

from Greenville, three hundred miles from Roseburg, and two hundred miles from Sacramento.

9. Young may have been referring to the conical, bark-covered Maidu *hubo*, a summer camp shelter.

10. In April 1901, Young wrote, "The attendance at Sunday School has been rather small, but the interest on the part of those attending has been great. One of the local pastors assisted in holding special meetings for tea afternoons. Several conversions in the S.S. [Sunday School] have included two or three drinking men who have thus given up the use of intoxicants." In July, "A good precedent [was] established in the marriage of an Indian couple by white pastor—the *first* instance among these people." As far as I have been able to tell, Young's was the first systematic Christian proselytizing to touch the Honey Lake Maidus. Its legacy is tremendous, considering that George Peconom would later speak of the Creator's journey through Mountain Maidu territory as a syncretistic symbology of the genesis of this world by Jesus Christ's hand. Viola Williams speaks similarly today.

11. See LaDuke and Churchill (1992), Nader and Ou (1998), and Collins (1998).

12. Recall, however, that Marshall's comments on *Cherokee Nation v. Georgia* in 1830 previewed the idea that "recognition" was within jurisdictional purview of the U.S. government.

13. In an interesting coda to this, Anderson also draws our attention to a comment in a Department of the Interior (DOI) internal memorandum comparing the Senate and House bills just before the final version was agreed upon.

Senate Section 18 restricts the definition of "Indian" for purposes of the Act (e.g., preference in Indian Service employment, land, loan, and educational benefits) more narrowly than does the House provision, setting up a criterion of one-half blood, instead of one-fourth blood as provided in the House bill, and *limiting recognized tribal membership to those tribes "now under federal jurisdiction."* [Anderson's italics]

This last phrase is, in the opinion of the Department [of the Interior], likely to provoke interminable questions of interpretation, and should be deleted. (1978, 10)

Despite such ominous foreshadowing, the language was left, and the Department of the Interior took on precisely these interminable interpretations in later years with its Federal Acknowledgment criteria.

14. Legal scholar Felix Cohen wrote, in 1953, "In place of the old Jeffersonian formula of 'consent' of the governed, one finds the Indian Bureau now using the formula of 'consultation.' In practice, 'consultation' means trying to persuade the Indians to go along with a Bureau program; if the effort fails, then the Bureau asks Congress to adopt the Bureau program anyway" (ACCIP 1997b, 13).

15. Forty-one rancherias had been Terminated by P.L. 671 on August 18, 1958, during the 85th Congress: Alexander Valley, Auburn, Big Sandy, Big Valley, Blue Lake, Buena Vista, Cache Creek, Chicken Ranch, Chico, Clod Springs, Cloverdale, Elk Valley, Grantona, Greenville, Guidiville, Hopland, Indian Ranch, Lytton, Mark West, Middleton, Montgomery Creek, Mooretown, Nevada City, North Fork, Paskenta, Picayune, Pinoleville, Potter Valley, Quartz Valley, Redding, Redwood Valley, Robinson, Rohnerville, Ruffeys, Scotts Valley, Smith River, Strawberry Valley, Table Bluff, Table Mountain, Upper Lake, and Wilton. For various reasons, the Tillie Hardwick suit (*Tillie Hardwick, et al., Plaintiffs, v. United States of American et al. Defendants*, No. C-79-1710-SW) in the end brought Restoration to only seventeen of these rancherias: Big Valley, Blue Lake, Buena Vista, Chicken Ranch, Cloverdale, Elk Valley, Greenville, Mooretown, North Fork, Picayune, Pinoleville, Potter Valley, Quartz Valley, Redding, Redwood Valley, Rhonerville, and Smith River.

16. Termination was, in fact, only put to an official end in 1988.

17. This 1790 legislation was continuous with British policies in the American colonies, which gave Native peoples particular rights in relation to the states in which they lived in order to ensure their loyalty to the crown for purposes of trade and warfare. But please note that the Indian Trade and Non-Intercourse Act of 1790 did not have any particular efficacy in California at this point because of the settlement, in 1963, of land claims cases brought by the Indians of California.

18. William Evans, however, recorded that Roxie Peconom remembered that the Mountain Maidu headman Servilicn had signed a treaty, "right after the Mexican War" (1978, 2).

19. The *Handbook* has been hailed as a work of legal genius. The Board of Authors and Editors of the 1982 edition quote Justice Felix Frankfurter, who said:

Only a ripe and imaginative scholar with a synthesizing faculty would have brought luminous order out of such a mish-mash. He was enabled to do so because of his wide learning in the various fields of inquiry which are relevant to so-called technical legal questions. Learning would not have sufficed. It required realization of any domain of law, but particularly the intricacies and peculiarities of Indian law, demanded an appreciation of history and understanding of the economic, social, political and moral problems in which the more immediate problems of that law are entwined. (Cohen 1982 [1942]: viii–ix).

20. OD letters were renamed Technical Assistance letters in the mid-1990s.

21. The Cabazon Band is one of the Desert Cahuilla peoples. They are located in Indio, near Joshua Tree National Park. Like several other Southern

California tribes, they were awarded a reservation in 1876 by President Grant's executive order. Today the Cabazon Band runs Fantasy Springs Casino, among other economic endeavors.

22. Connecticut's gaming compacts, for example, brought $332,418,314 to the total state General Fund of $591,761,174 in 2001.

23. See Spilde 2000, 86.

24. See the California Nations Indian Gaming Association press release, August 28, 2001.

25. In November 2004, Gov. Schwarzenegger's Proposition 68 attempted, unsuccessfully, to threaten the tribes' exclusive rights to gaming by proposing that they pay the 25 percent to the state, or else slot machine privileges would be extended to non-Indian–run racetracks and card clubs.

CHAPTER THREE

1. Jack Campisi is an anthropologist at Wellesley College and the State University College in Oneonta, New York, who has critiqued and tangled with the Federal Acknowledgment process for more than twenty-five years. He has been the director of the Mashantucket-Pequot Museum and Research Center Project since 1992. The statement I quote comes from an essay called "A Burden Too Heavy to Bear," which Yvonne Morales had in the belongings her brother Ron inherited at her death. No mention of date or publication was included on her copy.

2. BAR's suggestions for petitioners are as follows:

Start with genealogy. Hire a genealogist first. They will try to trace your ancestry to a historic tribe. A historian will next build on what the genealogist has found by placing the ancestors in a historical context. Finally, the anthropologist describes the social and political entity your ancestors maintained in the past, and you maintain today. Don't hire them all at once. Stagger their work. This is generally how BIA researchers work too. (1997, 29)

3. In a pretrial motion, the *Mashpee* plaintiff had suggested a continuance when it learned that the Department of the Interior was creating the Acknowledgment process (Quinn 1992, 57). The motion was denied, however, in part because of the "strong public interest in the prompt resolution" of the case and the uncertainties of when the DOI's procedures would be made available to the Mashpees. Indeed, the Mashpees, after deciding to undertake the DOI process once the trial was over, are still waiting on the department for their Acknowledgment as the Mashpee Wampanoag Tribe.

4. Shubow's reference is to the controversial instructions from Judge Skinner that jurors find that the Mashpees were a tribe (considering race, territory, community, and leadership) at each of six dates in history—1790,

1834, 1842, 1869, 1870, and 1976 —in order for a ruling in their favor. He insisted that if they were not a tribe at any of these points in history, they are not a tribe today.

5. Leanne Hinton's "Afterword: Linguistics and California Languages," in her *Flutes of Fire* (1994) lays out some of the history of the relationship between linguists and California Indian people and then offers a progressive vision for the future.

6. In one interview, Clara LeCompte (Mountain Maidu) told me, "I thought it was a 'Christmas Bonus.' I cashed it. But that doesn't mean it's okay they took the land." The Pit River bands, however, did not accept these checks, and in fact sued the state of California for land claims separately from the rest of the California tribes. The BIA tried to settle the matter in 1963, but sparked tribal division instead (see Bruce G. Miller 2004, 131).

7. Anthropologists who worked on behalf of the tribes included Alfred Kroeber, Omer Stewart, Robert F. Heizer, Edward Gifford, Samuel Barrett, and a number of unnamed graduate students. On the government's behalf, Julian Steward, William Duncan Strong, Harold E. Driver, Erminie Wheeler-Voegelin, Walter R. Goldschmidt, Joel M. Halpern, and Ralph L. Beals testified.

8. Please note that there was some additional legal activity through 1974.

9. The Pit Rivers Nation fought this, petitioning for separate land claims. Members were also part of the only tribe in the state to refuse the $633.00 compensation checks. But the prevailing trend was to administer California as a single unit.

10. To begin, please see Benedict Anderson (1977), Barsh (1991), Bee (1982), Beinart (1999), Campisi (1990, n.d.), Castile (1992), Collins (1998), Colson (1953), Cramer (2001), Davis (2001), Duthu (2001), Field (1999), Field et al. (1992), Fogelson (1989a), Gover (2001), Grabowski (1994), Greenbaum (1985), McCulloch and Wilkins (1995), B. G. Miller (2004), Roth (1992), Sarris (1998), Schiedermair (1990), Sheffield (1997), Sider (1993), Slagle (1979, 1986, 1987, 1990, 1998, 2000a, 2000b, 2001), Slagle and Davis (1989, 1995), Weatherhead (1980), Vizenor (2000).

11. See U.S. House 1992, 155.

12. There has been no formal explanation for this policy, but it appears that landless peoples were considered too assimilated to be included in the IRA— if they hadn't been noticed by earlier administrators who made provisions for homeless Indians, perhaps it was assumed that their cultures were in extreme decline or gone for good. Bud Shapard has testified before Congress that

no one has ever asserted that every viable Indian tribe in the country was asked to vote [on the IRA]! Thus it is obvious that there are a number of tribes which were ignored, some by accident, others by deliberate omission because they did not meet some unwritten, subjective criteria established within the BIA. A group in Michigan comes to mind which was not allowed to vote on the IRA and went unrecognized because the BIA investigator found that most of the members had radios in their homes. They were, therefore, considered "too civilized" to be an Indian tribe. (U.S. House 1992, 69)

13. The *Official Guidelines to the Federal Acknowledgment Regulations* even note that

there is a recurring problem of the self-appointed chief among petitioners. He or she may mail a lot of letters to public officials, march in local parades wearing a headdress or beadwork, and even make speeches about the group's history at the Kiwanis club. But almost nobody on his membership list knows or cares what he does. Do his or her actions demonstrate political activity and influence? Not according to the Acknowledgment regulations, the way they have been applied and court decisions. Leaders by definition must have followers. (1997, 49)

14. Steve "KC" Camacho is a white retired history teacher in Susanville and a friend who recorded many useful interviews with local Indian people and pioneer families.

15. Ron insists that I mention that Riddell eventually backed the Honey Lake Maidus' presence in the valley, with a letter of support for their Federal Acknowledgment petition.

16. By 2003, the Honey Lake Maidus had come around to this idea after seeing bones they believed were their ancestors' buried by Maidus from the Rancheria. They are, as Riddell envisioned, searching for someone to work up a DNA fingerprint of their tribe.

17. The only member of the three-person petition review team missing from our discussion at this point was a genealogist. BAR tries to spin its small size (there are three such teams of three, plus a chief administrator and one support staff person, making eleven total employees at BAR) as "comforting" rather than emblematic of the bottleneck of the nation's reluctance to recognize tribes. BAR's Federal Acknowledgment packet, for example, argues that "BAR does not qualify as a large, faceless, government bureaucracy. It is currently authorized to have 10 full-time employees. Sometimes, because of staff turnover and hiring procedures, it has fewer than that" (1997, 6).

18. The Tuscarora Gas Transmission Company owns a 229-mile interstate pipeline system that transports natural gas from Oregon to northeastern California and Nevada. Susanville's Sierra Pacific Resources (a.k.a. the local lumber mill) owns a 50 percent interest in Tuscarora. It is no coincidence that Ron's experience with Tuscarora led him to anthropology—private developers are another formidable force in Honey Lake Valley, often with their own teams of anthropologists.

19. Continuing in the vein of his relationship with Riddell, Ron has taken to calling Evans and aggressively asking him for his field notes. Evans always seems to have an excuse not to copy them for him.

20. Yahi refugees married into many local tribes, and thus the Yahi bloodlines have not been extinguished.

21. In 1996, Ishi's brain was tracked to specimen pot 3, tank 6 on a dusty shelf at a Smithsonian Institution warehouse, after a letter confirming that the organ was not, in fact, with the rest of his remains was discovered by Orin Starn, a Duke University anthropologist who was doing the research at the request of Art Angle, a Konkow Maidu from Enterprise Rancheria and leader of the Butte County Native American Cultural Committee. The discovery of an older generation of academic and personal betrayals of the Yahi man's last wishes necessarily renewed the disgust of Native Californians: Ishi is and always has been a symbol of something larger than himself.

22. The Achomawi and Atsugewi are among the eleven bands (and Alfred Kroeber, in fact, recognized them as eleven tribelets [1955, 98]) of the Pit River Nation.

23. Reflecting this, Heizer notes that "in 1955 Kroeber and I, in connection with our services on behalf of the Indians of California who were plaintiffs in a suit against the United States, went over the 1925 map of California tribes and made certain changes on the basis of information acquired in the intervening years. These changes are not very great, but they are worth mentioning" (1966, 15)—especially to the tribes whose territories were expanded/contracted. I assume that the case of Honey Lake Valley was not addressed.

24. Anthropologically, we could align Riddell's theories with cultural ecology and Dixon's with diffusionism, each theory, unsurprisingly, leading to its own version of Maidu boundaries.

CHAPTER FOUR

1. *Maidem* means "the man" in Mountain Maidu, hence his name means "Wooly Man."

2. *Munmunim* is also called "wormwood" by participants, though a botanist friend insists that it is actually mugwort.

3. *Wepum* means "coyote." Non-Indians in the area call Wepum Mountain "Round Mountain." Today, despite an ancient, ceremonial fire circle at its soft apex, Wepum Mountain has been cut away and is being mined for sand.

4. Roxie Peconom's grandmother, Momolo, was also from Honey Lake Valley.

5. Bill Simmons, personal communication, based on Steve Camacho's interview with Lucy Lowry.

6. The Bear Dance Foundation today is similarly adamant that drinking alcohol and using drugs will not be tolerated in the Lassen National Forest.

7. *Yah-Monee* means "Mountain."

8. Lowry and Harris are members of the Susanville Indian Rancheria. The Smiths and Pimentail are Konkow Maidus.

9. Mona's own tribe, the Strawberry Valley Maidus, was among those terminated tribes left out of the Tillie Hardwick class-action suit. Today, they are petitioning for Restoration, but remain un-Acknowledged.

10. Indian Heights Full Gospel Church is a small church that is arguably, by its history and current membership, a Honey Lake Maidu institution.

11. And proudly, in 2001, one girl!

12. From the book *Handgame!* (1993) put out by brother william and coyote man.

13. The Tyme Maidus are a Konkow people (from the foothills of the upper Sacramento Valley). Berry Creek Rancheria is located in Oroville, in Butte County.

14. A variation has it that the World Maker pinched off Bear's tail and threw the acorn bread at Rattlesnake's head and then stamped on it, leaving a diamond-shaped mark.

15. Roland B. Dixon described the rattlesnake as a flag in his 1905 depiction of the Bear Dance.

16. Sunday's Bear Dance is also called the *Wahdom buyan*, or "Spring Big Time," after Marie Potts (1977), or *panom wulu*, literally "bear dance," after Marvin Benner (1989). A *weda*, as I have mentioned before, is an intertribal gathering for a celebration involving dancing and the sharing of food, as opposed to a purely local, intratribal event. Viola Williams, while generally calling both the gathering and the dance "the Bear Dance" in English, made sure to teach me that the distinction of importance is between the terms *weda* and *Wedam:* the difference between *a* big time and *the* Big Time, the Mountain Maidu rite of spring.

17. This statement leaves aside Radley Davis at the sweat lodge, which is physically situated away from the circle and is a far less public part of the Bear Dance ceremony.

18. Among the oldest of prohibitions surrounding the Bear Dance, Ron tells me, is that of never fighting about or over the ceremony.

19. Gifford Pinchot, father of the modern Forest Service, is known for his ecologically questionable decisions about what "use" the nation's forest lands should have. For example, in a notorious debate with John Muir, he sided with the state's urban governors, who wanted to flood and destroy the

Hetch Hetchy Valley to create a reservoir and water delivery system for the thirsty, overgrown San Francisco Bay Area.

20. For another example, please see Buckley (2002, 170–201). Buckley writes insightfully of the Forest Service's commodification of Yoruk sacred sites, translating the meanings behind such terms as *cultural resources*.

21. A roundhouse is a ceremonial house. These days a roundhouse is a potent symbol of tradition and culture because so few remain standing, again, mostly because of the historical loss—and continuing lack—of land in Indian ownership.

22. The facilitator was hired after the long-awaited new forest supervisor, Ed Cole, witnessed the impossible state of affairs between his employees and the Bear Dance Foundation. What I saw was that she basically facilitated the Forest Service perspective. (See Nader and Ou 1998 and Nader 1990 for discussion of coercive adjudication processes involving American Indians.)

23. Attempts are made to employ Indian inmates, though in 2000, those who came out were predominantly black or Latino. The inmates I spoke with said they look forward to this work—chopping wood, raking, moving picnic tables—and expressed that they could feel the power of the site. Even though they weren't permitted to attend the ritual, they took some of it back with them.

24. Ike Lowry is Allen's brother. In the spring of 2001, a new council had been elected at the rancheria—an electoral routing of the longstanding Paiute power structure, which was causing all kinds of upset but was allowing these kinds of politically backed letters to be sent in the interest of some of the rancheria's Maidu members.

25. The Honey Lake Maidus have creation stories of the Maker's journey through Mountain Maidu country, and, in parallel, stories about Coyote's creation of various natural formations, such as what is known today as Bass Hill, on the north side of which is Lone Pine, where Lamb Samson held Bear Dances.

CHAPTER FIVE

1. ANA's competitive, sixty-five thousand dollar grants should be compared with Connecticut representatives Simmons and Johnson's H.R. 992 IH (2001), which proposed financing, with grants of $500,000, "efforts of states and local governments to challenge acknowledgement petitions and any other tribal claims, including those of recognized tribes, as third parties" (Slagle 2001, 31). Though not passed into law, H.R. 992 IH has had successive legislative reincarnations. I mention it here to offer the reader a sense of the value of not recognizing more Indian tribes, and to highlight the comparison between this value and that placed on extending Federal Recognition.

2. The Honey Lake Maidus no longer participate in the AIOLC programs because of a disagreement over insurance for the Bear Dance in the early 1990s.

3. In the non-Indian world Morales was a player and manager for the Susanville Merchants baseball team and a foreman at the lumber mill, as well as a coordinator of youth sports leagues.

4. In other words, the Bear Dance Foundation was the functioning arm of the tribe at this point in time. Members of the Bear Dance Foundation had wanted the grant run, at least in name, by the "Honey Lake Maidus," but they were advised that running the grant under the Bear Dance Foundation, a California-registered nonprofit organization, made the ANA funding more likely.

5. The status of Indian people from un-Acknowledged tribes who are "adopted" as nonvoting members of Acknowledged tribes to which they are related appears to be quite common among the Maidu peoples in California. Adoptees I have spoken with find this a frustrating and at times degrading position to be in.

6. The Lumbees, for instance, were denied Federal Acknowledgment in 1987 based on the BIA's reading of the language of Congress's 1956 Lumbee Act, which terminated their tribal status. Since 1987, the tribe has struggled with the dead weight of being denied Acknowledgment. It is extremely hard to reverse.

7. More fishing imagery: Fred A. Baker, who traveled through California and signed Indian people onto the 1928 Rolls, described his work in the heroic terms of a fisherman casting a broad net, allowing not a single individual to escape (see L. K. Miller 1998, 3).

8. In 2002, after over a year of visiting the archive, an archivist who did not recognize me insisted on investigating my authority to be conducting tribal research. Yet even though I did not have proof of my employment with me, and I could not get authorization over the phone because the tribal office was closed, I was allowed to access allotment files after he screened them for sensitive materials such as social security numbers.

9. Another way of thinking about this is that for a petition there is a tension between the realities of tribal affiliation and the impressions they make to outsiders. Looks take on a real importance.

10. Birth certificates identify the race of the parents and child, though this is (rightly, in my opinion) not considered conclusive evidence of racial affiliation by the BIA.

11. Jean-Baptiste Lamarck (1744–1829) is well remembered for his early theory of genetic inheritance, the "inheritance of acquired traits," since disproven. A popular caricature of this theory would have it that if a man builds up his muscles, his offspring will have well-developed muscles too.

12. Tellingly, according to anthropologist David Schneider, the latter system—of reckoning descent in terms of one's blood distance from one's relations—is the underlying principle of the "American system" (1968).

13. All this has changed since the opening of the Smithsonian Museum of the American Indian in September 2004. The symbolism of a hemispheric Native presence at the head of the Mall is truly powerful. That Native peoples are curating their own communities next door to the Capitol, with the strength of casino money, testifies to changes afoot that deserve careful consideration.

14. BAR would deny that simple multiplication can tell us how long it will take for number 223 to reach the front of the line. Petitioners move through the queue at varying speeds—some, for instance, receive a numbered place in line after writing a Letter of Intent to Petition, and then never send in a petition. The fact remains, however, that others send in their documentation and are left to wait an unbearably long time.

15. Back in California, this was no easy task because the San Bruno archive only possessed copies of the 1928 and 1955 rolls. One has to contact the notoriously hard-to-contact Sacramento BIA to arduously request, member by member, the 1944s and 1968s.

16. At the end of 2000, Democrat Maria Campwell was running for Congress against Republican Slade Gorton, a notorious foe of Indian sovereignty, in Washington State. While the Republicans whined about Al Gore's attempt at a recount in Florida, they had started their own recount in the opposite corner of the country.

17. Carole, who I would describe as youthful, hip, and loveably eccentric, has since passed away. I miss going for "early birds" with her.

18. That said, there were also tribe members, like Gina Garcia, who were vigilant in their support for the lawyers' work and my own.

19. Despite the cultural habit (see Kunkle 1974) of reckoning descent ambilaterally (that is, perceiving of oneself as equally related to one's mother's and father's kin), I felt I had to enforce a strict understanding of descent from those ancestors born in the Honey Lake Valley in order to make a solid case to BAR. As a consequence, Ron and his cousin John Peconom struggled with understanding why the Salems, related through Roxie Peconom's husband, John, Sr., were not included as Honey Lake Maidus in the petition.

20. The character Johnny in Greg Sarris's novel, *Watermelon Nights*, refers to the genealogical charts required by the BIA to prove tribal membership for federal recognition as "pedigree charts." He says, "If you ask me, [they] are no different from dog pedigrees" (1998, 5). The implication is that the state treats Indian people no better than dogs—*zoë*, or "bare life," in philosopher Giorgio Agamben's sense (1998).

21. Her children may have a "home" in their Honey Lake Maidu identity that she hasn't fully recognized. Her daughter's work, in high school, to have a local creek and park given a Mountain Maidu name seems a clue to that possibility.

22. Sarris is not only a novelist but also an English professor and the chair of the Federated Indians of Graton Rancheria.

CHAPTER SIX

1. Today, for instance, one finds a deeper sediment of paternal responsibility to Indian peoples embedded in the uproar over the federal government's abuse of individual trust accounts in Indian Country, though it is more overtly expressed in outrage over the BIA's unsound investment practices. That is, there is moral inflection within the critique, but the grounds for revision are neoliberal in principle.

2. The piñata image is borrowed from Diane Nelson's 1999 study of the relationships between Guatemala's indigenous peoples and the state.

3. Gerald Sider's *Lumbee Indian Histories* (1993) offers an excellent analysis of a different but similar set of Indian histories.

4. Recall that Ulleseit lives in Reno and is genealogically connected to both the Peconom and Jack lineages. She was a tribal council member-at-large. Chavez was the tribe's treasurer and a Jack lineage descendant from central California.

5. Ron later told me that his vision was that, after a period of "tribal hosting" of the Bear Dance, individual families would return to hosting it, in the old way. "In the old days," he said, "remember that Bob Tail [an Old Tom descendant] and Lamb Sampson [a Wetajam/Momolo descendant] were *both* holding Bear Dances."

6. Mark Edwin Miller writes, "The BAR findings are so complex and factual in nature that the IBIA will decide only procedural issues and remand the cases to the bureau for further review" (2004, 66).

7. Riddell's use of *Wadátkut* is noticeably different from Harold Dixon's use of *Wadakut*. I defer to Dixon's name for his people.

8. As Theresa Dixon requested, I am not identifying the eponymous location of the massacre, except in the general terms of its proximity to Eagle Lake.

9. Please see Joelle Fraser (2000) for a sketch of the political and moral economies of the Honey Lake Valley.

10. I met a number of these "amateur archaeologists" during my time in Susanville.

WORKS CITED

Advisory Council on California Indian Policy (ACCIP)

1997a *Final Reports and Recommendations to the Congress of the United States Pursuant to Public Law 102-416, Executive Summary.* Washington, D.C.: U.S. GPO.

1997b *The ACCIP Historical Overview Report: The Special Circumstances of California Indians.* Washington, D.C.: U.S. GPO.

1997c *The ACCIP Recognition Report: Equal Justice for California.* Washington, D.C.: U.S. GPO.

1997d *The ACCIP Report on California Indian Cultural Preservation.* Washington, D.C.: U.S. GPO.

Agamben, Giorgio

1998 *Homo Sacer: Sovereign Power and Bare Life.* Stanford: Stanford University Press.

Alexie, Sherman

1993 *The Lone Ranger and Tonto Fistfight in Heaven.* New York: Atlantic Monthly Press.

1996 Why We Play Basketball. In *Summer of Black Widows,* 21–28. New York: Hanging Loose Press.

Althusser, Louis

1971 Ideology and Ideological State Apparatuses (Notes Toward Investigation). In *Lenin and Philosophy and Other Essays,* 127–86. New York: Monthly Review Press.

American Indian Policy Review Commission (AIPRC)

1976 *Report on Terminated and Nonfederally Recognized Indians: Task Force Ten Final Report to the American Indian Policy Review Commission.* Washington, D.C.: U.S. GPO.

Anderson, Benedict
   1977   *Imagined Communities*. London: Verso.
Anderson, George E., W. H. Ellison, and Robert F. Heizer
   1978   Treaty-Making and the Federal Government in Califor-
           nia, 1851–1852. In *Treaty Making and Treaty Rejection by
           the Federal Government in California, 1850–1852*, 1–37.
           Socorro, N.Mex.: Ballena Press.
Anderson, Terry
   1978   "Federal Recognition: The Vicious Myth." *American
           Indian Journal of the Institute for the Development of Indian
           Law* 4, no. 5 (May): 7–19.
Angulo, Jaime de
   1990   *Indians in Overalls*. San Francisco: City Lights Books.
           (Orig. pub. 1950.)
Arentzen, Bernard
   1894   Letter to Commissioner of Indian Affairs. March 17,
           1894. National Archives and Records Administration,
           Letter no. 11072, box no. PI-163, E-91, Hm 1996.
Ashmore, Shayla
   1997   Mural Dedication. *Lassen County (Susanville, Calif.) Times*.
   2000   Centennial Mural for Susanville Supermarket Takes
           Shape. *Lassen County (Susanville, Calif.) Times*.
The Associated Press
   2000   Author and State Officials Warn Town about Recogniz-
           ing Tribe. www.msnbc.com/local/wjar/575530.asp.
Baldwin, Chris
   1977   Paradise Lost or Economic Gain? *Chico (Calif.) News
           and Review*.
Barlett, Donald L., and James B. Steele
   2002a   Playing the Political Slots Part Two: How Indian Casino
           Interests Have Learned the Art of Buying Influence in
           Washington. *Time Magazine*, December 23.
   2002b   Special Report, Indian Casinos: Wheel of Misfortune.
           Time Magazine, December 16, 44–58.
Barsh, Russel L.
   1991   Federal Acknowledgment: Another Viewpoint. *European
           Review of Native American Studies* 5, no.1:64–65.

Beals, Ralph L.
  1977   The Anthropologist as Expert Witness: Illustrations from
          the California Indian Land Claims Case. In *Irredeemable
          America: The Indians' Estate and Land Claims*, ed. Imre Sut-
          ton, 139–55. Albuquerque: University of New Mexico Press.
Beals, Ralph L., and Joseph Hester
  1974   Indian Occupation, Subsistence, and Land Use Patterns
          in California. In *Commission Findings of the Indian Claims
          Commission*. New York: Garland.
Bean, Lowell John
  1975   Power and Its Applications in Native California. *Journal
          of California Anthropology* 2, no. 1:25–33.
Bee, Robert L.
  1982   *The Politics of American Indian Policy*. Cambridge, Mass.:
          Schenkman.
  1992   Riding the Paper Tiger. In *State and Reservation: New
          Perspectives in Federal Indian Policy*. Tucson: University
          of Arizona Press.
Beinart, Peter
  1999   Lost Tribes: Native Americans and Government Anthro-
          pologists Feud over Indians Identity. *Lingua Franca*
          (May/June): 33–41.
Benedict, Jeff
  2000   *Without Reservation: The Making of American's Most Power-
          ful Indian Tribe and Foxwoods, the World's Largest Casino*.
          New York: HarperCollins.
Benedict, Ruth
  1934   *Patterns of Culture*. Boston: Houghton Mifflin.
Benner, Marvin
  1989   Jamani Maidu Wedam: Mountain Maidu Spring Rite.
          News from Native California 3:18–19.
  1996   Lassen National Forest. In *Working Together: California
          Indians and the Forest Service*, ed. U.S. Forest Service.
          Washington, D.C.: U.S. GPO.
Biolsi, Thomas, and Larry J. Zimmerman, eds.
  1997   Introduction: What's Changed and What Hasn't. In *Indians
          and Anthropologists: Vine Deloria Junior and the Critique of
          Anthropology*, 3–24. Tucson: University of Arizona Press.

Blu, Karen

  2001   Region and Recognition: Southern Indians, Anthropologists, and Presumed Biology. In *Anthropologists and Indians in The New South,* ed. J. Anthony Paredes and Rachel A. Bonney, 71–85. Tuscaloosa: University of Alabama Press.

Borneman, John

  1998   Toward a Theory of Ethnic Cleansing. *Subversions of International Order.* New York: SUNY Press.

Branch of Acknowledgment and Research

  1995   Letter to Ms. Clara LeCompte. October 27, 1995.

  1997   *The Official Guidelines to the Federal Acknowledgment Regulations.* Bureau of Indian Affairs.

  1998a   *Recommendations to the Assistant Secretary-Indian Affairs on California Indians and Acknowledgment (Draft).*

  1998b   What Is the Background of the Federal Acknowledgment Regulations? www.doi.gov/bia/arguide.html.

Brodeur, Paul

  1985   *Restitution: The Land Claims of the Mashpee, Passamaquoddy, and Penobscot Indians of New England.* Boston: Northeastern University Press.

Brown, Wendy

  1995   Finding the Man in the State. In *States of Injury.* Princeton, N.J.: Princeton University Press.

Bruff, J. Goldborough

  1949   *"Gold Rush": the Journals, Drawings, and Other Papers of J. Goldborough Bruff.* New York: Columbia University Press.

Bruner, E. M.

  1961   Mandan. In *Perspectives in American Indian Culture Change,* 187–277. Chicago: University of Chicago Press.

Buckley, Thomas

  1977   The Little History of Pitiful Events: The Epistemological and Moral Contexts of Kroeber's Californian Ethnology. In *Volksgeist as Method and Ethic: Essays on Boasian Ethnography and the German Anthropological Tradition,* vol. 8, *History of Anthropology,* ed. G. Stocking, Jr., 257–97. Madison: University of Wisconsin Press.

2002   *Standing Ground: Yurok Indian Spirituality, 1850–1990.*
        Berkeley: University of California Press.

Bureau of Indian Affairs

1897–   Records of the Greenville School and Agency, and Records
1956   of the Sacramento Area Office. San Bruno, Calif.: National
        Archives and Records Administration.

1901–   Quarterly Field Matron Reports. San Bruno, Calif.: National
1919   Archives and Records Administration.

1918   Records of the Greenville Agency, Administrative Records,
        General Correspondence File, Box 107, Letter from Miller
        to Raker, 1918. San Bruno, Calif.: National Archives
        and Records Administration.

1994   *25 Code of Federal Regulations.* Sec. 83.1–83.7. (Orig.
        pub. 1978.)

2001   Proposed Finding against Federal Acknowledgment of
        the Ohlone/Coastanoan Muwekma Tribe. 66 *Federal
        Register* Sec. 40712.

2002   Strategic Plan: Response to the November 2001 General
        Accounting Office Report, September 12, 2002, 1–19.

Burrill, Richard

1988   *River of Sorrows.* Happy Camp, Calif.: Naturegraph.

1990   *Ishi: American's Last Stone Age Indian.* Sacramento,
        Calif.: Anthropology Company.

Buzaljko, Grace

2003   Kroeber, Pope, and Ishi. In *Ishi in Three Centuries,* eds.
        K. Kroeber and C. Kroeber, 48–66. Lincoln: University
        of Nebraska Press.

California Indian Nations' Voice

1994   Cultural and Political Preservation Stressed at Mon-
        terey Meeting. Advisory Council on California Indian
        Policy newsletter. Vol. 1, 1–4.
        Indian Advisory Council Begins Work. Advisory Council
        on California Indian Policy newsletter. Vol. 1, 2–3.

California Nations Indian Gaming Association

2001   California's Gaming Tribes Share More Than $30 Mil-
        lion with Other Tribes. Press release. August 28, 2001.
        www.cniga.com.

Camacho, Steve, Ron Morales, William Simmons, and Viola Williams, eds.

Forth- Susanville Maidu: Creation. As told by Leona Peconom
coming Morales. Susanville, Calif.: Lassen Yah-Monee Maidu
        Bear Dance Foundation.

Campisi, Jack

1985   The Trade and Intercourse Acts: Land Claims on the
        Eastern Seaboard. In *Irredeemable America: The Indians'
        Estate and Land Claims*, ed. Imre Sutton, 337–62. Albu-
        querque: University of New Mexico Press,

1990   The New England Tribes and Their Quest for Justice. In
        The Pequots in Southern New England, eds. Laurence M.
        Hauptman and James D. Wherry, 179–93. Norman: Uni-
        versity of Oklahoma Press.

1991   *The Mashpee Indians: Tribe on Trial*. Syracuse, N.Y.: Syra-
        cuse University Press.

n.d.   A Burden Too Heavy to Bear. Paper presented at Welles-
        ley College, Wellesley, Mass.

Castile, Georges Pierre

1992   Indian Sign: Hegemony and Symbolism in Federal Indian
        Policy. In *State and Reservation: New Perspectives in Fed-
        eral Indian Policy*, eds. R. L. Bee and G. P. Castile, 165–86.
        Tucson: University of Arizona Press.

Clappe, Louise Amelia Knapp Smith

1998   *The Shirley Letters from the California Mines, 1851–1852*.
        Berkeley, Calif.: Heyday Books. (Orig. pub. 1852.)

Clark, Bruce A.

1999   *Justice in Paradise*. Montreal: McGill-Queen's University
        Press.

Clifford, James

1988   Identity In Mashpee. In *The Predicament of Culture: Twen-
        tieth-Century Ethnography, Literature, and Art*, 277–347.
        Cambridge, Mass.: Harvard University Press.

Cohen, Felix

1971   The Legal Status of Indian Tribes. In *Felix S. Cohen's
        Handbook of Federal Indian Law*, 268–73. Albuquerque:
        University of New Mexico Press. (Orig. pub. 1947.)

1982 Introduction to *Felix S. Cohen's Handbook of Federal Indian Law*, vii–xi. Reprint, Charlottesville, Va.: Michie, Bobbs-Merrill.

Collier, Mary E. T., and Sylvia Barker Thalman
1996 *Interviews with Tom Smith and Maria Copia: Isabel Kelly's Ethnographic Notes on the Coast Miwok Indians of Marin and Southern Sonoma Counties, California.* Second printing (Orig. pub. 1991). San Rafael, Calif.: Miwok Archaeological Preserve of Marin.

Collins, James
1998 *Understanding Tolowa Histories: Western Hegemonies and Native American Responses.* New York: Routledge.

Colson, Elizabeth
1953 *The Makah Indians: A Study of an Indian Tribe in Modern America.* Minneapolis: University of Minnesota Press.

Cook, Sherburne F.
1978 Historical Demography. In *California*, vol. 8, *Handbook of North American Indians*, ed. R. F. Heizer, 91–98. Washington, D.C.: Smithsonian Institution Press.

Cooper, James Fenimore
1947 *The Last of the Mohicans.* New York: Scribner. (Orig. pub. 1826.)

Cramer, Renée Ann
2001 The Politics of Recognition: The Contexts of Federal Acknowledgment Law. Ph.D. diss., New York University.

Das, Veena
1995 *Critical Events.* Delhi and London: Oxford University Press.

Davis, Dave D.
2001 A Case of Identity: Ethnogenesis of the New Houma Indians. *Ethnohistory* 48, no. 3:473–94.

Davis, Mike
1996 The Politics of Super Incarceration. In *Criminal Injustice: Confronting the Prison Crisis*, ed. E. Rosenblatt, 73–78. Boston: South End Press Collective.

D'Azevedo, Warren L.
1963 Washo Indians of California and Nevada. Anthropological Papers, no. 67. Salt Lake City: University of Utah, Salt Lake City.

DeBuys, William
  2000   In Search of a Politics of Union. In *(Paonia, Colo.) High
          Country News,* April.
Deloria, Philip
  1998   *Playing Indian.* New Haven, Conn.: Yale University Press.
Deloria, Vine, Jr.
  1995   *Red Earth, White Lies: Native Americans and the Myth of
          Scientific Fact.* New York: Scribner.
Deloria, Vine, Jr., and Clifford Lytle
  1983   *American Indians, American Justice.* Austin: University
          of Texas Press.
Deloria, Vine, Jr., and David E. Wilkins
  1999   *Tribes, Treaties, and Constitutional Tribulations.* Austin:
          University of Texas Press.
Dixon, Harold
  1994   Letter to Bureau of Indian Affairs' Branch of Acknowl-
          edgment and Research. May 20, 1994.
Dixon, Roland B.
  1983   *The Northern Maidu.* Vol. 17, part 3. New York: Bulletin
          of the American Museum of Natural History, AMS Press.
          (Orig. pub. 1905.)
Dobkins, Rebecca J.
  1997   The Life and Art of Frank Day. In *Memory and Imagina-
          tion: The Legacy of Maidu Indian Artist Frank Day,* 1–26.
          Oakland and Seattle: Oakland Museum of California.
Dobkins, Rebecca J., with Carey T. Caldwell and Frank R. LaPena
  1997   *Memory and Imagination: The Legacy of Maidu Indian Artist
          Frank Day,* ed. R. J. Dobkins. Catalog of an exhibition
          held at the Oakland Museum of California, March 15–
          August 3, 1997. Oakland: Oakland Museum of California.
          Distributed by the University of Washington Press.
Dorrington, Lafayette
  1927   Report from Superintendent L. A. Dorrington to Com-
          missioner of Indian Affairs E. B. Merritt. June 23. U.S.
          Department of the Interior. Indian Field Service. San
          Bruno, Calif.: National Archives and Records Adminis-
          tration, RG 75.

Downs, Chuck
    1978   A National Conference on Tribal Recognition. *American Indian Journal of the Institute for the Development of Indian Law* 4, no. 5 (May): 2–4.
Duane, Timothy
    1999   *Shaping the Sierra: Nature, Culture, and Conflict in the Changing West.* Berkeley: University of California Press.
DuBois, Cora
    1939   The 1870 Ghost Dance. *U.C. Anthropological Records* 3:v–vi, 39–40.
Duthu, N. Bruce
    2001   The Houma of Louisiana: Politics, Identity, and the Legal Status of "Tribe." *European Review of Native American Studies* 15, no. 2:37–40.
Dworkin, Ronald
    1977   *The Philosophy of Law.* London: Oxford University Press.
Eargle, Dolan H., Jr.
    2000   *Native California Guide: Weaving Past and Present.* San Francisco: Trees Company Press.
Eisler, Kim Isaac
    2001   *Revenge of the Pequots: How a Small Native American Tribe Created the World's Most Powerful Casino.* New York: Simon and Schuster.
Ellison, W. H.
    1978   Rejection of California Indian Treaties: A Study in Local Influence on National Policy. In *Treaty Making and Treaty Rejection by the Federal Government in California, 1850–1852,* Heizer, Elasser, and Anderson, 50–71. Socorro, N.Mex.: Ballena Press.
Erdrich, Louise
    1994   *The Bingo Palace.* New York: HarperCollins.
Evans, William S., Jr.
    1978   Ethnographic Notes on the Honey Lake Maidu. *Nevada State Museum Occasional Papers* 3, part 2.
Fairfield, Asa M.
    1998   *Fairfield's Pioneer History of Lassen County, California.* Clovis, Calif.: Word Dancer Press. (Orig. pub. 1916.)

Faleomavaega, Eni
  1997   Indian Federal Recognition Administrative Procedures
          Act of 1997. In *Congressional Record: Proceedings of the
          Debates of the 105th Congress, First Session.*

Fariss and Smith, eds.
  1882   *Illustrated History of Plumas, Lassen and Sierra Counties
          (with California from 1513 to 1850).* San Francisco: Fariss
          and Smith.

Fawcett-Sayet, Melissa
  1987   Sociocultural Leadership. In *Rooted Like the Ash Trees:
          New England Indians and the Land,* ed. R. Carlson, 153–54.
          Naugatuck, Conn.: Eagle Wing Press.

Feit, Harvey A.
  1991   The Construction of Algonquian Hunting Territories:
          Private Property as Moral Lesson, Policy Advocacy, and
          Ethnographic Error. In *Colonial Situations, vol. 7, History
          of Anthropology,* ed. G. Stocking, Jr., 109–34. Madison:
          University of Wisconsin Press.

Field, Les
  1999   Complicities and Collaboration: Anthropologists and
          the "Unacknowledged Tribes" of California. *Current
          Anthropology* 40:193–209.

Field, Les, Hank Sanchez, and Rosemary Cambra
  1992   A Contemporary Ohlone Revitalization Movement.
          California History (Fall): 413–31.

Fierman, S.
  1990   *Peasant Intellectuals: Anthropology and History in Tanzania.*
          Madison: University of Wisconsin Press.

Fogelson, Raymond D.
  1977   On the Varieties of Indian History: Sequoyah and Traveller
          Bird. *Journal of Ethnic Studies* 2:105–12.
  1989a   The Context of American Indian Political History: An
          Overview and Critique. In *The Second Newberry Library
          Conference on Themes in American Indian History: The
          Struggle for Political Autonomy,* 8–21. Chicago: Newberry
          Library Occasional Papers in Curriculum Series.

1989b The Ethnohistory of Events and Nonevents. *Ethnohistory* 36, no. 2:133–47.

Foster, George M.

2003 Assuming Responsibility for Ishi: An Alternative Interpretation. In *Ishi in Three Centuries*, eds. K. Kroeber and C. Kroeber, 89–98. Lincoln: University of Nebraska Press.

Foucault, Michel

1977 What Is an Author. In *Language, Counter-Memory, Practice*, ed. D. F. Bouchard, 113–38. Ithaca, N.Y.: Cornell University Press.

1979 On Governmentality. *Ideology and Consciousness* 6:5–21.

Fraser, Joelle

2000 An American Seduction: Portrait of a Prison Town. *Michigan Quarterly Review* (Fall): 775–95.

Fraser, Nancy

1997 From Redistribution to Recognition? Dilemmas of Justice in a "Postsocialist" Age. In *Justice Interruptus: Critical Reflections on the "Postsocialist" Condition*, 11–40. New York: Routledge.

Fried, Morton

1975 *The Notion of Tribe*. Menlo Park, Calif.: Cummings.

Gendar, Jeannine

1995 *Grass Games and Moon Races: California Indian Games and Toys*. Berkeley, Calif.: Heyday Books.

Gifford, Frank

1916 Letter to Alfred Kroeber. March 24, 1916. Bancroft Library, Records of the Department and Museum of Anthropology, CU-23.

Gold, Scott

2002 Indian Casinos on a Roll: The Number and Quality of the California Establishments Are up Markedly, and They're Poised to Give Nevada a Run for Its Money. *Los Angeles Times*. November 22.

Goodenough, Ward H.

1996 Culture. In *Encyclopedia of Cultural Anthropology*, vol. 1, eds. David Levine and Melvin Embers, 291–99. New York: Henry Holt.

Gover, Kevin
    1977   Gover: Recognition Study "Cooked." Indianz.com (accessed November 1, 2001).
Grabowski, Christine Tracey
    1994   Coiled Intent: Federal Acknowledgment Policy and the Gay Head Wampanoags. Vols. 1–2. Ph.D. diss., City University of New York.
Graburn, Nelson H. H.
    1998   Weirs in the River of Time: The Development of Canadian Inuit Historical Consciousness. *Museum Anthropology* 21:54–66.
    2001   "Learning to Consume": What Is Heritage and When Is It Traditional? In *Consuming Tradition, Manufacturing Heritage: Global Norms and Urban Forms in the Age of Tourism*, ed. Nezar Al Sayyad, 68–88. London: Routledge.
Gramsci, Antonio
    1980   State and Civil Society. In *Selections from the Prison Notebooks of Antonio Gramsci*, eds. Quintin Hoare and Gregory Nowell Smith, 206–76. New York: International. (Orig. pub. 1971.)
Green, Rick
    2001   An Assault on Scholarship. *New London (Conn.) Day.*
Greenbaum, Susan D.
    1985   In Search of Lost Tribes: Anthropology and the Federal Acknowledgment Process. *Human Organization* 44, no. 4:361–67.
Habermas, Jurgen
    1977   *The Public Sphere.* Cambridge, Mass.: MIT Press.
Hall, Stuart
    1986   Gramsci's Relevance for the Study of Race and Ethnicity. *Journal of Communication Inquiry* 10, no. 2.
Harmon, Alexandra
    1998   *Indians in the Making: Ethnic Relations and Indian Identities around Puget Sound.* Berkeley: University of California Press.
Heizer, Robert F.
    1966   *Languages, Territories, and Names of California Indian Tribes.* Berkeley: University of California Press.

Heizer, Robert F., ed.
1993   *The Destruction of California Indians: A Collection of Documents from the Period 1847 to 1865 in Which Are Described Some of the Things That Happened to Some of the Indians of California.* Lincoln: University of Nebraska Press. (Orig. pub. 1974.)

Hinsley, Curtiss
1979   Anthropology as Science and Politics: The Dilemma of the BAE, 1879–1904. In *The Uses of Anthropology: A Special Publication of the American Anthropological Association, No. 11,* ed. Walter Goldschmidt, 18–32. Washington, D.C.: American Anthropological Association.

Hinton, Leanne
1994   Afterword: Linguistics and California Languages. In *Flutes of Fire,* 249–54. Berkeley, Calif.: Heyday Books.

Hobsbawm, Eric, and Terence Ranger
1983   *The Invention of Tradition.* Cambridge, UK: Cambridge University Press.

Honey Lake Maidu Tribe
2001   Petition for Federal Acknowledgment. In the possession of the author.

Hopkins, Sarah Winnemucca
1994   *Life among the Piutes.* Reno: University of Nevada Press. (Orig. pub. 1883.)

Hunt, Leigh Ann
1996   *Rite of Spring: A History of the Mountain Maidu Bear Dance.* Master's thesis, California State University, 1991. Susanville, Calif.: Lassen County Historical Society.

Hurtado, A. L.
1988   *Indian Survival on the California Frontier.* Yale Western Americana Series, 35. New Haven, Conn.: Yale University Press.

Jacknis, Ira
2003   Yahi Culture in the Wax Museum: Ishi's Sound Recordings. In *Ishi in Three Centuries,* eds. K. Kroeber and C. Kroeber, 235–74. Lincoln: University of Nebraska Press.

Jackson, Helen Hunt
 1934   *Ramona.* Boston: Little, Brown. (Orig. pub. 1884.)
 1964   *A Century of Dishonor: A Sketch of the United States Government's Dealing with Some of the Indian Tribes.* Minneapolis: Ross and Haines. (Orig. pub. 1881.)
Jaimes, M. Annette
 1992   Federal Indian Identification Policy: A Usurpation of Indigenous Sovereignty in North America. In *The State of Native America: Genocide, Colonization, and Resistance,* ed. M. Annette Jaimes, 123–38. Boston: South End Press.
Jewell, Don P.
 1987   *Indians of the Feather River: Tales and Legends of Concow Maidu of California.* Menlo Park, Calif.: Ballena Press.
Judson, George
 1994   Not the Last of This Tribe. *New York Times.*
Kafka, Franz
 1971   In the Penal Colony. In *Franz Kafka: The Complete Stories,* ed. Nahum N. Glatzer. New York: Schocken Books. (Orig. pub. 1919.)
 1992   The Legend. In *The Trial.* Introduction by George Steiner. New York: Alfred A. Knopf. (Orig. pub. 1937.)
 1994   *The Castle.* London: Minerva.
Kamper, David
 2000   Introduction: The Mimicry of Indian Gaming. In *Indian Gaming: Who Wins?* Eds. Mullis and Kamper, vii–xiv. Los Angeles: American Indian Studies Center, UCLA.
Kelly, Isabel
 1971   *Southern Paiute Ethnography.* Anthropological Papers of the University of Utah Department of Anthropology, no. 69. Glen Canyon Series, no. 21. New York: Johnson Reprint. (Orig. pub. 1964.)
Kelsey, C. E.
 1971   *Census of Non-Reservation California Indians, 1905–1906,* ed. R. F. Heizer. Berkeley, Calif.: Archaeological Research Facility. (Orig. pub. 1906.)

King, Arden
    1941   Mountain Maidu Field Notes. Unpublished Manuscript. Anthropological Archives no. 216, The Bancroft Library, University of California, Berkeley.

Kovner, Guy
    2000   Senate Votes to Restore Tribal Status to Coast Miwok Indians After 42 Years. *(Santa Rosa, Calif.) Press Democrat.*
    2004   East Bay Casino Tribe Ready to Negotiate. *(Santa Rosa, Calif.) Press Democrat.* June 23.

Kroeber, Alfred L.
    1908   The Anthropology of California. *Science* 27:281–90.
    1925   *Handbook of the Indians of California.* Berkeley: California Book Company.
    1955   The Nature of the Land-Holding Group. *Ethnohistory* 2:303–14.
    1963   The Nature of Land-Holding Groups in Aboriginal California. In *Aboriginal California,* 81–120. Berkeley: University of California Press. (Orig. pub. 1955.)

Kroeber, Karl, and Clifton Kroeber, eds.
    2003   *Ishi in Three Centuries.* Lincoln: University of Nebraska Press.

Kroeber, Theodora
    1961   *Ishi in Two Worlds.* Berkeley: University of California Press.
    1964   *Ishi: Last of His Tribe.* Berkeley, Calif.: Parnassus Press.

Kunkle, Peter H.
    1974   The Pomo Kin Group and the Political Unit in Aboriginal California. *Journal of California Anthropology* 1, no. 1.:7–18.

Kurtz, Patricia
    1963   A History of Indians Valley, Plumas County, California, 1850–1920. Master's thesis, California State University, Chico.

Laclau, Ernesto, and Chantal Mouffe
    2001   *Hegemony and Socialist Strategy: Towards A Radical Democratic Politics.* London: Verso.

Lacy, Julie
    1977   *Beauty and the Bomb: An Ethnography of Cancer and the Military.* Master's thesis, University of Nevada, Reno.

LaDuke, Winonna, and Ward Churchill
   1992   Native North America: The Political Economy of Radio-
          active Colonialism. In *The State of Native North America:
          Genocide, Colonization, and Resistance*, ed. M. Annette
          Jaimes. Boston: South End Press.
LaPena, Frank R.
   1997   Frank Day: A Remembrance. In *Memory an Imagination:
          The Legacy of Maidu Indian Artist Frank Day*, ed. R. J.
          Dobkins, 27–34. Oakland: Oakland Museum of California.
LaRue, Don
   1996   *Washo Land.* Tahoe City, Calif.: Don LaRue Studio.
Lassen County (Susanville, Calif.) Times
   2000   Letter to the editor. March 3.
Levenson, Rosemarie
   1994   *The Short-lived Explorations of Isadore Meyerowitz: Gold
          Prospecting in Northeastern California with Peter Lassen.*
          Janesville, Calif.: High Desert Press.
Leventhal, Alan, Les Field, Hank Alvarez, and Rosemary Cambra
   1994   The Ohlone: Back from Extinction. In *The Ohlone Past
          and Present*, ed. L. J. Bean, 297–331. Ballena Press Anthro-
          pological Papers No. 42. Menlo Park, Calif.: Ballena Press.
Li, Tania M.
   2000   Articulating Indigenous Identity in Indonesia: Resource
          Politics and the Tribal Slot. *Comparative Studies in Society
          and History* 42:149–79.
Linton, R., M. Herskovitz, and R. Redfield
   1935   Memorandum on the Study of Acculturation. *Man* 35:
          145–48.
Locke, John
   1952   *The Second Treatise of Government.* New York: Liberal
          Arts Press.
Loeb, E. M.
   1933   *The Eastern Kuksu Cult.* Vol. 33, no. 2. Berkeley, Calif.:
          University Publications in American Archaeology and
          Ethnology.
Lowry, Sandra D.
   n.d.   *The Mountain Maidu Bear Dance.* Self-published pamphlet.

Lurie, Nancy O.
  1979   The Will-o'-the Wisp of Indian Unity. In *Currents in Anthropology: Essays in Honor of Sol Tax*, ed. R. Hinton. The Hague and New York: Mounton.
Magdaleno, Dena
  2000   Letter to the author. October 1.
Malkki, Liisa
  1995   *Purity and Exile*. Chicago: University of Chicago Press.
man, coyote, and brother william
  1993   *Handgame!* Berkeley, Calif.: Yerba Buena Press.
Manners, Robert A.
  1974   Introduction to the Ethnohistorical Reports on the Land Claims Cases. In *California and Great Basin*, ed. David Horr, 17–19. New York: Garland.
Margolin, Malcolm
  1999   Editor's Notes. *News from Native California* 13:2.
Marx, Karl
  1977   On the Jewish Question. In *Karl Marx, Selected Writings*, ed. D. McClellan. New York: Oxford University Press.
Mason, Clark, and Sam Kennedy
  2003   Casino Near Sears Point Proposed by Miwoks. *Santa Rose Press Democrat*. April 24.
Mason, W. Dale
  1977   *Indian Gaming: Tribal Sovereignty and American Politics*. Norman: University of Oklahoma Press.
McCulloch, Anne Merline, and David E. Wilkins
  1995   "Constructing" Nations within States: The Quest for Federal Recognition by the Catawba and Lumbee Tribes. *American Indian Quarterly* 19, no. 3. (Summer): 361–87.
McDow, George J.
  1965   Historical Mines on the Diamond Mountain Mining District. Susanville, Calif.: Lassen County Historical Society Publications (April):1–41.
McMillin, James H.
  1963   The Aboriginal Human Ecology of the Mountain Meadows Area in Southwestern Lassen County, California. Master's thesis, Sacramento State College.

McNamara, Eileen
    2000   Blumenthal: Ban Tribal Recognition. Process Needs to
            Be reformed, AG Says. *New London (Conn.) Day*.
Mead, Margaret
    1932   *The Changing Culture of an Indian Tribe*. New York:
            Columbia University Press.
Miller, Bruce G.
    1988   After the F.A.P.: Tribal Reorganization after Federal Recog-
            nition. *Journal of Ethnic Studies* 17:89–100.
    2004   *Invisible Indigenes: The Politics of Nonrecognition*. Lincoln:
            University of Nebraska Press.
Miller, Larissa K.
    1998   Introduction. In *Indian of California Census Rolls Authorized
            under the Act of May 18, 1928, as Amended, Approved
            May 16–17, 1933*. National Archives and Records Adminis-
            tration, 1–8.
Miller, Mark Edwin
    2004   *Forgotten Tribes: Unrecognized Indians and the Federal Acknowl-
            edgment Process*. Lincoln: University of Nebraska Press.
Mooney, James
    1896   *The Ghost Dance and the Sioux Outbreak of 1890*. Vol. 2.
            Fourteenth Annual Report of the Bureau of Ethnology.
Morgan, Henry Louis
    1877   *Ancient Society; or, Researches in the Lines of Human
            Progress from Savagery through Barbarism to Civilization*.
            New York: World Publishing.
Morgan, Wally
    2000   History Books Tell Only One Side of the Story. *Lassen
            County (Susanville,Calif.) Times*.
Moses, L. G.
    1984   *The Indian Man: A Biography of James Mooney*. Urbana
            and Chicago: University of Illinois Press.
Mullis, Angela, and David Kamper, eds.
    2000   *Indian Gaming: Who Wins?* Los Angeles: American
            Indian Studies Center, UCLA.
Mustric, Crystal
    1977   Hayden Hill Mine. *Lassen County (Susanville, Calif.)
            Times*.

1978   Nevada's Senator Reid Seeks Sierra Depot Blast Investi-
        gation. *Lassen County (Susanville, Calif.) Times*. March.
Nader, Laura
    1972   Up the Anthropologist: Perspectives Gained from Study-
            ing Up. In *Reinventing Anthropology*, ed. Dell Hymes,
            284–311. New York: Pantheon Antitextbooks.
    1990   *Harmony Ideology: Justice and Control in a Zapotec Moun-
            tain Village*. Stanford: Stanford University Press.
Nader, Laura, and Jay Ou
    1998   Idealizations and Power: Legality and Tradition in Native
            American Law. *Oklahoma City University Law Review*
            23:13–43.
National Association of Governors
    2000   Federal Recognition. www.nga.org/pubs/policy/edoc06.asp.
Nelson, Diane M.
    1999   *A Finger in the Wound: Body Politics in Quincentennial
            Guatemala*. Berkeley: University of California Press.
Ortner, Sherry
    1996   *Making Gender: The Politics and Erotics of Culture*. Boston:
            Beacon Press.
Owens, Louis
    2003   Native Sovereignty and the Tricky Mirror: Gerald
            Vizenor's "Ishi and the Wood Ducks." In *Ishi in Three
            Centuries*, eds. K. Kroeber and C. Kroeber, 373–87. Lincoln:
            University of Nebraska Press.
Pateman, Carol
    1988   *The Sexual Contract*. Palo Alto, Calif.: Stanford Univer-
            sity Press.
Potts, Marie
    1977   *The Northern Maidu*. Happy Camp, Calif.: Naturegraph.
Povinelli, Elizabeth A.
    2002   *The Cunning of Recognition*. Durham, N.C.: Duke Uni-
            versity Press.
Powell, John Wesley
    1891   *Indian Linguistic Families of America, North of Mexico*. In
            *Annual Report of the BAE to the Secretary of the Smithsonian
            Institution*. Vol. 7, part 1. Washington, D.C.: Smithsonian
            Institution Press.

Powers, Stephen
    1975   Centennial Mission to the Indians of Western Nevada
            and California. In *The Northern California Indians, Con-
            tributions of the University of California Archaeological
            Research Facility*, ed. R. F. Heizer, 191–99. Berkeley: Uni-
            versity of California Press. (Orig. pub. 1876.)
    1976   The Mai-du or Mai-deh. In *Tribes of California*, 282–312.
            Berkeley: University of California Press. (Orig. pub.
            1877.)
Pratt, Mary Louise
    1986   Fieldwork in Common Places. In *Writing Culture: The
            Politics and Poetics of Ethnography*, eds. James Clifford
            and George E. Marcus, 27–50. Berkeley: University of
            California Press.
Purdy, Timothy I.
    2000   *Fruit Growers Supply Company—Hilt, Susanville, Westwood,
            Burney: A History of the Northern California Operations*.
            Susanville, Calif.: Lahontan Images.
Quinn, William W., Jr.
    1977   Public Ethnohistory? Or, Writing Tribal Histories at the
            Bureau of Indian Affairs. *Public Historian* 10, no. 2:71–76.
    1978   The Southeast Syndrome: Notes on Indian Descendant
            Recruitment Organizations and Their Perceptions of
            Native American Culture. *American Indian Quarterly*
            (Spring 1990): 147–54.
    1990   Federal Acknowledgment of American Indian Tribes:
            The Historical Development of a Legal Concept. *American
            Journal of Legal History* 34, no. 4 (October 1990): 331–65.
    1992   Federal Acknowledgement of American Indian Tribes:
            Authority, Judicial Interposition, and 25 C.F.R. 83. *Ameri-
            can Indian Law Review* 17, no. 1:37–69.
Rathbun, Bill
    1988   Letter to the editor: Bear Dance. *Lassen County (Susan-
            ville, Calif.) Times*.
Rawls, James J.
    1984   *Indians of California: The Changing Image*. Norman: Uni-
            versity of Oklahoma Press.

Renan, Ernest
    1990   What Is a Nation? In *Nation and Narration*, ed. H. Bhaha,
            8–22. London and New Work: Routledge. (Orig. pub.
            1882.)
Reynolds, Linda A.
    1995   Tribal Governments and Communities in the Sierra
            Nevada Ecoregion: A Sierra Nevada Ecosystem Project
            Assessment. U.S. Forest Service. Unpublished draft.
Riddell, Francis A.
    1978a   Honey Lake Paiute Ethnography. Nevada State Museum
            Occasional Papers. Vol. 3, part 1.
    1978b   Maidu and Konkow. In *Handbook of North American
            Indians*. Vol. 8. Ed. R. F. Heizer, 370–86. Washington,
            D.C.: Smithsonian Institution Press.
    1995   Letter to William S. Simmons. August 14. Copy in the
            possession of the author.
Roessel, Faith
    1989   Federal Recognition: A Historical Twist of Fate. *Native
            American Rights Fund Legal Review* 14, no. 3:1–9.
Rose, Nikolas
    1999   *Powers of Freedom: Reframing Political Thought.* Cam-
            bridge, UK: Cambridge University Press.
Roth, George
    1992   Overview of Southeastern Indian Tribes Today. In *Indians
            of the Southeastern United states in the Late 20th Century*,
            ed. J. Anthony Paredes, 183–202. Tuscaloosa: Univer-
            sity of Alabama Press.
    1996   Working paper on previous acknowledgment in Califor-
            nia, 1887–1933 (draft). Branch of Acknowledgment and
            Research.
Rusco, Elmer R.
    2000   *A Fateful Time: The Background and Legal History of the
            Indian Reorganization Act*. Reno: University of Nevada,
            Reno Press.
Santiago, Chiori, and Judith Lowry
    1998   *Home to Medicine Mountain*. San Francisco: Children's
            Book Press.

Sarris, Greg
    1998   *Watermelon Nights*. New York: Hyperion.
    2001   First Thoughts on Restoration: Notes from a Tribal Chairman. *News from Native California* 14:12–15.
Scheper-Hughes, Nancy
    1977   Ishi's Brain, Ishi's Ashes: Anthropology and Genocide. *Anthropology Today* 17:12–18.
    2001   Ishi's Brain, Ishi's Ashes. *Anthropology Today* 17:12–18.
    2003   Ishi's Brain, Ishi's Ashes: Reflections on Anthropology and Genocide. In *Ishi in Three Centuries*, eds. K. Kroeber and C. Kroeber, 99–131. Lincoln: University of Nebraska Press.
Schiedermair, Bettina
    1990   "Federal Acknowledgment": Anthropological Import and Bureaucratic Application. *European Review of Native American Studies* 4, no. 1:47–50.
Schneider, David
    1968   *American Kinship: A Cultural Account*. Englewood Cliffs, N.J.: Prentice-Hall.
Sheffield, Gail K.
    1997   *The Arbitrary Indian: The Indian Arts and Crafts Act of 1990*. Norman: University of Oklahoma Press.
Shipley, William S.
    1963   *Maidu Texts and Dictionary*. Vol. 33. Publications in Linguistics. Berkeley: University of California Press.
Sider, Gerald M.
    1993   *Lumbee Indian Histories: Race, Ethnicity, and Indian Identity in the Southern United States*. Vol. 2. Culture and Class in Anthropology and History Series. Cambridge, UK: Cambridge University Press.
Simmons, William S.
    1986   *The Spirit of the New England Tribes*. Hanover, N.H.: University Press of New England.
    1988   Culture Theory in Contemporary Ethnohistory. *Ethnohistory* 35:1–14.
    n.d.   Indian Peoples of California. Unpublished manuscript.

Simmons, William S., Ron Morales, Viola Williams, and Steve Camacho
    1997   Honey Lake Maidu Ethnogeography of Lassen County, California. *Journal of California and Great Basin Anthropology* 19:2–31.

Slagle, Allogan
    1979   The American Indian Policy Review Commission: Repercussions and Aftermath. In *A Review of the American Indian Policy Review Commission: New Directions in Federal Indian Policy*, 115–32. Los Angeles: American Indian Studies Center, UCLA.
    1986   *Huss: The Tolowa People.* Arcata, Calif.: Humbolt State University, Center for Community Development.
    1987   The Native American Tradition and Legal Status: Tolowa Tales and Tolowa Places. *Cultural Critique* (Fall): 103–18.
    1990   Groundhog Day. *News from Native California* 4:47–50.
    1998   Groundhog Day. *News from Native California* 12:40–43.
    2000a Groundhog Day. *News from Native California* 14:56–59.
    2000b Groundhog Day: Changes at BAR. *News from Native California* 13:48–50.
    2001   Groundhog Day: McCaleb Denies Preliminary Recognition to Ohlone. *News from Native California* 15:16–17.

Slagle, Allogan, and Lee Davis
    1989   Unfinished Justice: Completing the Restoration and Acknowledgment of California Indian Tribes. *American Indian Quarterly* (Fall): 325–45.
    1995   The Special Circumstances of California Indians. Ed. Victoria Patterson. Advisory Council on California Indian Policy.

Snyder, Gary
    1991   Foreword to *The Maidu Indian Myths and Stories of Hanc'ibyjim*, ed. William S. Shipley, vii–x. Berkeley, Calif.: Heyday Books / Rick Heide.

Southall, Aiden
    1996   Tribes. *Encyclopedia of Cultural Anthropology*, ed. David Levine and Melvin Embers, 1329–36. New York: Henry Holt.

Speck, Frank
   1915   Family Hunting Territories and Social Life of Various
          Algonkian Bands of the Ottowa Valley. In *Bulletin of the
          National Museum of Ottowa.* Anthropological Series.
          Nos. 8–9:289–305.
Spicer, Edward H., ed.
   1961   *Perspectives in American Indian Culture Change.* International
          University Summer Research Seminar 1956, University
          of New Mexico. Chicago: University of Chicago Press.
Spilde, Katherine J.
   2000   Educating Local Non-Indian Communities about Indian
          Nation Governmental Gaming: Messages and Methods.
          In *Indian Gaming: Who Wins?* Eds. Mullis and Kamper.
          Los Angeles: American Indian Studies Center, UCLA.
Stegner, Wallace
   1992   Living Dry. In *Where the Bluebird Sings to the Lemonade Springs:
          Living and Writing in the West.* New York: Wings Books.
Steward, Julian H.
   1955   Theory and Application in a Social Science. *Ethnohis-
          tory* 2, no. 4:292–302.
   1970   The Foundations of Basin-Plateau Shoshonean Society.
          In *Languages and Cultures of Western North America:
          Essays in Honor of Sven S. Liljeblad,* ed. J. E. H. Swanson,
          113–51. Pocatello: Idaho State University Press.
Steward, Julian H., and E. Wheeler-Voegelin
   1977   The Northern Paiute. In *Paiute Indians I, Vol. 3,* ed.
          David A. Horr. Garland Series on the American Indian:
          Plateau and Great Basin.
Stewart, Omer C.
   1977   Kroeber and the Indian Claims Commission Cases. In
          The Kroeber Anthropological Society Papers, 181–90. Berke-
          ley: California Indian Library Collections Project.
Stiffarm, Lenore, and Phil Lane, Jr.
   1992   The Demography of Native North America: A Question
          of American Indians Survival. In *The State of Native
          America: Genocide, Colonization, and Resistance,* ed. M.
          Annette Jaimes, 23–53. Boston: South End Press.

Strong, Pauline Turner, and Barrik Van Winkle
1996   "Indian Blood": Reflections on the Reckoning and Refiguring of Native North American Identity. *Cultural Anthropology* 11, no. 4:547–76.
Sturm, Circe
2002   *Blood Politics: Race, Culture, and Identity in the Cherokee Nation of Oklahoma*. Berkeley: University of California Press.
Sturtevant, William, ed.
1978   California. Vol. 8. *Handbook of North American Indians*. Washington, D.C.: Smithsonian Institution Press / U.S. GPO.
1979   Tribe and State in the 16th and 20th Centuries. In *The Development of Political Organization in Native North America: 1979 Proceedings of the American Ethnological Society*, ed. Elisabeth Tooker, 3–16. Philadelphia: American Ethnological Society.
(*Susanville, Calif.*) *Lassen Advocate*
1887   A Grand Indian Dance Was Given at the Digger Camp . . .
1900   Henry Vanetti Killed by Walter Peconom. June 28.
1906   Indians of This Section. May 31.
1910   Walter Peconom Killed. July 29.
Taylor, Charles
1994   The Politics of Recognition. In *Multiculturalism*, ed. A. Gutmann, 25–74. Princeton, N.J.: Princeton University Press.
Theodoratus, Dorothea J., and Frank R. LaPena
1992   Wintu Sacred Geography. In *California Indian Shamanism*, ed. L. J. Bean, 211–25. Menlo Park, Calif.: Ballena Press.
Thomas, D. H.
1977   Harvesting Ramona's Garden: Life in California's Mythical Mission Past. In *Columbian Consequences: The Spanish Borderlands in Pan-American Perspective*. Vol. 3. Ed. D. H. Thomas, 119–57. Washington, D.C.: Smithsonian Institution Press.
Thomas, D. H., Jay Miller, Richard White, Peter Nabokov, and Philip J. Deloria
1993   *The Native Americans*. Menomonee Fall, Minn.: Inland Press.

Thompson, A. C.
    2000   King of Stumps. *San Francisco Bay Guardian*.
Thorp, Rebecca A.
    2000   The Changing Identity of the Strawberry Valley Band of
            Maidu Indians. Bachelor's thesis, University of California,
            Los Angeles.
Tocqueville, Alexis de
    1981   *Democracy in America*. New York: Modern Library,
            McGraw-Hill. (Orig. pub. 1835.)
Tolley, Sara-Larus
    2004   Review: Invisible Indigenes. *American Indian Culture
            and Research Journal* 28, no. 3:153–56.
Tureen, Thomas N.
    1976   Federal Recognition and the "Passamaquoddy" Decision.
            In *Final Report of the American Indian Policy Review Com-
            mission, Task Force Three, Federal Administration and
            Structure of Indian Affairs*, 1653–74. Washington, D.C.:
            U.S. GPO.
Uldall Hans J., and William S. Shipley
    1977   *Nisenan Texts and Dictionary*. Vol. 36. Berkeley: Univer-
            sity of California Publications in Linguistics.
U.S. Army
    1850   Reports Relating to the U.S. Army's Military Expedition
            against the Indians of the Pit River Area, California.
            Bancroft Library, Berkeley, Calif. MSS 91-35c.
    1993   Environmental Update, Sierra Army Depot, Herlong,
            Calif. Aberdeen Proving Ground, Md.: U.S. Army Envi-
            ronmental Center (July): 1–2.
U.S. General Accounting Office
    2002   Indian Issues: Basis for BIA's Tribal Recognition Deci-
            sions Is Not Always Clear. Statement of Barry T. Hill,
            Director Natural Resources and Environment. Before
            the Committee on Indian Affairs, U.S. Senate.
U.S. House
    1977   Committee on Interior and Insular Affairs. Subcommittee
            on Indian Affairs and Public Lands. *H.R. 13773 and Similar
            Bills (Including H.R. 12996) to Establish an Administrative*

Procedures and Guidelines to be Followed by the Department of the Interior in Its Decision to Acknowledge the Existence of Certain Indian Tribes. 95th Cong., 2nd sess., August 10.

1978   Committee on Interior and Insular Affairs. *H.R. 3430, to Establish Administrative Procedures to Extend Federal Recognition to Certain Indian Groups.* 100th Cong., 2nd sess., September 15.

1992a   Committee on Interior and Insular Affairs. *Federal Acknowledgment of Various Indian Groups: Hearing on H.R. 3958, H.R. 1475, H.R. 2349, H.R. 5562, H.R. 3607.* 102nd Cong., 2nd sess., July 8.

1992b   Committee on Interior and Insular Affairs. *Hearing on H.R. 3430, to Establish Administrative Procedures to Extend Federal Recognition to Certain Indian Groups.* 103rd Cong., 2nd sess.

1994   Committee on Natural Resources. Subcommittee on Native American Affairs. *Various Bills Involving Federal Acknowledgment: Hearing on H.R. 2549, H.R. 4462, and H.R. 4709.* 103rd Cong., 2nd sess., July 22.

U.S. Senate
1977   Select Committee on Indian Affairs. *Oversight Hearing on Federal Acknowledgment Process.* 100th Cong., 2nd sess., May 26.

1978   Select Committee on Indian Affairs. *To Transfer Administrative Consideration of Applications for Federal Recognition of an Indian Tribe to an Independent Commission.* 102nd Cong., 1st sess., October 22.

2000   Committee on Indian Affairs. *S. 611, To Provide for Administrative Procedures to Extend Federal Recognition to Certain Indian Groups.* 106th Cong., 2nd sess., May 24.

Vieira, Meredith
1990   The Coach. *60 Minutes.* CBS. Transcript. Vol. 23, no. 12:13–19.

Vizenor, Gerald R.
1977   *Manifest Manners: Postindian Warriors of Survivance.* Hanover, N.H.: Wesleyan University Press.

1995   Ishi and the Wood Ducks. In *Native American Literature: A Brief Introduction and Anthology,* ed. Gerald Vizenor, 299–336. New York: HarperCollins.

2000   *Chancers: A Novel.* American Indian Literature and Critical Studies Series. Norman: University of Oklahoma Press.

Ward, Chip

2000   *Canaries on the Rim: Living Downwind in the West.* The Haymarket Series. London: Verso.

Weatherhead, L. R.

1980   What Is an "Indian Tribe"? The Question of Tribal Existence. *American Indian Law Review* 8:1–47.

Weber, Max

1977   Bureaucracy. In *Economy and Society: An Outline of Interpretive Sociology,* ed. G. R. A. C. Wittich, 956–1005. Berkeley: University of California Press.

Williams, Sam

2022   Army Halts OB/OD at SIAD. *Lassen County (Susanville, Calif.) Times.* October 3.

Wolf, Eric R.

1974   American Anthropologists and American Society. In *Reinventing Anthropology,* ed. D. Himes. New York: Vintage Books. (Orig. pub. 1969.)

INDEX

Day, Frank, 122, 123
DeHaven, Cap and Emma, 164, 167
Department of the Interior (DOI):
    before 1978, 58–60; slight of
    hand, 63–64. *See also* Branch of
    Acknowledgment and Research
    (BAR); Bureau of Indian Affairs
    (BIA); Federal Acknowledgment
Devil, the, 146, 221, 234, 247n1
Diaz, Cindy, 135, 136, 138–39, 140
Dibbern, John, 91, 175, 176–78
Dixon, Harold ("Utie"), 210–12
Dixon, Roland B., 100–102, 113,
    146; linguistics, 74
Dixon, Theresa, 211
Dobkins, Rebecca, 122
Doctoring, 221, 237
Dorrington, Lafayette, 48–49
Dow and Hines, 29–31

Eagle Lake Massacre. *See* Papoose
    Massacre
Ecology and land use, 99, 136
Enterprise Rancheria, 209
Evans, William, 95, 99

Factionalism, 12, 91–92, 130, 132,
    144–45, 197, 205, 210, 220; and
    the archive, 161; and Bear Dance,
    137–38, 142–44, 211; and Coyote,
    195; and non-Indians, 210; role
    of anthropologists in, 70–71
Fairfield, Asa, 29–31, 214
Faleomaveaga, Eni, 80
Federal Acknowledgment (25 CFR
    part 83.7), 227–32; as inappro-
    priate to California tribes, 79,
    82; biogenetic requirements,

168, 193–94; the burden of the
    proof, 19; creation of, 81; the
    criteria, 82–83, 202–204; defini-
    tion of "community," 55, 92,
    204; description of, 12; docu-
    mentation for, 62–63, 165–66;
    geneaology, 183; and handgame,
    119; history of, 54, 58–59; and
    hope, 159; and Lafayette Dorring-
    ton, 48; Letter of Intent to Peti-
    tion, 180; reform, 66; summary
    of critique of, 202; violence and,
    168. *See also* Shapard, Bud
Federal Recognition: lower-case "r"
    recognition, 14, 42, 214; number
    of unrecognized tribes in
    California, 19. *See also* Federal
    Acknowledgment
Federated Indians of Graton
    Rancheria, 29, 67, 205
Field Matron, 250n7. *See also* Young,
    Edith
Fleming, Lee, 175
Food: acorn, 113, 121; and the Bear
    Dance, 113–16; onions and
    potatoes, 233, 234, 235; salmon,
    112–15; sugar, 194. *See also* Meat
Forest Service, 124, 126; collabora-
    tions with Indian people, 137;
    District Ranger, 132–34; Eagle
    lake Ranger District, 212; and
    factionalism, 130, 138; forms of
    communication, 135; Lassen
    National Forest, 104–105, 128,
    130; multi-use approach, 131;
    and non-Recognized tribes,
    129–30; relationship with
    Recognized Tribes, 132; Tribal

Relations Program, 124, 129, 135; Tribal Summit, 131. *See also* Andrews, Bob; Cole, Ed; Diaz, Cindy; Reynolds, Linda
Foucault, Michel, 15, 148, 163, 190
Freedom, 44, 148–49, 160; and the BAR's philosophy 178
Freedom of Information Act, requests, 223
Freid, Morton, 73
Frow, Dilly, 28, 57

Gaming, 66, 99, 203. *See also* Casinos; Handgame
Garcia, Amelia, 142
Garcia, Gina, 124, 128, 180–83, 187, 219
Genealogy, 161, 183, 190, 219, 253
General Accounting Office (GAO), 223
General Allotment Act of 1887, 44; Section 4 Allotments, 45, 174–75, 176, 177. *See also* Allotmments
Genocide, 18, 19, 34; relation to ethnocide, 39
Geography: BAR approach to, 92; Claims Commission and, 77; Honey Lake Maidu approach to, 37, 92–93; Honey Lake Maidu tribal boundaries, 93–94
George, Big Rosie, 109
Ghost Dance, the, 35
Gorton, Slade, 177
Gover, Kevin, 67, 177
Gramsci, Antonio: justice, 149–50; non–Indian hegemony, 16; war of position, 16
Greenville Rancheria, 161, 163

Guadalupe Hidalgo, Treaty of (1848), 20, 73
Guerrero, Lynne, 141, 142, 158, 200

Handgame, 117–19
Harris, Marvina, 126
Haskell Institute, 181
Heizer, Robert F., 74
Homeless Indians, 47–49
Honey Lake Maidus: and the Bear Dance Foundation, 190, 197; California Land Claims Commission, 76, 77; comparison with other California tribes, 210; The Creator, 85, 101; denying Papoose Massacre, 213; dispute with Paiute, 91, 93; draft constitution, 185–86; economic goals, 14, 99–100, 199; ethnogeography, 85; historical population numbers, 25–26; hope, 195; lineages, 28, 164, 196, 198; medicinal plants, 101; Mountain Meadows, 99, 100; petition, 16, 36–37, 112–13, 218; petition, rescinded, 218; and Fritz Riddell, 84, 85–91; sacred sites, 92–93; secrecy, 7, 84, 85, 188; summary of critique of BAR, 202; traditional healing, 221, 237; tribal boundaries, 83–84, 93–94, 156; tribal council, 185, 187, 199; tribal elections, 179; tribal history, 187–88; and Tuscarora, 95, 102
House of Representatives, 80, 217
Hunt, Leigh Ann, 110
Hupa, 104
Hutt, Linda, 112, 124, 142, 196, 200

Timbisha Shoshones of Death
Valley, 41, 208
Tobacco, 113
Tolowa Nation, 216
Tully v. the United States (1891),
60–61
Tureen, Tom, 60–61
Treaties of 1850–51, 21–22, 41, 60,
75
Tribal adoption, 158
Tribe: Coyote and, 14; definitions
of, 9, 53, 54–55, 71, 72, 73, 80;
economic/ecological views of,
98–100
Tribelet, 164; Kroeber and, 78;
political leadership and, 82
Tuscarora pipeline, 95, 102

Uldall, Hans, 145
Ulleseit, Margaret, 187, 199, 219

Valenzuela, Inez Chavez, 157, 167,
181, 182, 199
Violence, 146, 183, 184, 195, 220;
anthropologists and, 220; at
BAR, 175; factionalist, 197; and
the Honey Lake Maidu experience, 29–33; George Peconom
and Celia Jack, 181

Wadakut Paiutes, 91, 210, 211
Walker, Francis, 54
Washington, 116, 152, 172–78
Wdojykom, 187
Wetajam, 165; abandoned, 33; as
Rousche's Ranch, 7, 33
Williams, Dan, 111
Williams, Viola, 110, 122, 135, 137,
142, 178; on Papoose Massacre, 213
Wilson, George, 182
Wilson, Pete, 66, 67
Winnemucca, Chief, 91, 248–49n10
Wintu tribes. *See* Nomtipom Wintus
Woods, Clyde, 95, 100, 102
Woolsey, Lynne, 67
Wooly Maidem, 104
Wormwood. *See Munmunim*
Wozencraft, Oliver, 21–23, 41, 60

Young, Edith, 49, 196; and allot-
ments, 51–52; and Bear Dance,
51; and field reports, 50–59; and
Walter Peconom, 49, 52; and
Lamb Samson, 50; and Viola
Williams, 50
Young, Tom, 146
Yurok tribe, 104

Zunino, Mike, 142